YESTERDAY, TODAY, TOMORROW

VOLUME FOUR • 1940 to Present

By Ira Peck with Steven Deyle

HISTORICAL CONSULTANTS

Elaine Tyler May
*Professor of American
Studies and History
University of Minnesota
Minneapolis, Minnesota*

Bruce Palmer
*Associate Professor of Historical Studies
University of Houston
Houston, Texas*

IRA PECK is a professional writer. Born in New York City, he attended public schools there and Harvard College, where he majored in history. As a journalist, he worked as a newspaper reporter and a magazine editor. He has written numerous biographies and historical books for young people.

STEVEN DEYLE is a professional historian and teacher. He has received degrees in American history from the University of California—Santa Cruz and Columbia University. He was a historical consultant and contributing writer for Scholastic's *African American History: Four Centuries of Black Life*.

ON THE COVER

The painting called *The Right to Know* appeared as an illustration in *Look* Magazine on August 20, 1968. Printed by permission of the Estate of Norman Rockwell. Copyright © 1968 Estate of Norman Rockwell. The following caption appeared with the painting: "We are the governed, but we govern too. Assume our love of country, for it is only the simplest of self-love. Worry little about our strength, for we have our history to show for it. And because we are strong, there are others who have hope. But watch us more closely from now on, for those of us who stand here mean to watch those we put in the seats of power. And listen to us, you who lead, for we are listening harder for the truth that you have not always offered us. Your voice must be ours, and ours speaks of cities that are not safe, and of wars we do not want, of poor in a land of plenty, and of a world that will not take the shape our arms would give it. We are not fierce, and the truth will not frighten us. Trust us, for we have given you our trust. We are the governed, remember, but we govern too."

For reprint permission, grateful acknowledgement is made to:
Joan Daves, agent to the estate of Martin Luther King, Jr., for the excerpt from I HAVE A DREAM by Martin Luther King, Jr., copyright © 1963 by Martin Luther King, Jr.

Scholastic Inc. ISBN 0-590-35705-0

12 11 10 9 8 7 6 5 4 3 2 1   7 0 / 9 1 2 3 4 5 / 9

PUBLISHER
ELEANOR ANGELES

EDITORIAL DIRECTOR
CAROLYN JACKSON

PROJECT EDITOR
DEBORAH GORE

SKILLS EDITOR
MOLLIE COHEN

MANAGING EDITOR
KEVIN GILLESPIE

ASSISTANT EDITOR
LISA KEATING

EDITORIAL ASSISTANT
LISA CRAWLEY

PRODUCTION
CLAUDIA BRUCE
VIRGINIA DUSTIN
MIDGE MARONI

◆

DESIGN DIRECTOR
CAMPION PRIMM

ART DIRECTOR
JUDITH ORLICK

PHOTO & ILLUSTRATION
RESEARCHERS
PHOTOSEARCH, INC.

CARTOGRAPHER
DAVID LINDROTH

ILLUSTRATOR
CHIP WASS

COVER DESIGN
ROSEMARY INTRIERI

CONTENTS

YESTERDAY, TODAY, TOMORROW

By the summer of 1938, more and more Americans were getting their news from the radio. Every evening, millions of families gathered around their sets to learn what had happened that day. Often news reports were beamed directly from world capitals. "We take you now to Berlin," a newscaster would say. Then another, more distant voice would crackle through the airwaves.

Such newscasts were proof of how small the world had become. In the summer of 1938, they also revealed how troubled the world was. Europe was on the brink of another war. As World

Adolf Hitler's campaign of hate pulled Germany from poverty to power—at a tremendous cost. Here, he salutes his followers at a 1938 Nazi rally in Nuremberg, Germany.

WORLD

1940	1941	1944
1940 Selective Service Act calls men to military service.	**1941** Japan attacks Pearl Harbor, December 7. — U.S. Lend-Lease Bill provides weapons to Great Britain. — United States and Great Britain declare war on Japan.	**1944** Allies invade German-occupied France, June 6.

WAR II

1945

1945

U. S. drops A-bomb on
Hiroshima and
Nagasaki, Japan.

Japan
surrenders,
August 14.

UNIT 1

War I had shown, a conflict in Europe could threaten peace around the world.

Beginning of War

In 1919, the Treaty of Versailles forced Germany to give up large amounts of territory, and to pay heavy damages for its role in World War I. The treaty also required Germany to accept the blame for starting the war.

Four years later, the German economy collapsed. Many people could not find work. German money became worthless. When their economy collapsed again in the 1930s, Germans felt angry and helpless. Some believed that their government was too weak to deal with Germany's problems. Many people began to look for extreme answers. Some joined a party led by Adolf Hitler. This party was the National Socialist, or Nazi, party.

Hitler's Rise to Power

Hitler and the Nazis rose to power by appealing to German nationalism. They also preyed upon people's prejudices. They preached hatred, especially of Jewish people. They blamed the Jews for Germany's defeat in World War I.

The Nazis came to power in 1933. Hitler was named head of the German government, and soon made himself dictator of Germany. He banned all other political parties. Then he began jailing and

World War II was one of the most destructive wars in history. Here is Winston Churchill (1874–1965) surveying the aftermath of a bombing in London.

killing those who disagreed with him.

Hitler made it his special goal to wipe out all Jewish influence in Germany. He took away the citizenship of German Jews. But this was only the beginning. Between 1941 and 1945, he directed one of the most terrible criminal periods in human history. Under his leadership, the Nazis murdered six million European Jews, and six million other people, mostly Poles and Soviets.

As Hitler became more powerful, he began to look beyond Germany's borders. In one fanatic speech after another, he called for a German empire that would rule the entire world. At the same time, he began rearming Germany.

In 1936, German forces marched into the Rhineland, the area of western Germany bordering France. The Treaty of Versailles had ordered that this area be **demilitarized** (kept free of armed forces). This meant that, although the land was German territory, there could be no German troops there. In March of 1938, Hitler sent German troops to take over German-speaking Austria. Britain, France, and the Soviet Union protested but took no action.

In September 1938, Hitler announced his plan to seize the Sudetenland (soo-DAY-ten-land), a western part of Czechoslovakia that contained a large German-speaking population. Hitler would go through with this plan, he said, unless the area was given to him peacefully. Despite protests from the Czechoslovakian government, leaders from

Britain and France reluctantly gave in. They let Hitler take this land. They hoped that this would prevent war.

Around the World

Germany was not the only country in the 1930s run by a power-hungry dictator. The Italian **fascist** (one who believes in rigid, militaristic, one-party dictatorship) leader Benito Mussolini also preached about greatness for his people. He marched armies into Ethiopia in Africa, and Albania in Eastern Europe.

In Asia, meanwhile, military leaders had become a powerful force in Japanese life. In 1931, Japanese troops seized the Chinese province of Manchuria. Fighting between China and Japan continued throughout the 1930s. Full-scale war be-tween the two countries broke out in 1937.

These events worried many Americans. Yet they were in no mood to fight another war. Many of them now believed that the United States had been drawn into World War I by mistake. They thought that the United States should isolate itself—that is, stay clear of alliances with foreign governments.

European War

The war in Europe began on September 1, 1939. On that day, without warning, Nazi Germany attacked Poland. Germany wanted to have more territories in the East. German dive bombers and tanks quickly smashed all Polish opposition. The Nazis overwhelmed the Poles with a new form of warfare. They called it

The European Theater in World War II

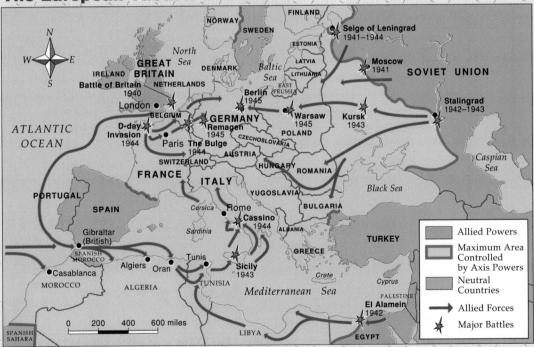

Which countries came under Axis control during World War II? From what direction(s) did the Allies invade Axis-occupied Europe?

blitzkrieg, or "lightning war."

Germany, Italy, and Japan formed a war partnership known as the **Axis.** In 1940 and 1941, the Axis grew in strength. Germany took control of much of Europe. It also sent armies to North Africa. Japan was on the march in the Pacific.

In June 1941, three million German troops attacked the Soviet Union. Soviet armies were caught off guard. By early fall, the Soviets had lost 2,500,000 troops. German forces advanced along a front more than 1000 miles long. In the North, they moved toward Leningrad. In the South, they pushed into the Ukraine. Their principal goal was the capture of Moscow, the Soviet capital. However, a brutal winter set in and prevented their taking Moscow. The German advance stopped, and the Soviets counterattacked.

In the spring of 1942, the Germans resumed their offensive. In the South, they headed for Stalingrad. Soviet forces surrounded the German army, which was trying to capture the city, and forced it to surrender.

The German defeat at Stalingrad was a great turning point in World War II. The tide of Nazi conquest began to recede. From then until the end of the war, Nazi Germany would be on the defensive.

The Soviet Union, under the leadership of Joseph Stalin, joined Britain, Canada, Australia, France, and other nations in fighting Germany. These nations became known as the **Allies.** By 1941, Britain had

Military and Civilian Casualties in World War II

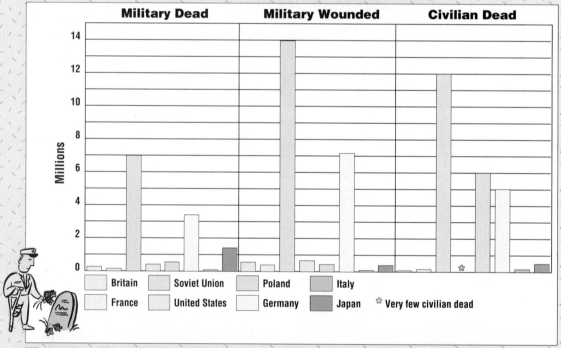

What nation suffered the most civilian deaths during World War II? The most military deaths? Why were there so few American civilian deaths? How might the number of Soviet casualties in World War II have affected their attitude towards war? How might American attitudes towards war be different?

a new prime minister, Winston Churchill, who led Britain through its darkest years in fighting Nazi Germany. Some Americans believed the United States should join the Allies. Others said the United States should not get involved in other countries' wars.

Pearl Harbor

On December 7, 1941, Japan forced the U.S. into action. Japanese war planes attacked the U.S. naval base at Pearl Harbor, Hawaii. The next day, the United States declared war on Japan. Three days later, Germany and Italy declared war on the United States.

American forces were soon fighting a war on three continents. At first, the United States suffered military setbacks. In the South Pacific, Japan had taken over most of the important islands and coastal regions. In 1942, however, American ships and planes reversed Japan's momentum.

American forces landed in North Africa late in 1942. They joined the British in defeating Germany's Afrika Korps. Meanwhile, in Eastern Europe, the Soviets suffered huge losses, but finally stopped Hitler's armies.

In 1943, Allied troops invaded Italy and forced it to surrender. The next year, other Allied forces crossed the English Channel from Britain into Nazi-held France. The invasion hastened the end for the Nazis. It took almost a year more of fighting, but finally the Allies defeated the Nazis, and Hitler was dead.

Results of War

On the home front, the war affected most Americans. Almost everyone knew someone fighting in the war. Most of the economy shifted toward the war effort. Many consumer goods, such as sugar, coffee, gas, and tires, became strictly limited.

Many new jobs were created as a result of the war. In addition, millions of women went to work in these new war-related industries.

One of the saddest effects of the war on the home front was the nation's treatment of Japanese Americans. Due to the unfounded fear that people of Japanese descent might try to help Japan win the war, many Japanese Americans were forcibly moved to military camps. Called **relocation centers**, these centers in isolated areas of the West were nothing more than prison camps. They were surrounded by barbed wire and watchtowers. More than 110,000 people were rounded up, about 70,000 of them U.S. citizens.

Franklin D. Roosevelt did not live to see the end of the war. He had been the American member of the Allied leaders known as the Big Three that also included Churchill and Stalin. FDR died before the Allies defeated the Axis. The Big Three had met throughout the war years to plan strategy against the Axis. When FDR died suddenly in April of 1945, Vice-President Harry S. Truman followed him as president.

Truman decided to use the atomic bomb against Japan. The bomb ended the war in the Pacific, but it began a new, deadly era in human history.

At war's end, most of the Allies were exhausted, and the Axis powers were in ruins. Some 45 million people had died. Among them were 400,000 Americans. The United States had become the most powerful nation in the world. However, the United States could no longer think of returning to its isolated past.

1 RISE OF A DICTATOR

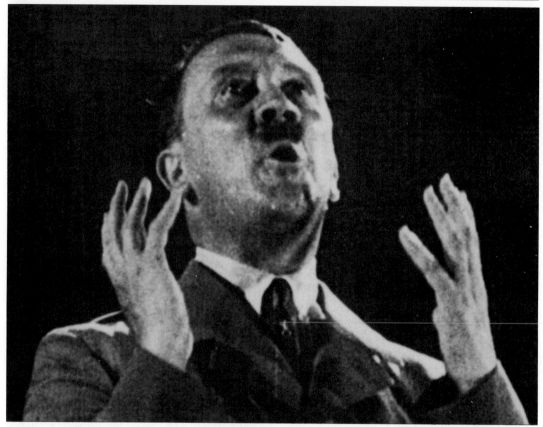

A moody and bitter man, Adolf Hitler (1889–1945) devoted all his interest and energy to politics. His impassioned speeches, fired by hatred and suspicion, swayed many Germans to support his cause.

In fiery political speeches throughout Germany in the late 1920s, Adolf Hitler proclaimed his dark vision of humanity's future. An extremely powerful and appealing speaker, he screamed and shouted his evil message to a growing number of followers.

Hitler preached that the strong must trample and rule the weak. Only violence and war could once again make Germany a mighty empire, he said. He longed to see his political party, the National Socialists, or **Nazis,** rule Germany and make Germans into what he called a master race. The fact that Hitler almost achieved his dream is one of modern history's most brutal, tragic chapters.

Hitler was born in 1889 on the Austrian–German border, the son of a customs officer. He grew up shy, sickly, and prone to hysterical outbursts. He quit high school to become a painter. Twice he failed an entrance exam to the Academy of Fine Arts in Vienna. Hitler then worked as a commercial artist in a series of odd jobs. Soon he fell into poverty and lived in a run-down men's residence. Much of Hitler's hatred for society is believed to have been fueled by these grim years in Vienna.

World War I, he said later, gave him a way out of despair. The war promised great adventure. Wounded twice while serving in the German army, he became a corporal and was awarded an Iron Cross. Yet Germany's surrender in 1918 devastated him.

Hitler's Two Enemies

After World War I, Hitler became involved in politics. He ranted about Germany's two great enemies. One enemy, he said, was the group of "traitors" who had "stabbed Germany in the back." These were the politicians who had surrendered at the end of the war, and signed the Treaty of Versailles. Hitler raged at the huge cash payments the treaty required of Germany as repayment for the Allies' war costs. Such concessions humiliated Germany, he argued.

The other enemy, claimed Hitler, was the Jews. Hitler strongly promoted the anti-Jewish ideas of his time. He believed that this small but powerful minority group was to blame for Germany's economic woes. Hitler's exceptionally extreme hatred of both the Versailles Treaty and Jews became the basis of his political platform.

Why did so many Germans believe his message? Hitler rose to power during the Depression of the 1930s. He promised jobs, food, the return of dignity—and greatness—if he were in power.

In 1923, the Nazis planned an over-

World War I left Germany riddled with poverty. By the 1920s, money was nearly worthless, and food supplies scarce. In this 1923 photograph, German housewives wait in long lines hoping to buy meat for their families. Such impoverished conditions fed the bitterness that led to World War II.

throw of Germany's government. But when the Nazis tried to take power in Munich, the police stopped them and arrested Hitler. He was thrown into prison, where he wrote his famous autobiography, *Mein Kampf* (mine kahmf), which means "my struggle." In his book, Hitler revealed his plans to retake the lands Germany had lost in the Versailles Treaty. Germany would also seize "living space" in Eastern Europe, and in the Soviet Union. Finally, Hitler vowed to deal with what he called the Jewish question.

Rise of Nazism

After his release from prison, Hitler devoted his life to building the Nazi party into Germany's strongest political force. He won the support of many conservative military leaders and businessmen. They believed that only Hitler's severe measures could save Germany from a communist takeover.

In the 1932 election, Hitler ran against German President Paul von Hindenburg. Hitler received almost 40 percent of the vote. In 1933, Hindenburg appointed him **chancellor** (high state official). Within months, Hitler turned the government into his own personal dictatorship. He became the *führer*, or "leader."

Overnight, Germans lost their civil rights. Labor unions and all other political parties except the Nazi party were outlawed. Hitler lashed out at democrats and communists alike. German Jews were forbidden to marry non-Jews, teach, or work as doctors. Hitler's secret police, the *Gestapo*, shot or jailed thousands of his "enemies."

The Nazis shut down opposing newspapers, and burned books they hated. They drove Jews and other minorities from their jobs and businesses. Many Germans fled this shocking reign of terror.

The Third Reich

In 1934, Hitler began to prepare Germany for an upcoming war. "Conquest is not only a right, but a duty," he told the German people. Today, Hitler bragged, the Nazis rule Germany. Tomorrow, he promised, they would control the world. Hitler rebuilt the German army and air force. War production made the factories busy, and the economy picked up. Many Germans started to think of Hitler as their hero. He called his German empire the **Third Reich,** after two earlier German empires.

In 1936, Hitler moved on to the rest of his plan. He sent troops into the Rhine-

Hitler spread his hatred of Jews across Germany. Attacks on Jews increased, and many Jewish homes and businesses became targets of violence. This photograph shows a Jewish family being expelled from their home in March 1939.

land, the demilitarized area of Germany bordering France. When France and England failed to react, Hitler grew bolder. He annexed Austria, a German-speaking country south of Germany.

How did Americans react to Hitler? At first, most did not take him seriously, though many were concerned. In 1937, President Roosevelt began to warn the public of Hitler's menace. However, the United States did not act. Was not the country safe, protected by two oceans? The best course, most Americans believed, was to stay neutral.

"The German student fights for the Führer and the People," declares this German propaganda of the 1930s. One group manipulated to help spread Hitler's word and support his work was Germany's young people—the "Hitler Youth."

CHAPTER CHECK

WORD MATCH
1. Nazis
2. Gestapo
3. chancellor
4. führer
5. Third Reich

a. the German empire under Hitler from 1933 to 1945
b. the German political party during Hitler's time in power, National Socialists
c. Hitler's secret police
d. high official of state
e. title meaning "leader" in German

QUICK QUIZ
1. Who were Hitler's two "enemies" and why was he able to win people to his cause?
2. Name some steps Hitler took to eliminate any political opposition.

THINK ABOUT IT
1. Why do you think so many people believed Hitler when he said that Jews were to blame for Germany's economic problems?
2. What do you think Hitler meant when he said, "Conquest is not only a right, but a duty"?

2 "PEACE FOR OUR TIME"

Neville Chamberlain, shown here before a cheering throng on September 30, 1938, believed Hitler to be a reasonable man. Chamberlain hoped their agreement would preserve peace, but instead, it paved the way to war.

It was September 30, 1938. A huge crowd had gathered at an airport near London. They waited for a plane from Munich (MEW-nick), Germany. As the plane slowed to a stop, the crowd began to cheer loudly. The door of the plane opened. There stood Neville Chamberlain, the British prime minister. In his hand was a piece of paper. He held it up for the crowd to see. Then the prime minister stepped to some microphones. "I think that it is peace for our time!" he said.

More cheers: "Good old Neville!"

Crowds in Paris

Another crowd had gathered at an airport in Paris. When the plane came in, the Parisians rushed up to it, even before it had stopped. Then Édouard Daladier (ED-wahr duh-LAHD-yay), the French head of government, appeared. Crowds began dancing and cheering.

Daladier turned to a man at his side. "The fools," he said with sadness. "They don't know what they are cheering."

Crowds in Czechoslovakia

There were crowds in the cities of Czechoslovakia that day, too. These crowds did not cheer. Some people had tears running down their faces. September 30, 1938, was a sad day for the people of Czechoslovakia.

Why were the crowds in London and Paris so happy? They believed that their leaders had saved them from a war with Nazi Germany. Chamberlain and Daladier had made a deal with Adolf Hitler.

The price of this bargain was the Sudetenland, land along the German border that belonged to Czechoslovakia. Hitler had wanted this area for a long time. He gave many warlike speeches about it at Nazi party meetings in Germany.

"The people of the Sudetenland are Germans!" he screamed. "The Sudetenland must be turned over to Germany!" If it were not, he warned, Germany would go to war.

The war's impact hit Britain sooner than most people had expected. These two children wear gas masks to protect themselves during an air raid drill in 1939.

Fears of War

By the summer of 1938, Europeans were sure that war would break out any moment. People were very scared.

The British and the French wanted to prevent war. On September 29, 1938, Chamberlain and Daladier flew to Munich. They had a **summit** (highest level, for top officials only) meeting with Hitler. Benito Mussolini, the Italian dictator, also went to Munich. He was Hitler's ally, and he agreed with everything Hitler said.

Hitler told the British and French that, if they gave the Sudetenland to Germany, there would be no war. He also said that this would be his final demand for territory. He would ask for nothing more. Chamberlain and Daladier argued with Hitler for hours. Finally they gave in. Early in the morning of September 30, 1938, they agreed to let Hitler take over the Sudetenland. In other words, they decided to give in to Hitler to keep peace. Ever since this agreement, their policy has been known as **appeasement.**

No Defense

Now Czechoslovakia was doomed. The Sudetenland was mountainous. The mountains were vital to Czechoslovakia's defense. Without the Sudetenland, the Czechs had no hope of defending their country from invasion.

Unlike the Czechs, people in London and Paris cheered. Most people in these cities thought that peace had been saved. The price of peace, a part of Czechoslovakia, was not too high, many English and French people said. Besides, they were not ready for war. Neither England nor France was as powerful as Nazi Germany in 1938.

Czechoslovakia had been a small democracy. Its government had been on good terms with the United States. Now thousands of Czech Americans wept over the fate of their homeland. Some other Americans began to worry more about the threat of war. Yet most Americans were relieved that the peace had been maintained—at least for a while.

The Czechs and Slovaks, on the other hand, believed that the price of peace was too high. To keep Hitler quiet, they said, England and France had betrayed them. England and France would learn how wrong they had been. There would be no way of stopping a man like Hitler from making more demands.

The Czechs and Slovaks were right. The English and the French

Despite his promises of peace to Chamberlain and Daladier, Hitler continued to prepare for war. This parade of Nazi troops in 1938 was a show of military force—and a source of pride for Hitler and his followers.

had been wrong. In a few months German armies marched in and took over most of the remainder of Czechoslovakia.

Hitler wanted more land. Germany was more powerful than ever. The leaders of France and Britain had made a terrible mistake. World War II began with this mistake.

As German troops marched into their Sudetenland hometown in 1938, these people saluted—and wept. Czechoslovakia, now part of Hitler's new empire, was only the first nation to fall.

CHAPTER CHECK

WORD MATCH

1. Neville Chamberlain
2. appeasement
3. Édouard Daladier
4. summit
5. Benito Mussolini

a. the Italian dictator
b. the British prime minister
c. highest level, for top officials only
d. the French head of government
e. the policy of giving in to keep peace

QUICK QUIZ

1. What promise did Hitler make if he was given the Sudetenland?
2. What was the American position toward the European situation at that time?

THINK ABOUT IT

1. When he returned from Munich, many Parisians greeted Daladier with cheers. What do you think Daladier meant when he said, "The fools. They don't know what they're cheering about"?
2. British and French leaders thought they could appease Hitler by giving him the land he demanded. Do you think government leaders should divide a territory without asking the people who live there what they want? Why or why not?

CHAPTER 3 BLITZKRIEG

Once Hitler decided to take Poland, his troops moved with terrifying speed and force. Tanks of Germany's panzer divisions [above] roll into Poland during the blitzkrieg of 1939.

The Polish farmer bent to grab a handful of soil from her field. As she did, she heard a sound on the road behind her. Motors! She heard clanking like moving tractor treads. Whose tractor was this? Where was it going? Why was it moving now?

The farmer turned to get a glimpse of the tractor. She soon saw that it was not a tractor at all, but a German tank. Then came another tank, and another. The farmer hurried toward her house. Oddly, the first thought to cross her mind was the date. It was her son's fourth birthday—September 1, 1939.

These tanks were part of a new kind of war. The Germans called it **blitzkrieg.** Blitzkrieg means speed and surprise— it referred to armies that traveled fast, or Nazi bomber planes that brought sudden death and destruction. The Germans smashed Polish cities and towns. Dive bombers swooped low and bombed, and shot both soldiers and civilians alike.

On the ground, German tanks and motorcycles raced along Polish roads. Nazi troops, taking orders by radio and telephone, spread fire and death. Polish soldiers fought back bravely, but they had old guns. The Polish army was not prepared for such a war. Hitler wanted to defeat Poland so Germany could have more territories in the East.

Hitler miscalculated world reaction. Britain and France declared war on Germany on September 3, 1939. But they did not help Poland. The Germans crushed the Polish army within a month. Poland's suffering worsened in mid-September, when Soviet armies moved in and grabbed eastern Poland. The Poles surrendered on September 27. Germany and the Soviet Union had signed a secret agreement before the war. They now divided Poland between them.

Military Buildup

To most Americans, the war still seemed far away. They were not in any danger—or so they thought. Still,

Poland was devastated by Germany's attack. These Jewish children of Poland's Warsaw ghetto suffered from starvation and other war horrors.

President Roosevelt was worried. He was sure that Germany, Italy, and Japan planned to take over all of Europe and Asia. FDR did not want the United States to sit back and let this happen.

"When you see a rattlesnake getting ready to strike," he said, "you do not wait till he has struck before you crush him."

Slowly, President Roosevelt persuaded Congress to help the Allies. First, the United States allowed Britain and France to buy American guns. Then the President asked for—and received—money to start building thousands of warplanes.

In June 1940, the Nazis crushed France. Britain stood alone. If it were beaten, the United States would be without any friendly nations in Western Europe. In September, FDR sent Britain 50 old U.S. destroyers to help its fleet. In return, Britain gave the United States the right to lease naval bases in the Caribbean, and in part of North America.

The United States also began building up the size of its army and navy. Under a 1940 law, all men between the ages of 21 and 35 were required to sign up as candidates for military service. Then certain of these men were chosen by lot from the larger group and **drafted** (called into the armed forces). This was the first peace-time draft in U.S. history. President Roosevelt approved it because he believed the country had to be ready to defend itself.

Lend-Lease

In the meantime, German bombers pounded Great Britain. German tanks fought the British in North Africa. Roosevelt knew that Britain needed more weapons. He also knew that the British did not have money to pay for them. Roosevelt proposed to Congress that the United States lend or lease weapons to Britain. He suggested that Britain could pay for the weapons later. Congress agreed to this **lend-lease** idea in March 1941. The United States soon sped weapons to the defense of Great Britain.

In the fall of 1940, Roosevelt ran for president for the third time. His Republican opponent, Wendell Willkie, also spoke "for Britain and against Hitler." Some Republicans said, however, that Roosevelt was leading the country into war. Some Democrats, on the other hand, said that Republicans wanted to ignore Hitler. Willkie campaigned hard, but Roosevelt won easily. He was the first president to be elected to a third term. He is still the only president ever to have served more than two terms.

By 1941, U.S. factories were busy day

Nazi Germany on the March, 1935–1939

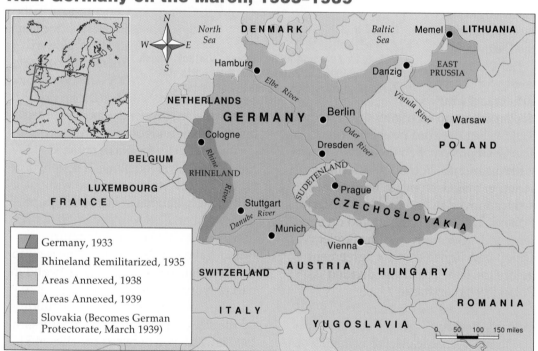

Germany, 1933
Rhineland Remilitarized, 1935
Areas Annexed, 1938
Areas Annexed, 1939
Slovakia (Becomes German Protectorate, March 1939)

In which countries did Germany annex territory between 1938–1939? Why do you think France was upset by the remilitarization of the Rhineland in 1935?

and night turning out various guns, weapons, and other war materials. Our aim, FDR said, was to give Britain any aid "short of war."

Millions of Americans agreed with the president, including a Kansas newspaper editor, William Allen White. Americans, said White, must show that we are "not too blind or too timid to help those who are fighting tyranny abroad."

Fear of German air raids drove many Londoners into stations of "the underground"—their subway system. The crowd gathers at one station in hopes of getting a good night's sleep in safety.

CHAPTER CHECK

WORD MATCH
1. blitzkrieg
2. lend-lease
3. drafted
4. Poland
5. Soviet Union

a. called to serve in the armed forces
b. U.S. policy allowing Britain to borrow weapons, or pay for them later
c. lightning-quick war, characterized by speed and surprise
d. country with which Germany signed a secret agreement promising not to fight
e. country bordering Soviet Union and Germany that Hitler attacked in 1939

QUICK QUIZ
1. Which country was divided in two in 1939? Who controlled each part?
2. What was the response of Britain? Of France? Of the United States?

THINK ABOUT IT
1. How was the war in Europe a 1940 presidential issue? What were the positions of each party?
2. The 1940 draft was enacted when the United States was not at war. Do you think a draft could be enacted today? Explain.

4 THE HOLOCAUST

This is the concentration camp at Auschwitz, Poland, where millions of European Jews were sent to their deaths during World War II. Auschwitz remains a bitter reminder of Hitler's campaign of hate.

In 1940, a 12-year-old Jewish boy in Hungary, Elie Wiesel (EHL-ee wee-ZEHL), became friends with a village character called Moishe (MOY-shuh) the Beadle. Moishe, a popular usher in the Jewish temple, lived on the villagers' charity and spent his days discussing religious philosophy.

Moishe's life was violently interrupted in 1944. Hungary was allied with Nazi Germany. The police had been ordered to expel all foreign Jews from the country. Moishe, who was not Hungarian, was crammed into the cattle car of a train, and Wiesel never expected to see him again.

Several months later, Moishe reappeared to tell the villagers what had happened. The Jews had been taken to Poland where the Gestapo, the German secret police, loaded them into trucks. The prisoners were driven to a forest, where they were forced to get out and dig huge graves.

The Gestapo then murdered the Jews and shoved them into the fresh graves. Somehow, Moishe had managed to survive.

Wiesel's village did not believe Moishe's story. The villagers thought he wanted pity or had lost his mind. Perhaps the truth was too terrible for them to believe.

Later in 1944, Wiesel and his family were rounded up with their neighbors and sent by cattle car to a **concentration camp** (a prison camp for those the Nazis considered enemies). Only then did Wiesel and his family and neighbors begin to sense the terrible reality of what came to be called the **Holocaust,** the slaughter of Jews and other peoples by Nazis during World War II.

The Final Solution

During Hitler's rise to power, one crucial plank in his political platform had been **anti-semitism** (violent prejudice against Jews). He and his advisors plotted what they called the **Final Solution.** First they planned to destroy the entire Jewish population of Germany, and then, of all Europe. As Hitler gained more power, he put his brutal ideas into action.

The Final Solution was only part of Hitler's dream of a "new order." Documents confiscated after the war show that he envisioned a Nazi-ruled Europe. A vast slave labor force would serve the Germans, whom he thought of as the "master race." People who were "undesirable" or "subhumans" would be

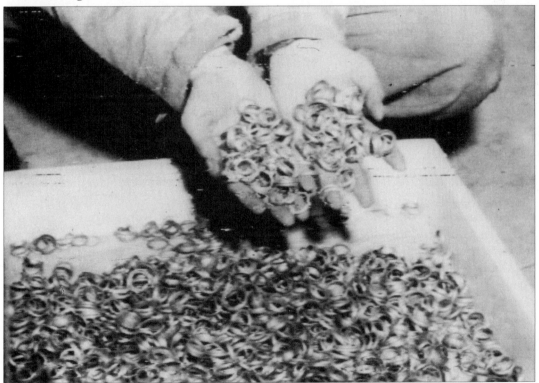

Part of Hitler's Final Solution called for the murder of millions of innocent men, women, and children. These rings were among the personal items stolen by the Nazis from the Jews they killed.

"eliminated." This category included Poles, Soviets, gypsies, the handicapped, and homosexuals, as well as Jews.

Auschwitz

Wiesel and his family were sent to Auschwitz, Poland, site of one of the most infamous death camps in history. Four huge gas chambers killed thousands of people each day. Experts estimate that two and one-half million people died in gas chambers there. At least 500,000 people there died of starvation, abuse, and disease during the war.

When Wiesel and his family arrived in Auschwitz, men were ordered to the left, women to the right. It was the last time Wiesel ever saw his mother and sisters. The male prisoners then filed past the notorious Dr. Joseph Mengele who used human beings as guinea pigs in hideous medical experiments. With the point of a finger, Mengele indicated which men would labor in the camp work force, and which would die.

"Never shall I forget that night, the first night in camp which has turned my life into one long night. . . . ," Elie Wiesel wrote in his autobiography *Night.* "Never shall I forget that smoke. Never shall I forget the little faces of the children whose bodies I saw turned into wreaths of smoke beneath a silent blue sky."

Under the Third Reich, **genocide** (deliberate murder of entire groups of people) became a massive industry. Germany's largest corporations competed to design and build efficient death camps. For example, the chemical company I.G. Farben developed Zyklon B, a crystal that could kill hundreds of people in a gas chamber within minutes. Prisoners direct-

ed to these chambers often mistakenly thought they were being led to showers.

Desperate Courage

When Wiesel was chosen to be a worker, a veteran prisoner told him, "You've already escaped the greatest danger—selection [death]. So now muster your strength and don't lose heart. . . . Have faith in life." During the war, Wiesel and other Jews drew on tremendous courage for day-to-day survival.

Such courage had been shown in the Warsaw ghetto uprising. In 1940, some 400,000 Polish Jews were sealed off within Warsaw's Jewish section. If they tried to leave, they were told they would be killed. Many died from hunger and disease. When some in the ghetto fought back, German tanks and artillery moved into the area. These brave Jews used what little ammunition they had to defend themselves. They hid in cellars and sewers and fought off the Nazis for four weeks. About 60,000 Jews lost their lives during this uprising.

In 1942 alone, the Nazis sent more than 300,000 Jews to concentration camps to be killed. In 1943, the remaining survivors of the Warsaw ghetto were slaughtered.

Crimes Against Humanity

The campaign to exterminate the Jews continued until the war ended in 1945. When Allied troops entered the concentration camps, they found piles of skeletons, and inmates nearly starved to death. People around the world reeled in horror.

After the war, some Nazis were brought to trial in Nuremberg, Germany, for their "crimes against humanity." There it was estimated that the Nazis had exterminated at least 5,700,000 Jews—one half of all

Jews in Europe— and six million other people.

　　Survivors such as Elie Wiesel have devoted their lives to educating others about this horrifying chapter of history. Wiesel has recorded his memories of how the Holocaust shaped the rest of his life: "One day I was able to get up, after gathering all my strength. I wanted to see myself in the mirror hanging on the opposite wall. I had not seen myself since the ghetto. From the depths of the mirror, a corpse gazed back at me. The look in his eyes, as they stared into mine never left me."

Hitler's defeat saved millions of people from certain death. When the war ended, American troops freed these rejoicing survivors of Dachau, a concentration camp in Germany.

CHAPTER CHECK

WORD MATCH
1. concentration camp
2. Holocaust
3. genocide
4. Final Solution
5. anti-semitism

a. violent hatred and prejudice towards Jews
b. where Nazis held as prisoners those considered enemies
c. the slaughter of the Jews by Nazis during WWII
d. deliberate murder of entire nation or ethnic group
e. Hitler's plan to destroy entire Jewish population of Europe

QUICK QUIZ
1. Describe the extent of Hitler's Final Solution.
2. What happened to the Jews of Warsaw's ghetto in 1940? How did they react?

THINK ABOUT IT
1. Why do you think the people of Elie Weisel's village refused to believe Moishe the Beadle? Do you think people today would believe such a story? Why or why not?
2. After the war, some Nazis were put on trial for "crimes against humanity." Why do you think the crimes they were accused of were called that? Do you think it was important to put some Nazis on trial? Why or why not?

5 "THIS IS NO DRILL"

December 7, 1941—U.S. sailors rescue a fellow seaman from the flaming water near the U.S.S. *West Virginia* following the Japanese attack on Pearl Harbor. President Roosevelt called it "a day that will live in infamy."

General Hideki Tojo (hih-DECK-ee TOE-joe) had been following a plan to take over most of Asia. Tojo was one of the proud military leaders who ran Japan. Tojo and other leaders thought Japan had a special right to rule Asia. Besides, Japan needed oil, tin, and rubber for its many factories. Asia had a large supply of such materials.

The plan to rule Asia had begun long before Tojo became Japan's **premier** (head of government) in 1941. It had started a full 10 years earlier. In September 1931, Japanese armies had marched into Man-churia, in northern China. In less than four months, they had complete control. Tensions between the Chinese and the Japanese worsened. In 1937, the two Asian powers went to war. By the end of 1940, Japan had marched into much of China, and the French colony of Indochina.

Embargo on Iron

U.S. leaders had grown more and more concerned. It seemed clear to many of them that the Japanese had to be prevented from taking more land. By 1940, the United States had stopped selling

AMERICAN ADVENTURES

scrap iron to Japan. The next year, 1941, it stopped selling the Japanese oil. Such a ban on commerce and trade is called an **embargo.** These U.S. embargoes set back Japanese plans.

The United States held peace talks with the Japanese in November 1941. The talks did not accomplish anything. The Japanese wanted a free hand in China. The United States wanted them out of China. Neither side would give in.

General Tojo secretly set November 25 as the last day for a peaceful agreement. After that, he planned to order the bombing of Pearl Harbor. Although Hawaii was not yet a state, Pearl Harbor was the main U.S. naval base in the Pacific. By smashing the U.S. Pacific fleet, Japan could grab whatever territory it wanted in Asia before the United States could strike back.

On November 26, a large Japanese fleet secretly sailed toward Pearl Harbor. A few days later, the Japanese admiral got a message. It said: "Climb Mount Nitaka." This was a code meaning, "Attack Pearl Harbor." In Washington, D.C., the Japanese ambassador continued to hold "peace" talks with the U.S.

Blips on a Screen

Japan set the date for the attack— Sunday, December 7, 1941. That Sunday morning, the weather over Pearl Harbor was clear. Two U.S. Army privates were watching their **radar** (device using

General Hideki Tojo (1848–1948), Japan's leader, approved the plan to attack Pearl Harbor. This move drew the U.S. into war.

radio waves to discover and locate moving objects) screen. This new equipment was supposed to spot planes from far away.

At 7:02 A.M., the men noticed a blip on the screen. This little spot on the radar screen meant that planes were approaching. The soldiers phoned their command post. The only man on duty there was new at his job. He said, "Don't worry." The blips were probably U.S. planes.

At 7:55, the first Japanese planes attacked and dropped their bombs. U.S. warships, lying in anchor along Battleship Row in Pearl Harbor, were easy targets. So were the planes neatly lined up on the airfields. Minutes later a Navy loudspeaker blared, "Air raid, Pearl Harbor. THIS IS NO DRILL."

Not everyone could hear the announcement. A few guessed that it was a Japanese attack. Others thought U.S. planes were bombing the place by mistake. Still others thought it was a practice drill.

Finally, the men on the ships realized that this was not a drill. The Japanese attacked ferociously. U.S. sailors climbed up ladders, trying to reach their battle stations. On some ships, they found the ammunition boxes locked. On shore there was great confusion, too. Despite the difficulties and complete surprise, many men fought bravely against the attackers.

A Base on Fire

By 10 A.M., it ended.

The last of the Japanese planes had left. The great U.S. base at Pearl Harbor was a burning wreck. When the smoke cleared, America learned of the devastation of the Japanese attack—2400 people dead and 1200 wounded. Besides inflicting a great loss of lives, the Japanese had sunk 18 ships, including the six largest ships in the fleet. They had destroyed 188 U.S. planes.

In just two hours, most of the U.S. Pacific fleet had been put out of action. Half the planes in Hawaii had been

Japanese Expansion to 1942

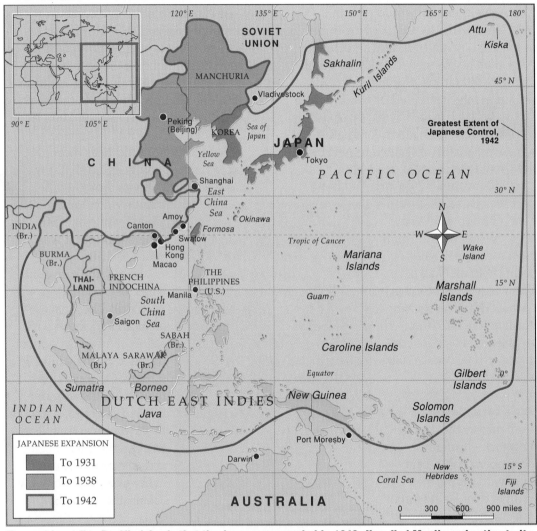

Name at least five Pacific islands that the Japanese occupied in 1942. Now find Manila and estimate its location using the latitude and longitude lines on your map.

AMERICAN ADVENTURES

destroyed. The Japanese had caught the United States completely off guard.

The next day, President Roosevelt called Congress together and reported the great damage done by the Japanese attack. He asked Congress to declare war on Japan. Within 40 minutes, the voting was over. The United States entered World War II.

These Imperial Marines were part of the powerful military force that Japan had built in just a few years. Japan's goal was to rule all of Asia, and to crush any opposition to its plan.

CHAPTER CHECK

WORD MATCH
1. embargo

2. Pearl Harbor

3. Asia

4. premier

5. radar

a. a head of government

b. continent Japan wished to rule exclusively

c. where Japan bombed U.S. Navy base in Hawaii

d. a ban on commerce and trade

e. device using radio waves to discover and locate moving objects

QUICK QUIZ
1. On what issue did the U.S. and Japan disagree? What was the Japanese goal?

2. What was the importance of Pearl Harbor to the U.S.?

THINK ABOUT IT
1. By 1941, the U.S. had stopped selling scrap iron and oil to the Japanese. Why do you think the U.S. did this?

2. When the Japanese attacked Pearl Harbor, there was no declaration of war between the U.S. and Japan. What do you think about one country attacking another by surprise, without a declaration of war?

"THIS IS NO DRILL"

6 THE WAR AT HOME

U. S. ARMY
OFFICIAL POSTER

SOLDIERS *without guns*

The people on the home front were an important part of the war effort. This World War II poster encouraged women to become part of the fight, and to help win the war by doing the jobs the men had left behind.

One Sunday afternoon in May of 1943, thirty-eight planes flew over Birmingham, Alabama, dropping 10,000 bombs. First aid workers rushed out to tend the wounded, and 40,000 civilians guarded their property. When the two-hour raid was over, Birmingham's civil defense leaders agreed. Their city was more than ready to face an attack by enemy forces.

The people of Birmingham never had a chance to find out if they were right. The Sunday afternoon raid was only a drill. The "bombs" dropped by Civil Air Patrol planes were made by schoolchildren who filled them with flour to simulate smoke. The "wounded" were Boy Scout volunteers covered with catsup "blood." Similar drills were held in cities all over the country. But neither Birmingham nor any other city on the United States mainland was ever actually bombed during World War II.

The real bombing raids and battlefields may have been far away in Europe, Africa, Asia, and the Pacific islands. But to Americans at home, the war was part of their everyday lives. The war often caused changes in their families and their work, the way they ate, and even where they lived.

Unequal Opportunities

Fighting the war required the labor of millions of people. About 12 million Americans joined the armed forces—more than twice as many as had served in World War I. The war industries demanded still more. Between 1941 and 1945, some 15 million Americans moved from their rural homes to seek jobs in shipyards, munitions factories, airplane factories, and other war-related shops. Even more found war jobs close to home.

The desperate need for workers led to expanding opportunities for some groups like African Americans, women, and the disabled, who had all been excluded from well-paying jobs before the war.

Because black men and women faced discrimination in the U.S. military, many of them sought jobs in the rapidly expanding war industries. Blacks served in all of the armed forces. The army accepted black soldiers, but segregated them in all-black units under the command of white officers. Still, by the end of the war, nearly three quarters of a million black soldiers were serving their country. White women were **recruited** (newly employed) for

Recycling became a major aspect of the war effort. These women sort empty toothpaste tubes so the metal can be reused.

clerical and nursing jobs in the military. But strict **quotas** (number of people of a particular race or gender allowed specific jobs) kept all but a few black women out of these jobs.

African Americans found far greater opportunities on the home front. In 1941, President Roosevelt ordered government agencies and manufacturers with defense contracts to stop racial discrimination. He created the Fair Employment Practices Committee (FEPC) to enforce this order. While the FEPC did not end discrimination, it did help black Americans get better-paying jobs while the war lasted. Thousands of blacks migrated to America's industrial cities where, as skilled workers, they could earn good wages, although never equal to those white workers earned.

Enter the Women

Black Americans were not the only ones who found new opportunities in war work. The federal government sponsored propaganda —newsreels, posters, magazine articles, even popular songs—to encourage women to take jobs in war industries. Women were hired to do all kinds of jobs that only men had done before the war.

An advertisement run by the Pennsylvania Railroad boasted of the kinds of jobs women were doing for the nation's railroads: "You see [women] . . . even in baggage rooms, train dispatchers' offices, in shops and yards and as section hands."

In the advertisements and newsreels, these women were portrayed as patriotic housewives who answered their nation's need for workers. They got their nickname, Rosie the Riveter, from the capable and efficient women workers in the film of the same name. In reality, three out of four women employed in war industries had also worked before the war. They were mostly maids, waitresses, clerks, or low-paid factory workers. War work brought them better-paying, more interesting jobs. Many women, both single and married, expected to continue to make use of their training as welders, pipe fitters, or electricians after the war. They wanted to support themselves and their families. But with the end of the fighting, the women were fired. Their jobs were given to returning veterans.

"Make It Do, or Do Without"

Wartime jobs brought many workers more money than they had ever had before. But there were fewer things to spend it on. Most raw materials went into the war effort, and people at home faced shortages and **rationing** (dividing up of goods during times of scarcity) of many basic supplies. Sugar, coffee, tires, gasoline, nylon, even shoes were hard to come by. The government issued ra-

tion coupons for all of these goods.

Even when goods weren't rationed, the government encouraged people to use less so the soldiers could have more. "Use it up, wear it out, make it do, or do without," became the slogan of the day. People took pride in showing how clever they could be about "making do." In a Rockford, Illinois school, students organized a "patriotic patches" club. Only those who wore patched hand-me-downs from an older brother or sister could join.

Using less of needed supplies was one way those at home could support the war. Another way was through **recycling** (treating materials to be used again). In communities all over the country, collection centers sprang up. Children and adults took part in drives to collect scrap iron, aluminum, rubber, and even kitchen grease, which could be used in making gunpowder for the war effort. Decorative iron fences, birdbaths, and lawn ornaments disappeared from some neighborhoods, to be melted down for bullets.

Part of "the war at home" involved forcing millions of Japanese Americans to live in desolate "relocation" centers like this one.

Victory Gardens and War Bonds

Just as during World War I, keeping food production high was a major concern. With so many farm workers in the armed forces, the federal government encouraged people to grow their own vegetables. "Victory gardens" sprang up all over the country. By the end of the war, almost a third of America's fresh vegetables came from these gardens.

People also showed their support for the war by buying war bonds. When Americans "bought" bonds, they actually were lending money to the government to help pay for the war. Movie stars promoted bonds and neighbors went door-to-door selling them.

Homelessness

Many people would later remember World War II as a time when everyone pulled together and made sacrifices without grumbling. In some ways this was true. But there were also many real problems and there was real suffering. Almost 50,000 of America's 185,000 doctors were in the Army, leaving the civilian population desperately short of medical care.

The great migration of workers to cities with war industry factories led to severe housing shortages. Men and women with well-paying jobs sometimes found themselves living in automobiles or tents while they searched for housing. Day-care facilities provided by the government were inadequate. It was difficult for women working in factories to find appropriate care for their children.

In some cities, black families arriving to work in defense plants faced hatred and resentment from the white population. In the summer of 1943, rioting of whites against blacks in Detroit resulted in the deaths of 34 people and the injury of 800 more.

After the War

With the war over, many Americans turned their hopes for security and the good life toward their private lives. After 20 years of insecurity and sacrifice, they wanted stability. For many, this meant a home and family. They began marrying younger and having more children, creating what we now call the **baby boom.**

CHAPTER CHECK

WORD MATCH
1. quotas
2. recruited
3. rationing
4. recycling
5. baby boom

a. newly employed
b. dividing up of goods during times of scarcity
c. treating or processing materials to be used again
d. the number of people of a particular race or gender allowed
e. sudden rise in birthrate after WWII

QUICK QUIZ
1. Name some of the wartime industries created by the U.S. involvement in World War II. How did the war change the face of the American work force?
2. What hardships did the war create for Americans at home?

THINK ABOUT IT
1. What was meant by, "Use it up, wear it out, make it do, or do without?" How do you think people would react to such an idea today?
2. Do you think that civilians should have been forced to give up their jobs after the war to returning veterans? Explain.

7 D-DAY AND KAMIKAZES

Just after midnight on June 6, 1944, Allied forces struck the coast of German-held France. Out of stormy weather and the chaos of battle, the Allies forged a victorious landing that turned the tide of the war.

In the spring of 1944, nearly three million Allied soldiers crowded into southern England. Some of the men had finished parachute training. Others had completed mock combat exercises. They were waiting for the order to invade France.

The Nazis were expecting the Allies to attack occupied France. The Allies, however, would have to cross the English Channel (body of water between Great Britain and France). Troops, tanks, ammunition, food, and medical equipment also had to be transported across the water, and landed right in front of the German Army.

There were other problems. In only a few harbors, could supplies be unloaded quickly and easily. Weather conditions and tides had to be exactly right. The Allies also ran the risk of the Germans learning of their plans.

These were chances General Dwight D. Eisenhower decided to take. Eisenhower, known as Ike, was the Allied commander. By the end of May, he knew that the tides would be best on June 5, 6, and 7. But storms were forecast for those days. Only the evening of June 5 might be clear. On that night, he sent the first wave of Allied

AMERICAN ADVENTURES

troops to the beaches of Normandy in France. Approximately 4000 ships carried 175,000 men. Planes and gliders carrying more men and equipment flew overhead. They covered 35 miles in their journey, arriving the next morning. This event would be known as **D-day** (the invasion of Western Europe by the Allies on June 6, 1944).

Disaster Day?

The crossing was rough. A storm blew in, and many boats and planes went off course in the fog and clouds. Many of the planes overshot their drop sites by two miles. Some of the men who parachuted out of these planes were completely lost. They didn't know the countryside, and the maps didn't always help. Some carried over 100 pounds of equipment and could not move, especially in marshy, flooded areas.

Anticipating an invasion, Nazi Field Marshal Erwin Rommel had ordered German machine-gunners to hide in the sand dunes. "As we went in toward the beach, there was no sign of life or resistance," remembered one soldier. "There was an intense quiet, so quiet that it was suspicious." Once the boats were in range, the Nazis opened fire.

Many of the boats were hit. Some soldiers had to disembark in very deep water and couldn't reach the shore. Some boats were ripped apart by German mines. Gradually, the remainder of the troops reached the shore, where land mines, iron

spikes, and rolls of barbed wire turned the fields of Normandy into deathtraps.

On June 6, at a landing site known as Omaha Beach, the Americans were attacked by a top German unit. "It seemed that everything went wrong," one soldier said. Another said, "It seemed we had entered hell itself. The whole beach was a great, burning fury. All around were burning vehicles, piled-up bodies. . . . The water was burning." The Americans gained little ground at Omaha Beach.

Allies Dig In

But as troops poured in, the Allies wedged their way onto French soil. The terrible confusion of the first days did not stop the flow of troops. Artificial harbors were floated into positions offshore so boats with supplies and troops could continue to dock.

Most important, Nazi resistance was not as strong as it might have been. Field

Dwight D. Eisenhower (1890–1969), Supreme Commander of Allied Forces, addresses troops just before they began their part in the D-day invasion.

Marshal Rommel had been in Normandy before the invasion, but the weather had been so bad that he was sure the invasion would be postponed. Just before the Allies landed, Rommel had left to meet with Hitler to discuss the Nazi defense.

When Hitler learned of the Allies' offensive, he was convinced it was a fake. He thought the real invasion would strike on another part of the coast. He refused to let Rommel take reinforcements back to Normandy. The landing was safe.

Soon after the successful landing, the Allies broke through German lines and chased the German army across France. In August, they liberated Paris from four years of German rule. In October, the weary Allies crossed the Rhine River into Germany and the end of the war seemed near.

War in the Pacific

Halfway around the globe, fighting continued in the Pacific. Both the Americans and the Japanese relied on air power. Fighter pilots bombed strategic targets and aircraft carriers were introduced as floating runways for the planes. By October 1944, when the war in Europe seemed near an end, the Japanese were in trouble.

The Pacific battles had been fierce and destructive. In the months after Pearl Harbor, the Japanese had conquered much of the Pacific region. Their conquests included the Philippines, Hong Kong, Indonesia, Indochina, and many small islands.

Not until June 1942, did the United States begin to change the course of the war. When the Japanese attacked the U.S. base on tiny Midway Island, the Americans were ready. They had stopped and decoded a secret Japanese message. U.S. ships sped to Midway's defense and American planes sank four Japanese aircraft carriers. The Battle of Midway, Japan's worst naval defeat of the war, halted the Japanese advance.

In February of 1943, the U.S. armed forces defeated the Japanese on Guadalcanal in the Solomon Islands. After Guadalcanal, the U.S. strategy was to move toward Japan by "island hopping." The Americans did not try to capture all of Japan's important outposts. Instead, they attacked certain islands that they could use as bases to advance closer toward Japan.

The strategy worked. By the spring of 1945, American forces were beginning to close in on Japan itself. The Japanese military commanders were growing desperate. There had to be some way to turn back the American forces. One Japanese admiral, Masafumi Arima, suggested **kamikaze** (aerial attack of an enemy ship in which pilot kills himself) to his commanders. But they did not approve his idea. On October 13, Arima decided his time had come. He aimed his plane into the U.S. aircraft carrier *Franklin.* More than 1000 sailors were killed or wounded.

Even though this first kamikaze flight did not destroy its target, the crash convinced Japanese commanders that kamikaze missions might work. The Japanese were running out of supplies and trained pilots. Unskilled pilots could be sacrificed to damage the enemy as much as possible.

In Japanese, kamikaze means "divine wind." Japanese leaders during World War II hoped that a new kind of kamikaze would push back the Americans. Kamikaze planes had enough fuel for pilots to reach their targets, but not enough to get them back to Japan. The pilots believed they would die with honor when they crashed their planes.

Japan's kamikaze pilots were a serious threat to Allied forces in the Pacific. This kamikaze attacker just missed crashing into the U.S.S. *Sangamon.*

At the Battle of Leyte Gulf in late October, the kamikazes sank only one destroyer. But American sailors in the Pacific realized they faced a new threat. At the fighting on Iwo Jima in February 1945, waves of kamikazes struck hard. They sank one aircraft carrier and 700 men were killed or wounded. Two months later, the Americans attacked Okinawa. The kamikazes attacked many ships, including the U.S. aircraft carrier *Bunker Hill.*

The Americans knew the kamikazes had to be stopped if America was going to take Japan. American bombers tried, but failed, to stop the kamikazes before they left the ground. Americans bombed kamikaze airfields, airplane factories, and the countryside. The American bombing missions continued, but the Japanese would not surrender.

CHAPTER CHECK

WORD MATCH

1. D-day

2. Guadalcanal

3. kamikaze

4. English Channel

5. Normandy

a. body of water connecting Great Britain and France

b. where U.S. defeated Japanese in the Pacific

c. the invasion of Western Europe by Allies on June 6, 1944

d. where U.S. troops landed to defeat Germans in France

e. aerial attack of an enemy ship in which pilot kills himself

QUICK QUIZ

1. What order did Hitler give to Rommel that had a great impact on the Allies' invasion of Europe?

2. Besides enemy defenses, what made D-day landing so difficult and dangerous?

3. After Pearl Harbor, the Japanese conquered much of the Pacific. What military event halted the Japanese advance in the Pacific?

THINK ABOUT IT

1. Why do you think the Allies chose to attack Europe where they did? Why do you think the Nazis expected them to do this?

2. Why do you think the kamikaze was such an effective weapon?

8 A-BOMB

This U.S. Air Force photograph shows the mushroom cloud over Hiroshima, Japan, three minutes after the A-bomb was dropped on that city. "My God, what have we done?" said a crewman on the *Enola Gay*.

At 7 A.M. on the morning of August 6, 1945, the people of Hiroshima (hear-uh-SHE-muh), Japan, began their day in the usual way. Some of them were eating breakfast. Others were on their way to work. Japan was still at war with the United States and its allies, but people did the same things they did on any other day.

Just then, air raid sirens sounded. The people of Hiroshima were not surprised. The warning sounded every morning when a U.S. weather plane flew over their land. So far, Hiroshima had been lucky. Almost every other large Japanese city had been bombed by Allied air raids. Hiroshi-

ma, with 245,000 people, had never been bombed. The people were beginning to wonder how long their luck would last.

Suddenly, the all-clear signal sounded. Japanese radar watchers had spotted three U.S. planes flying toward Hiroshima. Yet they did not believe it was a bombing raid. A raid usually included a larger group of planes.

Darkness After Dawn

Suddenly, at 8:15 A.M., a blinding flash of light cut across the sky. It was brighter than sunlight. The center of this great ball of light was as hot as the surface of the sun. A great column of heat and dust began to climb miles into the sky. Clouds of smoke and dust turned day into darkness.

What had happened? A U.S. plane, the *Enola Gay*, had dropped the first atomic bomb. The target hit was Hiroshima.

Such a bomb had been under development in the United States for four years. Scientists had begun their work in 1941. From the beginning, the project had been top-secret. After 1943, it had been carried out in a scientific and military unit known by its code name, the Manhattan Project.

Harry Truman knew nothing of the Manhattan Project until after he became president in April 1945. He learned then that the bomb would have more power than 20,000 tons of TNT. It would have more than 2000 times the power of the biggest dynamite bomb used so far. Truman did not interfere with the project. He and his top advisers thought that using the bomb might shorten the war.

Split the Skies

In mid-July 1945, the bomb was tested in the desert near Alamogordo (ah-lah-moe-GORE-doh), New Mexico. One observer described the test. "It was as though the earth had opened and the skies had split," he wrote. The test proved a success. A few days later, Truman gave temporary permission to use the bomb on Japan.

The Allies made one last attempt to end the war. Late in July, the United States, Britain, and China offered Japan new peace terms. Under these terms, Allied troops would occupy Japan. War criminals would be punished. Japan would not be enslaved or destroyed. Japan was told that its only other choice was "prompt and utter destruction." It would not surrender.

Japan's refusal sealed its fate. To top-level U.S. officials, the use of the bomb would mean fewer Americans would die than if the U.S. invaded Japan. A month earlier, the United States had driven the Japanese from the island of Okinawa (oh-kee-NAH-wah). In that fighting, 11,260 Americans and 160,000 Japanese had died. Any invasion of Japan itself promised to be even bloodier. No one could predict how long it would take to win.

So the United States dropped the bomb on Hiroshima. In the center of the city, almost every building was destroyed. The temperature rose so high that steel bubbled away as if it were boiling water. Burned-out streetcars and automobiles filled the streets. Even houses on the far edge of the city were badly damaged.

In a matter of seconds, the atomic bomb reduced most of the bustling city of Hiroshima, Japan, into a smoking wasteland.

Burials From the Blast

Thousands of people were buried alive in the ruins. Some were able to dig themselves out. Fires burned throughout the city. The people who had lived through the blast began to run from the blazing city. They were dazed and in shock. Many of them bled from their heads, chests, and backs. Some sat or lay down in the streets, vomited, and waited to die.

Soon the wounded began to crowd into hospitals. For many, there was no hope. Many doctors had been killed, and hospitals had been wrecked.

About two weeks after the blast, thousands of people suddenly became sick.

The Pacific Theater in World War II

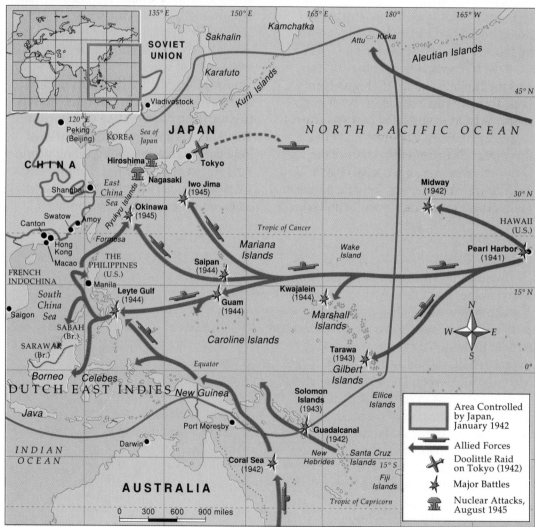

How far had the U.S. advanced into Japanese-occupied territory by October 1944? List the Pacific islands where battles took place during World War II.

AMERICAN ADVENTURES

Their hair began to fall out. They became weak with fever. Soon their gums bled, and red spots appeared on their skin. Old wounds opened up or would not heal. These people were suffering from a new disease—**radiation sickness.** Many died. In all, between 70,000 and 80,000 people died from the blast, or its effects, within a year. About an equal number were injured.

The Japanese kept on fighting after August 6. United States leaders grew more determined than ever to bring the war to an end. On August 9, the United States dropped a second atomic bomb. The target was the city of Nagasaki (nah-guh-SAH-kee). This city was also almost completely destroyed. On August 10, President Truman warned that more A-bombs would be dropped unless the Japanese surrendered.

On August 14, the Emperor of Japan said his country would surrender. After six years of fighting, World War II came to an end.

In February of 1945, Allied leaders Winston Churchill, Franklin D. Roosevelt, and Josef Stalin met in the Soviet seaport Yalta to make plans for post–war Europe.

Today, people in the United States and other countries argue over whether the United States should have dropped the bomb. Was the atomic bomb too horrible to drop even on enemies? Was it necessary to kill or maim so many civilians? Was the war really shortened? No matter how one answers these questions, all the worlds' people hope that these will be the last atomic weapons ever used.

CHAPTER CHECK

WORD MATCH

1. radiation sickness
2. Hiroshima
3. Manhattan Project
4. Nagasaki
5. Okinawa

a. city in Japan where U.S. dropped first atomic bomb
b. city in Japan where U.S. dropped atomic bomb that ended WWII
c. secret code name for unit developing the atomic bomb
d. caused by being subjected to an atomic explosion
e. island where U.S. defeated Japan in June 1945

QUICK QUIZ

1. Why did President Truman and his advisors think the Manhattan Project should be continued?
2. Describe the peace terms offered to the Japanese before the first A-bomb was dropped, and after the second bomb was dropped.

THINK ABOUT IT

1. Why do you think the Japanese refused to surrender after the first bomb? Do you think a second should have been used? Explain.
2. What consequences of using atomic weapons do you think were unforeseen by their advocates? You might want to do more research.

WORLD WAR II

History Detective

1. I played on the emotions of a whole country. I promised jobs, food, and power. While in prison I wrote of my plan to rebuild Germany. Who am I? What did I write?

2. We were the secret police who forced the German people to follow the ideas of the Führer. Who are we?

3. This policy allowed the U.S. to give the British needed weapons while still remaining free from fighting. What was this policy?

4. Due to a French and British deal made with Hitler, my mountainous land was given to Germany. This left me vulnerable to Nazi takeover. Where am I?

5. This technique of air battle convinced the U.S. that the Japanese would go to any length for victory. What is it?

6. I was the top secret project which changed history by producing a bomb 2000 times more powerful than any used before. What am I?

Voices From the Past

When Anne Frank was 13 years old, she went into hiding in a small attic at the back of a factory building in Amsterdam, Holland. She was one of a few lucky Jews able to hide from Nazi troops who were taking all Jews to prison camps. This was 1942, and the Holo-caust had begun. Anne and her family hid for two years before they were found. She kept a diary which has become very famous. Here is part of *Anne Frank: The Diary of a Young Girl.*

July 15, 1944: It's twice as hard for us young ones to hold our ground, and maintain our opinions, in a time when all ideals are being shattered . . . But I still believe people are really good at heart . . . I can hear the approaching thunder . . . and feel the sufferings of millions and yet, if I look up into the heavens, I think that it will all come out right, that this cruelty too will end, and that peace and tranquility will return again.

1. What do you think Anne meant by "approaching thunder"?

2. The Holocaust was disastrous for all Jews. What do you think Anne meant when she said that the young were effected the most?

Hands–On History

Being a Radio Reporter—During World War II, events happened very quickly. But for the first time the American public could be kept informed as history was being made. This was because of radio. Choose one of the events in this chapter—the Atomic bomb, fighting in the Soviet Union, Pearl Harbor, or D-day— and write a news bulletin that you could read on the air to the American public.

YESTERDAY'S NEWS

The American Adventures Newspaper

Spokane, Wash., March 17, 1942—A steady stream of proud Americans have gone to the courthouse and done their duty by registering with the Selective Service. Will they be drafted? Chances are good that they will be. Will they see action? That is doubtful. Only about 16% of those who volunteer or are drafted will see military action. The real task is for the government to train everyone—15 million all together. New soldiers have only three months to become prepared GIs. Later this year, women will also be recruited for the war effort. The Army's Women's Auxilary Army Corps (WACC) and the Navy's Women Accepted for Volunteer Emergency Service (WAVES) will fill clerk and typist positions to enable more men to fight in battle. The young people of Spokane and every community are rising to service when their country needs them!

2.

Who Will Do the Work at Home?

Detroit, Mich., August 3, 1943—The war has caused major changes in industrial America. Factories that used to make automobiles, toys, or appliances have now shifted to making war materials. So who will do all this work? The answer is: every able-bodied American. The work force has risen from 46 million to 53 million as women and older people have pitched in while our boys are off fighting—even some children have pitched in where possible! Industrial production in the U.S. has skyrocketed to an all-time high. Many wonder how life will change after the war when many people who hadn't worked before find they have money for the first time. **3.**

Movie Review of *Casablanca*

Hollywood, Calif., April 21, 1943—*Casablanca* may be the best picture to come along in several years. Humphrey Bogart and Ingrid Bergman give flawless performances as they try not to give in to their love for one another. The story is set in 1941, and the tension of the war is the background for the action, but Bogart hides from it all. "I stick my neck out for nobody," he tells Bergman. But he will have to stick his neck out to save her. This picture is an odds-on favorite for Best Picture of the Year, and maybe an all-time classic. Not bad, when you consider both Bogart and Bergman agree they "could not understand the storyline of the movie" when they were making it.

You Be the Reporter

Match each question with its news item above.

1. Write a title for this story.

2. Write a caption for this cartoon.

3. Finish this article by predicting what people might do with the extra money they make in the war, and how this will effect America.

SYNTHESIZING INFORMATION

Imagine that you and your family are suddenly ordered to leave your neighborhood, your school and friends, and most of your possessions for an unknown place. You have no idea when you can return home again. Perhaps most difficult of all, you will be living as a prisoner, even though you are innocent of any wrongdoing. That is what happened to many Japanese Americans during World War II.

In 1941, when Japan bombed Pearl Harbor, there were many people from Japan, or of Japanese background, living on the Pacific Coast of the United States. Although they were loyal to the United States, these people soon became mistrusted by many other Americans. In 1942, the U.S. government forced about 117,000 Japanese Americans, including about 70,000 **nisei** (U.S. citizens of Japanese origin), to leave their homes for relocation and **internment** (confinement) in special camps.

What was it like to be relocated as a Japanese American during World War II? To find out, read the following first-hand accounts of some Japanese Americans who personally lived through the experience. From their different stories, you can **synthesize** (pull together) some facts and details to form your own idea of what the experience was like.

Below, two Japanese Americans describe what it was like to be uprooted and sent away. Read both accounts and answer the questions that follow on a separate sheet of paper.

> *The government didn't tell us whether we would be able to come back or not. . . . So I told my wife that perhaps the best thing would be to sell our furniture and buy food and medicines and things like that. . . . We didn't know if there would be doctors or hospitals in the camp. So we took in as much medicine and baby food as possible.**

> *All we wanted to do was to be left alone on the coast. . . . My wife and I lost $10,000 in that evacuation. She had a beauty parlor and had to give that up. I had a good position worked up as a gardener, and was taken away from that. We had a little home and that's gone now.**

1. What detail in the first account tells you that this family included young children? What was this man's primary concern?

2. What were these relocated Japanese Americans forced to give up or leave behind? Be specific.

3. The Japanese Americans felt uncertain about what the camps would be like.
(a) Why do you think this was so?
(b) What statement from these accounts suggests this to you?

*From *Coming to America: Immigrants from the Far East* by Linda Perrin. Copyright © 1980 by Linda Perrin. Reprinted by permission of Delacorte Press, a division of Bantam, Doubleday, Dell Publishing Group, Inc.

Read the following three accounts of Japanese Americans describing what life was like in the internment camps. Then answer the questions that follow.

The . . . usual pattern of living was radically changed when the entire family was squeezed together in the same small room. . . tensions occasionally erupted into heated quarrels, emotional arguments, and petty bickering. . . .

. . . everything was rigidly regimented and monotonous: the same buildings, always the familiar surroundings, set hours for meals, regular routines, prescribed procedures, the next day the same as the one before. Daily existence was devoid of the pleasure of surprise. . . .*

The first thing we did in our camp—we built our churches. The Buddhist people got together and built their Buddhist church, and the Christian people built their own church. And the older nisei who were out of college or high school, they started teaching the children. And so we set up schools. . . . Pretty soon the young people started playing baseball . . . and it was just like outside. *

The barrack was built in such a way that there was no ceiling above each room—just one high ceiling. . . . When a person cannot have privacy, that is really bad. . . . When a lot of bread and vegetables were carted in in cardboard, you ought to have seen those people go after those cardboard boxes! They used them to make partitions so as to make a little privacy.*

4. What physical conditions made life in the camps difficult? Be specific.

5. How was life difficult emotionally for the internees (people in the camps)? How do you know?

6. What did the internees do to make life in the camps similar to the life outside?

7. What aspect of living in the camps do you think would have been the most difficult to endure? Explain your answer.

In December 1944, when the U.S. Army told them they were free to leave the camps, some internees were filled with doubts about the future. Here's how one woman described her family's reaction to the news:

In our family the response to this news was hardly joyful. For one thing we had no home to return to. Worse, the very thought of going back to the West Coast filled us with dread. What will they think of us, those who sent us here? How will they look at us. Three years of wartime propaganda—racist headlines, atrocity movies, hate slogans, and fright-mask posters—had turned the Japanese face into something despicable and grotesque. . . .**

8. How did this woman's family feel about returning to the West Coast? Why?

9. According to the writer, what had war-time propoganda done to the image of Japanese Americans?

10. What was it like to be relocated as a Japanese American during World War II? Explain in at least two paragraphs, using details from the first-hand accounts you've just read.

**Excerpt from *Farewell to Manzanar* by Jeanne Wakatsuki Houston and James D. Houston. Copyright © 1973 by James D. Houston. Reprinted by permission of Houghton Mifflin Co.

LOOKING AHEAD

The audience at the San Francisco Opera House rose to its feet. Applause and cheers filled the hall. But no opera singers were taking bows onstage. The cheers were for something else.

Americans had much to be happy for on this pleasant June night in 1945. The war with Germany was over. In the Pacific, the Japanese were being pushed back. The United States was now the strongest and richest country in the world. Peace was in sight.

During World War II, the Allies had laid plans for a new world organization. Now, in 1945, diplo-

With World War II behind them, Americans looked toward the future. This 1956 newspaper display showed how new technology could ease work and improve leisure time.

POST-WAR

1945   1950

1945
Harry S. Truman becomes president.

1948
Berlin Airlift

1948
Marshall Plan provides aid to war-torn Europe.

1949
North Atlantic Treaty Organization (NATO) forms.

1950
Korean War begins.

1953
Dwight D. Eisenhower becomes president.

AMERICA

UNIT 2

1955

1953
Korea and U.S. sign armistice.

1954
Chords record first rock 'n' roll song— "Sh-boom."

mats from 50 countries had just approved the charter of the United Nations (U.N.). They hoped the U.N. would help settle differences with words rather than guns.

The Cold War

No one could know, in June 1945, how difficult it would be to keep peace. Only a few months after World War II, the United States began quarreling with its ally, the Soviet Union. The two countries had entered a "cold war."

In this "war," Soviet and U.S. troops did not shoot at each other. Their war was one of words, threats, military buildup, and diplomatic actions. Both nations took part in an arms race—a race to see which could build the most powerful military forces. Both nations worked to win the support of governments around the world.

The Soviet Union and the United States had very different ways of life. In 1945, the communist Soviet government controlled almost all aspects of its citizens' lives. The government ran the educational and political systems and the economy. The Communist party was the only political party allowed. Many of the rights of American citizens, such as free speech, were denied to Soviet citizens. In the United States, however, most land and businesses were owned and controlled by private individuals or corporations.

In World War II, the United States and the Soviet Union had worked together to defeat Nazi Germany. When the war ended in 1945, the alliance began to fall apart. Soviet troops, who had driven the Germans from Eastern Europe, refused to leave. Josef Stalin, the Soviet dictator, wanted to make sure that communist governments came to power there. These actions angered the United States. The Allies had agreed earlier that the people of Eastern Europe would choose their own governments in free elections after the war.

U.S. leaders were very upset. The Soviet Union, however, had suffered massive death and destruction in two world wars. It wanted to be sure that it would not soon be threatened again. To ensure this, Soviet leaders saw to it that Eastern European countries had friendly governments. This policy was similar to the United States', which did not permit hostile governments in the Western Hemisphere. U.S. forces were placed in Latin America and the Caribbean after the war. Soviet armies stayed in Eastern Europe to keep it under Soviet control.

By 1946, disagreement between the United States and the Soviet Union had grown serious. That spring, British leader Winston Churchill said that the Soviet Union had lowered an "iron curtain" between Eastern and Western Europe.

President Truman decided to "get tough" with the Soviets. He said that the United States must be ready to "help free peoples" remain safe from communism. Truman's plan became known as the Truman Doctrine. It was part of a larger policy, called **containment,** to stop the spread of communism throughout the free world.

Dispute Over Germany

The next major area of dispute was Germany. At the end of World War II, Germany had been divided among the four main Allies. The city of Berlin was in the middle of the Soviet zone. Because Berlin had been the capital of Germany, it too was divided into four zones.

In 1948, the United States, Britain, and

France wanted to make Germany a united country again. To prevent this, the Soviets blockaded Berlin. They cut off all road and train traffic. The United States and Britain had to deliver essential supplies to Berlin by air until the Soviets lifted the blockade. The blockade occurred, in part, as a result of the formation, in 1949, of the North Atlantic Treaty Organization. NATO is an alliance of some Western European countries. After the blockade failed, the Western countries approved basic laws for the establishment of the Federal Republic of Germany (West Germany). East Germany was named the German Democratic Republic.

Fear of Communism

After a long civil war ended in China in 1949, communists took control of Asia's largest country. Soon afterward, the Soviet Union tested its first atomic bomb. Both events frightened many Americans. Some wondered where communists would strike next.

By 1950, fear of communism had many Americans believing that Soviet communists were conspiring to take over the United States. Some thought communists had entered every area of American life, from the local stores and factories to the national government. Hundreds of American citizens were wrongly accused of being communist supporters, disloyal to their country.

One U.S. senator even thought there were communist "traitors" in the U.S. government. Senator Joseph McCarthy of Wisconsin believed these traitors were doing everything they could to hurt the United States. McCarthy had no proof for his charges, but many people believed him.

In 1950, the Cold War turned "hot" in Asia. The armies of communist North Korea invaded non-communist South Korea. U.S. troops went to help the South. After the United States threatened the border China shared with North Korea, China entered the war. It took three years of fighting and more than 33,000 American deaths before a truce was reached.

No longer would the United States keep itself removed from the affairs of Europe and the rest of the world. Americans believed that they had to be prepared to fight anywhere on the globe to keep communism from spreading.

Post–War Changes

America changed after the war in other ways as well. The nation experienced great prosperity. The economy grew faster than ever before. Between 1945 and 1960, the amount of goods Americans produced more than doubled. Many people became wealthier than they

John D. Rockefeller's $8.5 million gift enabled the U.N. to buy land and build its world headquarters [above] in New York City.

had ever hoped to be.

Cities continued to grow, even though many people left their urban neighborhoods. By 1953, one out of five Americans had flocked to the suburbs. The suburbs offered a different style of life. People needed cars to get almost anywhere. Many people came into the city to work or shop, and returned to the suburbs at night. "Rush-hour" traffic jams became common.

Advertisers aimed many new products at consumers. Americans bought a new product—television sets. The emergence of

Less than five years after World War II ended, President Truman again sent U.S. troops to fight overseas. Tensions between communist and non-communist forces had exploded into war in Korea.

television contributed to the home-centered American lifestyle after the war. Older people began staying at home more for entertainment. Kids with cars looked for entertainment away from home.

The war had put many women to work. After the war, returning servicemen took many jobs away from women. Other women quit work to become full-time homemakers and mothers. Still, by the end of the 1950s, one third of all married women worked outside the home.

The post-war years seemed marked by

Europe After World War II

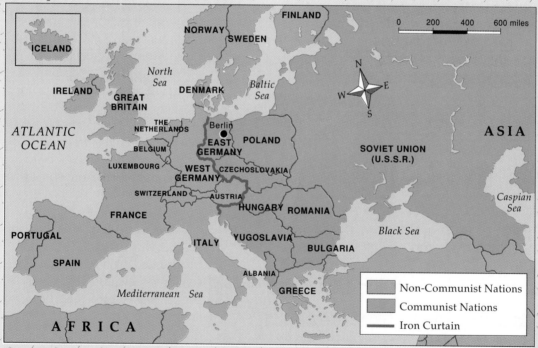

Which European nations had communist governments in 1949? Which had non-communist governments?

AMERICAN ADVENTURES

a desire for **conformity** (wanting to be like everyone else). Some people rebelled. Young people listened to rock 'n' roll musicians and created their own "youth culture."

Other Americans saw problems. They pointed out that the wealth of the 1950s was not shared by all Americans. Millions of Americans still lived in poverty. Many African Americans did not have full legal rights in many parts of the United States.

Other critics also had questions. How could a country with such great power and wealth be so afraid of a communist takeover? Were Americans too concerned with making money?

These questions had just begun to form in the 1950s. In the 1960s, they would become national issues.

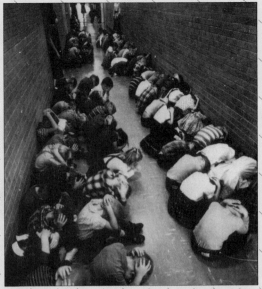
During the 1950s, schools held air raid drills like this one—in case the Soviet Union attacked.

NATO and Warsaw Pact Nations

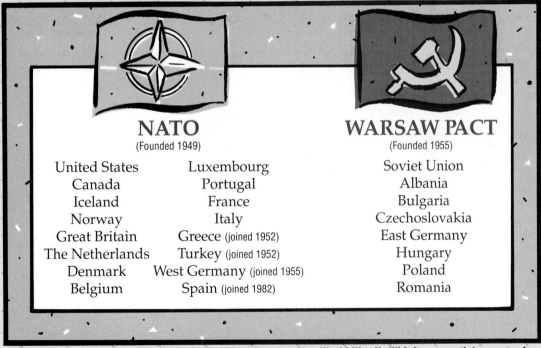

NATO
(Founded 1949)

United States	Luxembourg
Canada	Portugal
Iceland	France
Norway	Italy
Great Britain	Greece (joined 1952)
The Netherlands	Turkey (joined 1952)
Denmark	West Germany (joined 1955)
Belgium	Spain (joined 1982)

WARSAW PACT
(Founded 1955)

Soviet Union
Albania
Bulgaria
Czechoslovakia
East Germany
Hungary
Poland
Romania

Compare this chart with the map on page 636 of Europe after World War II. Which communist-governed European nation does not belong to the Warsaw Pact? Research this nation's history in your library to learn why it did not join the Warsaw Pact.

LOOKING AHEAD,

9 BERLIN AIRLIFT

The Brandenburg Gate, erected in 1791, is Berlin's most famous landmark. It stands just inside East Berlin near the east-west border. Before the Berlin Wall was built, this gate was the main crossing point for east-west traffic.

In 1948, West Berlin was in danger. Soviet troops had surrounded the city, cutting off supplies. Without daily shipments of food, coal, and medicine, the lives of two million people were in peril.

In June, the Soviets banned all railroad, highway, and canal traffic between the western zones of Germany and West Berlin. They also forbade the shipment of supplies from the Soviet zone into West Berlin. Without fresh supplies, the people of West Berlin would be reduced to hunger and misery within a month. The Soviets feared even a partially restored Germany. Josef Stalin believed that the **blockade** (shutting off an area to stop communication and trade) would force the United States, Britain, and France to give up their plans for a West German state. At least, he could force the three countries out of Berlin.

There remained one way that supplies could reach the city—by air. A written agreement with the Soviet Union in 1945 had given the Western Allies the right to use three air lanes over the Soviet zone leading into Berlin. On June 25, General Lucius D. Clay, commander of the U.S. forces in Germany, ordered an **airlift** (system of carrying supplies when ground routes are cut off) of food, coal, and other supplies into West Berlin.

Division of Germany

In 1948, a dispute concerning Germany almost brought about a war between the United States and the Soviet Union. After its defeat in World War II, Germany was divided into four **zones of occupation** (areas of a country controlled by the military) by the United States, Great Britain, France, and the Soviet Union. The former capital of Germany, Berlin, was also divided into four zones. But Berlin was deep

inside the Soviet zone. It was separated from the Western zones by more than 100 miles of Soviet-controlled territory.

In March 1948, as part of the formation of NATO, the United States, Britain, and France announced plans to unite their zones. They did not want Berlin to be controlled by the Soviets, even though it was in Soviet-controlled territory. The Western powers set up a separate West German government.

Berlin Airlift

No one really believed that the blockade could be defeated with supply shipments by air. When asked about the airlift, Clay snapped his fingers and said, "I wouldn't give you that for our chances."

Divided Berlin

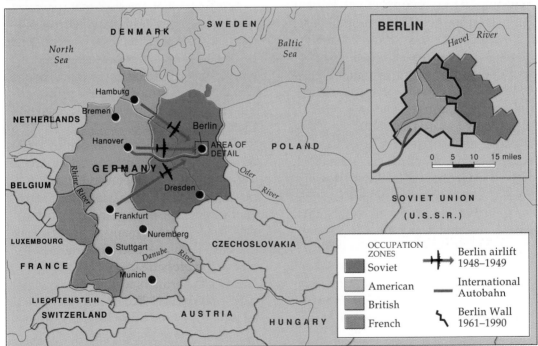

Germany was divided among the Allies after World War II. So was the city of Berlin. Berlin lay deep within the Soviet zone. In 1948, the Soviet Union set up a blockade to prevent the Allies from moving in and out of Berlin. What nation(s) controlled the western part of the city? What nation(s) controlled the eastern part?

West Berlin needed huge amounts of supplies to keep going. Before the blockade began, about 13,500 tons of food and other goods arrived each day by truck and by rail. Even if the people of West Berlin used dehydrated foods, U.S. experts estimated that they would need 4500 tons of food a day to avoid starvation.

This job was far beyond the means of Clay's tiny air force. He had only about 100 transport planes. Most of them were old, twin-engine planes that could carry no more than two and one half tons of cargo at a time. On the first day of its operation, the airlift flew only 80 tons of supplies into West Berlin's Tempelhof (TEM-pel-hof) Airport.

The next day, Clay asked President Harry S. Truman for help. Truman responded quickly. He ordered the U.S. Air Force and Navy to give the airlift their full support. From all over the world, U.S. planes flew toward Germany. These larger planes could each carry up to 10 tons of cargo. In all, about 225 such planes arrived in Germany. The British Royal Air Force also sent planes to help.

One British pilot described the first days of the airlift this way:

As more planes and crews arrived, the airlift began expanding rapidly. Planes were flying around the clock. By July 11, the daily average of deliveries was over 1100 tons. By September 18, it reached nearly 7000 tons. But this astonishing success created problems. Air Force bases were so overcrowded that pilots had to share the same beds, sleeping in five-hour shifts. There were not

The Soviet Union was determined to keep control of its sector of Berlin. East Berliners had staged strikes that had nearly shut down industry in the area. In June 1953, Soviet tanks moved in to break up rioting by German protesters.

enough mechanics or spare parts. One plane was flown for three days without a door.

At Tempelhof, the steel-mat runways were falling apart from the constant landings and takeoffs. But the airport could not be closed for repairs because the city would starve. So each time a plane landed, work crews swarmed over the runway. They beat the mats back into place before the next plane landed.

Every 90 seconds, a plane either landed or took off in Berlin. Strict air discipline was essential. If a pilot failed to land his plane on the first try, he could not circle for another attempt. He had to fly his plane back to western Germany and start again.

West Berlin needed a new airport to relieve the pressure. A site was chosen, and 17,000 Berliners went to work with picks and shovels. But the workers needed bulldozers and other heavy equipment that could not fit in the planes.

A team of experts in Frankfurt, West Germany, cut up the big machines and flew them to West Berlin, where they were reassembled. Before long, 81 bulldozers, rock crushers, and tractors were at work. By November, the new airport was in operation.

The endless roar of planes became a normal part of life in Berlin. A favorite pastime of Berlin children was to go to Tempelhof Airport and watch the planes land—especially after American pilots had dropped candy attatched to tiny parachutes from their planes.

Blockade Cracks

On April 16, the airlift flew over 12,900 tons of supplies into West Berlin. By this time it was clear to Soviet leaders that the blockade had failed. The Soviet Union agreed to call it off without any conditions. The Western Allies would again have free access to Berlin. On May 12, 1949, the blockade ended, 321 days after it

began. By that time, the airlift had flown in more than 1,500,000 tons of supplies in nearly 200,000 flights.

The Berlin airlift was costly. The United States and its allies spent $200 million to keep it going, and 55 airmen lost their lives in plane accidents. But West Berliners did not starve, nor did West Berlin fall under Soviet control.

The Berlin airlift flew in enough food and fuel to enable West Berliners to resist Soviet attempts to take control.

CHAPTER CHECK

WORD MATCH
1. blockade
2. zones of occupation
3. airlift
4. Berlin
5. Tempelhof

a. system of transporting supplies when ground routes are cut off
b. former capital of Germany
c. shutting off an area to stop communication and trade
d. areas of a country controlled by the military
e. West Berlin's airport where airlifts landed

QUICK QUIZ
1. What four nations controlled Germany after World War II? In which zone was Berlin located?
2. What was the purpose of the Berlin airlift? Did it succeed?

THINK ABOUT IT
1. How were the actions of the Soviet Union and the United States during the blockade and airlift typical of the Cold War?
2. What did British leader Winston Churchill mean by an "iron curtain"? How do you think such a label affected the Cold War?

10 THE HUNT FOR COMMUNISTS

During the 1950s, Senator Joseph McCarthy [above, at map] led a campaign to clear the nation of "disloyalty". His witch hunt tactics ruined the careers and lives of many innocent Americans.

After World War II, fear of communism gripped the United States. To many Americans, it appeared that the United States, the most powerful country in the world, was losing the Cold War. How was it possible? Were traitors within the United States to blame? President Harry Truman responded to those fears with a crackdown against communists in the United States.

In March 1947, Truman issued an Executive Order calling on the Federal Bureau of Investigation (FBI) to investigate the loyalty of all federal employees. Persons whose loyalty was doubted would be fired.

Later, the U.S. Attorney General issued a list of 90 organizations that were considered disloyal. Membership in any one of them was enough to arouse suspicion that a person was a communist.

These measures increased the hysteria over communist infiltration in the government. In 1948, a former state department official, Alger Hiss, was accused of spying for the Soviet Union during the 1930s. Hiss denied the charge, but after two long trials he was convicted in January 1950, of **perjury** (lying under oath). He was sentenced to five years in a federal prison.

The verdict against Hiss convinced even more people that the U.S. government was riddled with dangerous communists. It did not matter that the Hiss case was concerned with events that had taken place during the 1930s.

McCarthy's Rise

At this time, a senator from Wisconsin, Joseph R. McCarthy, began to play upon the fears of many Americans. In 1946, McCarthy was elected by a large margin to the Senate as a Republican. Part of his success was due to false claims he made about his record in World War II. McCarthy had served as a Marine intelligence officer in the Pacific. Most of his work was done at a desk. He did fly on several bomber missions, but only as an observer who sat in the tail gunner's seat. His slogan was: "Congress needs a Tail Gunner." McCarthy took Wisconsin by storm.

By 1950, however, his career seemed to be on the skids. There was ample evidence that McCarthy had struck up friendships with lobbyists for special interest groups. His defense of Nazi soldiers convicted of murdering U.S. prisoners during World War II made headlines. The Nazis claimed that they had been tortured by Army officers into making confessions. A Senate committee later cleared the Army of this charge.

Now McCarthy

Not everyone favored McCarthy's efforts. These protesters were among the many who opposed the jailing of Americans accused of disloyalty.

needed an issue to restore his political fortunes. He began his new career as an anti-communist watchdog on February 9, 1950. That day he spoke to a Republican women's group in Wheeling, West Virginia, about the Cold War. The danger to the United States, he said, came chiefly from "the traitorous actions of those who have been treated so well by this nation." This was especially true, he said, of people in the State Department where foreign policy was executed. Then he held up a piece of paper and declared:

I have here in my hand a list of 205 [persons] who were known to the secretary of state as being members of the Communist party and who nevertheless are still working and shaping the policy of the State Department.

Later, however, McCarthy made conflicting statements about the accusation. He declared that what he had really said was that there were 205 "bad risks" in the State Department. This might include others besides communists. Soon after, the figure of 205 was crossed out on copies of his speech and the number 57 inserted instead. He claimed that he had a list of the 57, but he ignored reporters' requests for a copy of it.

Despite the confusion, McCarthy was making headlines and his charges could not be ignored. An investigation was begun by a Senate committee. McCarthy named several people who, he said, had "communist affiliations" and had penetrated the government. He was unable to prove, however, that any of them were, in fact, communists. His method was simply to link them to organizations that may have had some communist members, or had been branded as "communist fronts." This was the technique of "guilt by association." It assumed that anyone associated with such groups had to be communist.

The House Un-American Activities Committee (HUAC) investigated the Hollywood film industry. HUAC was determined to find communists at any cost. The slightest hint of favoring the communists was seen as a disloyalty to America. Very little could actually be proven about someone's loyalty, but many careers were destroyed. These "witch hunts" were similar to McCarthy's investigations of government employees.

McCarthyism

In time, the reputations and careers of many innocent people were ruined by McCarthy's reckless charges. His technique came to be known as **McCarthyism.** It is defined by one dictionary as "public accusation of disloyalty . . . in many instances unsupported by proof or based on slight, doubtful, or irrelevant evidence."

The Senate committee issued its

The 1954 Army–McCarthy hearings [above], telecast live across the nation, exposed the unfair tactics that McCarthy used to brand people as communist traitors.

report in July 1950. A majority of its members, who were Democrats, agreed that "the charges made by Senator McCarthy were groundless and that the Senate and the American people had been deceived."

Such criticism did not stop McCarthy. Many people believed what he had to say and regarded him as a hero. As time went on, he became even bolder. In June 1951, he attacked General George C. Marshall, who had been the U.S. chief of staff in World War II. Later Marshall became secretary of state under President Truman. He held that office when communist forces triumphed in China, despite massive U.S. aid to the opposing Nationalist government forces. McCarthy saw the communist victory as "the product of a conspiracy" to deliver the world to communism. At the center of this conspiracy, he placed General Marshall. The attack on Marshall, whom President Truman called "the greatest living American," was proof that no one was safe from McCarthyism. McCarthy accused Presidents Franklin D. Roosevelt and Harry S. Truman of "20 years of treason."

Senate Hearings

Re-elected to the Senate in 1952, McCarthy continued to make reckless charges against all those he considered "disloyal." Government leaders who disliked McCarthy generally were afraid to speak out against him. They did not want to be accused of siding with communists.

In 1954, McCarthy took on an organization that was not afraid to fight back—the U.S. Army. That year, the Army gave an honorable discharge to a dentist who had refused to answer questions about his political beliefs. But McCarthy wanted the man **court-martialed** (brought to trial in the military system). He then questioned General Ralph W. Zwicker, a World War II hero, to find out who was responsible for discharging the dentist. When Zwicker appeared uncooperative, McCarthy told Zwicker that he was "a tremendous disgrace to the Army."

Soon after, the Army struck back. It accused Senator McCarthy of seeking favored treatment for one of his aides, who had just been drafted. McCarthy accused the Army of "blackmail." Finally, a Senate committee held hearings on the Army's charges. The hearings were shown on national television and were watched by millions of Americans for weeks. Most of them did not like what they saw. McCarthy was exposed at his worst—disrupting the proceedings, bullying witnesses, insulting fellow senators, introducing fake evidence, and ruining the reputation of innocent people.

It did not matter that the committee was divided in its report on the Army's charges. What mattered was that Americans had seen McCarthy in action. McCarthy's popularity dropped sharply after the hearings.

Even before the committee's report was issued, the Senate moved to curb McCarthy. A 1954 resolution condemned him for conduct "contrary to senatorial traditions." McCarthy was disgraced. He continued to make speeches, but few listened to him any more, and no one feared him. His four-year reign of terror was over.

In a few years, Joseph R. McCarthy gained tremendous power —then met ruinous defeat.

CHAPTER CHECK

WORD MATCH
1. George C. Marshall
2. perjury
3. Alger Hiss
4. McCarthyism
5. court-martialed

a. brought to trial in the military system
b. State Department official accused of spying for the Soviet Union
c. lying under oath
d. public accusation of disloyalty, often unfounded
e. secretary of state accused of supporting communism in China

QUICK QUIZ
1. What was the purpose of loyalty investigations during the Truman administration? How did they lead to hysteria?
2. How did Senator Joseph McCarthy use fear of communism to further his desired political objectives? What finally stopped him?

THINK ABOUT IT
1. Why do you think Senator McCarthy was so successful at first? What do you think is the best way to deal with accusations like the ones he made?
2. Do you think any restrictions should be placed on Americans whose political beliefs differ strongly from the majority of their fellow citizens? Explain.

11 WAR IN KOREA

This U.N. guard patrols non-communist South Korea's side of the demilitarized area on the 38th parallel. The building in the background is a border station for communist North Korea. Tensions between the two regions erupted into war in 1950.

Orange flames lit the Korean sky at 4 A.M. on June 25, 1950. Loud explosions shook the ground. The army of communist North Korea was attacking South Korea, using Soviet-made tanks and guns.

Korea had been divided into North and South since the end of World War II. North Korea was communist, while South Korea (the Republic of Korea) was anti-communist. North Korean leaders wanted to unite the country by force.

President Harry S. Truman heard the news at his home in Independence, Missouri. He boarded his plane, the *Independence,* and flew back to Washington, D.C. For most of the flight, Truman remained alone. He wanted time to consider what had happened—and what might happen next.

Less than a year earlier, communists had come to power in mainland China. This development shook many Americans. Some members of Congress criticized Truman for being "soft" on communism. They urged a "get-tough" policy in Asia.

AMERICAN ADVENTURES

Korea was seen as less important to the defense of the United States than some other countries. Although the government of South Korea was not communist, it was not democratic either. The U.S. government also suggested that Korea was outside the area of U.S. vital interests. This seemed to signal that it would not send U.S. troops into the conflict.

On the other hand, the Republic of Korea had been established by the United Nations. If North Korea succeeded in its attack, the U.N. would suffer a serious blow. Moreover, President Truman felt that if the United States did nothing to stop the attack, the communists might try to take over other countries.

Taking Action

Truman ordered U.S. planes and Navy ships to help South Korea. He said nothing about sending soldiers.

The Security Council of the United Nations had already called for an end to the fighting. Truman's aides put pressure on the Council to go still further. The Security Council passed a U.S. resolution calling on member-nations to help South Korea.

More pressure for sending troops came from General Douglas MacArthur, a World War II hero and the U.S. commander in Japan. He told Truman that U.S. troops would be needed to save South Korea. Truman learned of MacArthur's warning shortly before 5 A.M. on Friday, June 30. By noon, he had made up his mind. He ordered General MacArthur to send U.S. troops to help South Korea. Later, other members of the United Nations sent small forces. Although the army was made up mostly of U.S. soldiers, it was called the U.N. Army.

Punishing the Enemy

The Korean War was a seesaw fight. At first, the North Koreans drove troops far into South Korea. But near Pusan (POO-sahn), the American and South Korean troops stopped the advance. General MacArthur came up with a daring plan. United Nations troops would land at Inchon (IN-chahn), behind North Korean lines. The result was that the North Korean army was caught in a trap. Many of its soldiers gave up. The U.N. forces then raced north to the 38th parallel, the line dividing North and South Korea. President Truman ordered MacArthur to cross the 38th parallel to destroy the North Korean army.

Communist China warned that it would not sit by if North Korea was invaded. MacArthur told Truman that China was bluffing, and U.N. forces advanced

Although the U.S. never declared war on Korea, more than 54,000 Americans died there in fighting. Here, U.N. forces in Korea aid a U.S. infantry by firing on the enemy.

into North Korea. By November 21, they reached the Yalu River (the border between communist China and North Korea). Chinese troops had already begun to help the North Koreans. On November 26, the Chinese and North Koreans began a major attack. In bitter cold weather, they routed the U.N. forces out of North Korea and drove them back into South Korea. There wasn't enough food or medicine. Many U.S. soldiers were either killed, wounded, or severely frozen.

The Korean War, 1950–1953

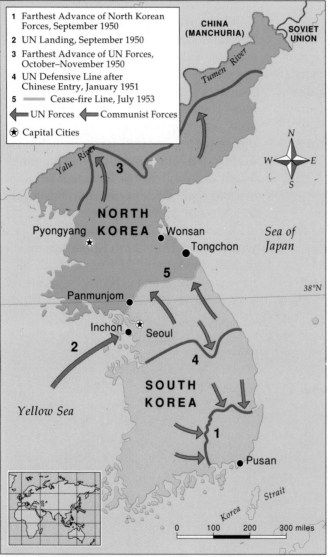

The Korean War front seesawed back and forth until June 1951. Which side controlled Seoul in August 1950? In November 1950? In February 1951? In July 1953?

Feuding Over Policy

General MacArthur wanted to bomb bases inside China. President Truman and his advisers were against this. They were afraid such an action might lead to a third world war. They thought that if the United States bombed China, the Soviet Union —China's ally—would probably attack the United States.

MacArthur argued hard for bombing China. He wanted to win completely in Korea. "There is no substitute for victory," he said. Finally, on April 11, 1951, Truman fired MacArthur for publicly disagreeing with him. Many people in the United States were angry with Truman. As president, however, Truman was commander-in-chief of the U.S. armed forces. He believed it was his duty to maintain control of the military.

Meanwhile, U.S. troops began advancing north again. By June 1951, the battle line was a few miles north of the 38th parallel. Then the war came to a stalemate—neither side could win a decisive victory.

Reaching a Truce

By the early summer of

1951, all the big nations were ready for a truce in Korea. Peace talks soon began, and they dragged on for two years. The fighting did not stop until July 27, 1953.

Even then, no final peace came to Korea. Soldiers continued to stand guard along the demilitarized zone that separated the North from the South. From time to time, shooting still broke out along the border. U.S. ground troops remained in South Korea to guard against any future attack.

In 1977, President Jimmy Carter set forth plans for removing these troops. By doing so, he hoped to avoid getting the United States involved in another ground war in Asia. Carter and his advisers hoped to have all U.S. ground troops out of South Korea by 1982. But U.S. troops remained in South Korea, and other forms of U.S. aid continued.

The Korean War caused many deaths and great damage. More than a million Korean civilians were killed. Several million lost their homes. The armed forces of both North and South Korea also suffered heavy losses. The United States alone had more than 33,000 dead and more than 100,000 wounded. Neither side could say it had won the war.

Korean civilians—innocent bystanders in a clash between world powers—suffered the most.

CHAPTER CHECK

WORD MATCH
1. North Korea   **a.** boundary between North and South Korea
2. South Korea   **b.** a division of the U.N. responsible for keeping peace
3. Security Council   **c.** boundary between Korea and China
4. 38th parallel   **d.** the anti-communist Republic of Korea
5. Yalu River   **e.** communist portion of Korea that wanted to unite entire country

QUICK QUIZ
1. How and why was the United Nations involved in the Korean conflict? What was the role of the United States?
2. What was resolved in the Korean War? What were the casualties?

THINK ABOUT IT
1. What did General MacArthur mean when he said there is "no substitute for victory"? Do you agree?
2. What do you think might have happened if President Truman had allowed China to be bombed in 1951?

12 THE SUBURBAN DREAM

Could the suburbs be the new paradise? During the 1950s, many Americans hoped so. Young families left the cities by the thousands and moved into new homes like this one in Levittown, New York.

A cold March wind was blowing across the potato fields of Long Island, New York. The gray sky threatened to bring snow. But on this raw day in 1949, more than 1000 people stood in line outside a small building. Some had been there for four days. They were anxiously waiting for William J. Levitt, a successful home-builder, to open his sales office.

Levitt was doing something unique. In the past, homes in **suburbs** (developed living areas on the outskirts of cities) were built a few at a time, and they were costly. But Levitt had developed a revolutionary way of mass-producing homes so they could be built inexpensively and sold at affordable prices.

Assembly-Line Houses

First, Levitt bought 1200 acres of farmland near Hicksville, Long Island. After the land was cleared, trucks moved rapidly over newly made roads. Every 100 feet, they stopped and dropped off identical bundles of lumber, bricks, pipes, shingles, and copper tubing. Near the bundles, giant machines scooped out narrow trenches around rectangles measuring 25 by 32 feet.

This took just 13 minutes. Then trucks loaded with cement poured four-inch foundations in the rectangles for each house.

Then workers in crews of two or three each did a special job—laying bricks, raising beams, painting, and shingling. This combination of workers and machines made it possible to build homes faster and more cheaply than ever before.

Now even Americans with limited incomes could afford to move from cities to suburbs like Levittown. In time, 17,300 homes were built on the Long Island site. They were divided into neighborhoods, each one with a school, a playground, and a swimming pool at its center.

Mass production enabled Levitt to sell his homes for as little as $7000, with no money down, and $65 a month in house payments. (Today they are each worth $175,000 or more.) The houses looked almost identical, but buyers didn't mind. The price was right. Soon after, two more Levittowns were built, one in Pennsylvania followed by another in New Jersey.

Life in Levittown

Levittowns were one answer to the severe shortage of housing that existed after World War II. During the war, hardly any new homes were built. Returning servicemen and their families often had to live with relatives. Some lived in old army barracks, garages, and even cars. The prospect of owning their own homes in Levittown communities appealed to them strongly.

Were they disappointed with life in these suburbs? Did they find it dull? Did they find that they had traded old problems for new ones? One person who tried to answer these questions was Herbert J. Gans, a sociologist who lived in Levittown, New Jersey, during its early years. Gans questioned his neighbors at great length and wrote about them in a book called *The Levittowners.*

Gans found that most of the Levittowners who began moving in from 1958 to 1960 were young couples who needed more space to raise their children. One out of five couples had three children, and one out of ten had four or more.

Large families were the rule in the 1950s when the country was having a "baby boom." Between 1950 and 1960, the U.S. population soared from 151 million to 179 million. Levittown houses were designed with children in mind. Each house had three or four bedrooms, each large enough to serve as a playroom as well.

Few Levittowners missed city life. One of them spoke for most Levittowners when she said, "We like quiet things —visiting neighbors, sitting out front in summer, having people drop by."

This feeling about Levittown was not shared by its teenagers. For some of them, Levittown

Vast tracts of suburban land were developed into ideal neighborhoods of row after row of identical homes.

was "endsville." Their most common complaint was that there was "nothing to do after school." But teenagers could go to luncheonettes, shopping centers, community centers, or bowling alleys.

A major complaint of the teenagers was the lack of transportation to meet friends after school or go outside Levittown.

Suburban Problems

Levittown offered fresh air, and the pleasures of backyard barbecues and gardening. But those who came to Levittown hoping to find a trouble-free community were disappointed.

Some of the problems that arose in Levittown stemmed from conflicts between people with different backgrounds. Most of them were members of the lower-middle class or the working class. They held **white-collar** (office) jobs in Philadelphia offices, or **blue-collar** (factory) jobs in the area. Some Levittowners were members of the middle class. They were mainly teachers, social workers, and a few doctors and lawyers.

Another problem that caused bitter disputes among Levittowners had to do with racial desegregation. Neither of the first two Levittowns sold homes to blacks. Would Levittown, New Jersey, which opened in 1958, also discriminate against them? William Levitt told reporters that he personally sympathized with minorities. But, he said, "Most whites prefer not to live in mixed communities." This was a typical defense of segregation at the time. Levitt feared that if he integrated the new Levittown, it would hurt the sale of homes to whites.

Urban Growth, 1950–1960

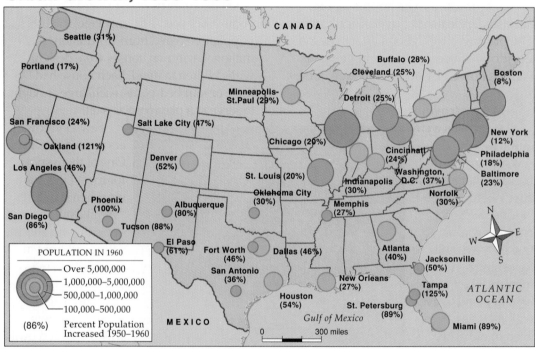

Which U.S. city experienced the highest percentage increase in population between 1950 and 1960? By what percent did Oklahoma City's population grow between 1950 and 1960?

While people in suburbs [above left] enjoyed barbecues in their own backyards, city life was much different. In many urban areas [above right] the poor lived in slums, like this one in Cleveland, Ohio, and had few comforts.

Some Levittowners supported integrating the community, but others strongly opposed it. Before long, two black families went to court to force Levittown to sell them homes. They charged that keeping out blacks violated the state's law against discrimination. Until then, the law was seldom enforced.

To avoid a long court battle and bad publicity, Levitt decided to desegregate voluntarily. In June 1960, the first black families moved in quietly, without any fuss. Integration was successful in Levittown. Other builders also decided to integrate. Civil rights laws in the 1960s made it illegal to discriminate against blacks. In time, more and more blacks would come to share the American dream of owning a home in the suburbs.

CHAPTER CHECK

WORD MATCH
1. Herbert J. Gans
2. blue-collar
3. William J. Levitt
4. suburbs
5. white-collar

a. describing jobs in industry, such as factory jobs
b. creator of mass-produced, low-cost housing
c. developed living areas on the outskirts of cities
d. describing jobs in offices
e. sociologist who wrote *The Levittowners*, describing life in these communities

QUICK QUIZ
1. What techniques allowed builders to keep prices moderate in Levittown? What other facilities did the builders provide?
2. What triggered the growth of the suburbs in the 1950s? What family trend determined the size of many new houses?

THINK ABOUT IT
1. What problems did city dwellers leave behind when they moved to the suburbs? What problems did they take with them?
2. How is the housing crisis of the 1950s like the housing crisis of the 1990s? How is it different?

13 TV'S GOLDEN ERA

Television first took hold in America during the 1950s. Lucille Ball and Milton Berle, the queen and king of TV comedy, kept millions of people at home—a fundamental change in Americans' lifestyle.

On January 19, 1953, Lucy Ricardo gave birth to a son. She named him Ricky, Jr. Lucy's husband was also called Ricky, and they were seen on television by millions of people every Monday night on the "I Love Lucy" show.

Although the Ricardo characters were fictional, their impact on the television viewing public was so great that about one million fans sent gifts, telegrams, and letters. Many even telephoned the television network to congratulate Lucy on the birth of her TV son (and the birth of her real-life son).

"I Love Lucy" went on the air in October 1951, with actress Lucille Ball playing the part of Lucy, a funny, lovable, redheaded housewife with a penchant for getting into hopelessly confusing situations. Actor Desi Arnaz (Ball's real-life husband) played Ricky, a handsome Cuban American band leader.

By exaggerating everyday things "to the point of happy hysteria," as she recalled, Ball became one of the most popular women in television. In one segment, Lucy tried to bake bread, but ended up with an inflated 13-foot loaf that leaped from the oven to attack her.

Lucille Ball ranked among America's most creative comics, but "I Love Lucy" also established many new technical standards in television. The shows were taped before a live audience. The tapes were of a higher quality than ever before and were able to be rerun.

The program attracted a devoted following in America and overseas. Even in the 1990s, "I Love Lucy" is in **syndication** (sold to a number of broadcast stations) in more than 80 countries, with an estimated audience in the tens of millions.

Mr. Television

In the early 1950s, Monday nights were "I Love Lucy" nights. Tuesday nights viewers crowded around their sets to watch "The Texaco Star Theater," starring Milton Berle. Berle, a stand-up comic, became known as Mr. Television and Uncle Miltie. In his skits, he surprised his audiences by dressing up as Cleopatra, Napoleon, Santa Claus, the Easter Bunny, and other characters. Berle would do anything for a laugh, including screaming in a high-pitched voice, telling old jokes, and goofing around with his guests.

Just three years before Berle's first

People not only rearranged their social lives to watch television, they also rearranged their furniture. Early television sets were so large and bulky that people had to make room for them in their homes.

year on the air, only 14,000 U.S. homes had television sets. Screens were small (10 inches), with greenish, flickering pictures. As the growing demand for TVs forced manufacturers to produce better sets for less money, TV screens grew, picture quality improved, and Americans kept on buying them.

By 1950, more than five million television sets had been sold in the United States. People who couldn't afford to buy their own TVs would watch at friends' houses or stand in front of the windows of appliance stores. Food manufacturers **capitalized** (used something to one's own advantage) on the boom by creating frozen TV dinners so that people wouldn't have to interrupt their TV watching by getting up to prepare dinner. The number of TV sets in the United States soared to 60 million by 1960.

A Shrinking World

Television changed the way people lived, how they thought, and even influenced the way they voted. No longer did families spend time talking, or gather around the radio listening to local, state, or national events. Now they could watch television news shows that covered political events, speeches, and conventions. TV showed viewers what was going on across town as well as what was happening on the other side of the continent. TV made people and events around the world seem less foreign.

Candidates' TV appearances became even more important than their political positions. How candidates looked on TV became as important as what they said. For example, in the 1952 presidential campaign, the Republican candidate, General Dwight D. Eisenhower, made 50 campaign advertisements for TV. His Democratic opponent, Illinois Governor Adlai Stevenson, decided not to make TV ads, although some of his speeches were carried on network TV. With the help of his TV campaign, Eisenhower won the election.

The Birth of TV Advertising

Advertisers hoped to sell their products to the millions of TV viewers. Networks sold air time to advertisers, who broadcast commercials across the country. The strategy was a success. For example, one cosmetic company increased its sales of lipstick by 90 times in two years of TV advertising.

No one anticipated the impact TV would have on American culture and morals. People rearranged their lives to stay home and watch TV. Television became part of the environment, a primary source of amusement, information, and education.

People hurried home from school or work to watch the tube, as it was nicknamed. They went out less often in the evenings, which hurt many businesses. Many movie houses closed, and libraries and book stores reported a drop in patronage. Once-popular newspapers and magazines were forced out of business, including the original *LIFE* Magazine, which was famous for its photography.

Many people criticized this trend. They said that television's "golden age" in the 1950s created a lazy society. TV viewers tended to be less active in social organizations and less likely to take part in sports or go out in the evenings. Some critics called the TV an "idiot box," implying that only unintelligent people watched it. They said most TV shows were silly. Others said TV news was often too brief to give the real story.

Yet, despite the criticism, television was also praised as educational. It showed viewers parts of the world and other cultures they would never have seen before.

In the 1950s, however, television was watched primarily for entertainment. In the coming decade, it would bring into American living rooms events more powerful than anyone imagined.

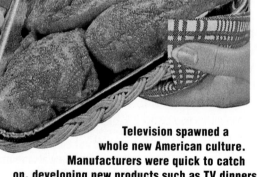

Television spawned a whole new American culture. Manufacturers were quick to catch on, developing new products such as TV dinners [above] to go with it.

Americans would see some of their leaders killed and a war fought in Asia. Near the end of the 1960s, they would see a man walk on the moon.

Children born during the baby boom of the 1950s, were the first to grow up with TV. Many experts worried that the "boob tube" or "idiot box" would lead to a new generation of zombie-like adults.

CHAPTER CHECK

WORD MATCH
1. syndication   **a.** used to one's own advantage or profit
2. Milton Berle   **b.** star of popular Monday night situation comedy TV show
3. capitalized   **c.** sold to a number of broadcast stations
4. Lucille Ball   **d.** star of popular Tuesday night comic variety TV show
5. TV's golden age   **e.** period of great popularity during the 1950s

QUICK QUIZ
1. What technical innovation enabled the "I Love Lucy" show to remain popular for so many years? What else may be responsible for its enduring popularity?
2. Name at least three ways in which television changed the living habits of millions of Americans.

THINK ABOUT IT
1. In what ways might the growth of the suburbs have contributed to the popularity of television?
2. How has television made the world seem smaller? In what other ways might it affect the way people look at the world?

14 "LONG LIVE ROCK 'N' ROLL"

If Elvis Presley is the king of rock 'n' roll, Chuck Berry is its granddaddy. Elvis, the Beatles, and other white rock stars said Berry influenced their work.

Hail, hail rock 'n' roll,
Deliver me from the
days of old.
Long live rock 'n' roll
The beat of the drum is
loud and bold,
Rock, rock, rock 'n' roll,
The spirit is there body
and soul

Chuck Berry sang these words in his 1950s hit "School Days." Berry, one of the most important musicians in the history of rock music, is often called the first folk poet of rock 'n' roll. His songs captured the feelings and attitudes of teens in the 1950s.

Born in St. Louis, Missouri, on October 18, 1926, Charles "Chuck" Berry began singing in his church choir when he was six. He took up the guitar in high school, and later formed his own band. Visiting Chicago in 1955, Berry recorded "Maybellene." It replaced "Rock Around the Clock" as the number one song on the rhythm-and-blues charts and was one of the top 50 pop singles of 1955. Over the next four years, Berry reached the peak of his popularity with songs such as "Roll Over Beethoven" and "Johnny B. Goode."

At first, many adults opposed the new music of Berry and other singers. A 1956 *Time* magazine article reported: "In San Antonio, rock 'n' roll was banned from the city swimming pool jukeboxes because, said the city council, its primitive beat attracted 'undesirable elements' given to practicing their spastic [movements] in . . . bathing suits."

Roots of Rock 'n' Roll

Rock 'n' roll evolved from the blues, a style of music developed mainly by rural black musicians. Rhythm and blues updated and urbanized the blues. Black radio stations picked up the rhythm-and-blues tunes, and soon the music captured a large following among blacks during the late 1940s.

Eventually, a growing audience of white teenagers, dissatisfied with the popular music of the period, became interested in rhythm and blues. They were drawn to its pounding beat and its direct lyrics, which spoke of real life, love, and longing.

Out of a combination of rhythm and blues and country, or "hillbilly", came a new style. In the mid-1950s, a Cleveland, Ohio disc jockey named Alan Freed, called this new music, that featured an amplified beat and electric guitar, rock 'n' roll. Teenagers quickly claimed the music as their own. It gave them an outlet for their discontent and

a sense of group identity. When young people eagerly responded to the music, radio stations switched to the new sound, and the rock 'n' roll craze spread.

Top 10 #1 Rock Songs, 1955–1958

Artist	Song	Year
Bill Haley and His Comets	"Rock Around the Clock"	1955
Kay Starr	"Rock and Roll Waltz"	1956
Elvis Presley	"Heartbreak Hotel"	1956
Elvis Presley	"I Want You, I Need You, I Love You"	1956
Elvis Presley	"Don't Be Cruel" / "Hound Dog"	1956
Elvis Presley	"Too Much"	1957
Elvis Presley	"All Shook Up"	1957
The Crickets	"That'll Be the Day"	1957
Elvis Presley	"Jailhouse Rock"	1957
Danny and the Juniors	"At the Hop"	1958

How many hits did Elvis Presley have between 1955–1957? How many of the songs listed above do you recognize?

Cover Versions

The first rock 'n' roll record was "Sh-Boom," recorded in 1954 by a black group, the Chords. The fate of "Sh-Boom" and the Chords would be repeated many times. The Chords' "Sh-Boom" was such a hit on the rhythm-and-blues radio stations that pop stations began to play it. Then a white group called the Crew Cuts recorded the song. Their version surpassed the original in sales, reaching the top 10 on the music charts in one week.

This process happened again and again. Black musicians would record hits, then white rock 'n' roll performers would take the songs and make "covers," selling far more records. For example, Bill Haley and His Comets rose to fame with "Rock Around the Clock," a rhythm-and-blues song first released by black singer Sonny Dae. Haley's version sold more than 17 million copies worldwide and was the first rock 'n' roll record to reach number one in the United States.

Songs performed by white artists usually sold better than those by blacks. Many white audiences were not used to the sound of black rhythm and blues. Radio stations and record promoters also preferred white musicians. Blacks were not entirely shut out of the rock 'n' roll market, however. By 1956, black artists like Fats Domino, Little Richard, and Chuck Berry climbed to the top of the charts.

"Elvis the Pelvis"

Berry wrote songs that spoke for the youth of the 1950s, but Elvis Presley was their idol. Across the country, from the newspapers, pulpits, and classrooms, there was outrage. Adults denounced the young man with the defiant sneer and wriggling hips whom they called "Elvis the pelvis." In some small towns, people even gathered to burn his records.

In 1956, Elvis Presley earned his nickname for the wild way he danced while singing his rock 'n' roll songs on network television. Presley provoked such a sensation because he was the first white performer to perform rock 'n' roll to a national audience.

During his childhood, Elvis listened to the music that shaped his singing style: gospel, rhythm and blues, and country. When he was 13, in 1948, the Presleys moved to Memphis, Tennessee, hoping to leave their poverty behind. After he graduated from high school, Elvis took a job driving a truck. One of the stops on his route was Sun Records, a small company that released Presley's first records in 1954. These recordings were a

Elvis Aron Presley (1935–1977) sparked an uproar when he came on the scene in the mid–1950s. His look, sound, and style upset many older people, but captured the imaginations of young people worldwide, and assured rock 'n' roll a firm place in music history.

raw mix of blues and country, and they earned Elvis a loyal regional following.

In 1956, he entered the national spotlight. His scandalous, gyrating appearances on TV during his performance of "Heartbreak Hotel" shocked audiences. With his long sideburns, unconventional clothes, and rebellious air, he was the defiant hero of America's teens. His expressive wails, groans, growls, and croons conveyed the vitality of rock 'n' roll.

Within two years, Presley sold 28 million records. "Don't Be Cruel," "Jailhouse Rock," and "Hound Dog" are among his many hits. Another song, "Love Me Tender," is also the title of a 1956 movie that was the first of his 33 films.

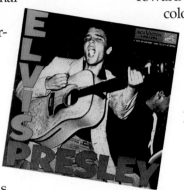

During his lifetime, Elvis Presley sold more than one-half billion albums, recorded 38 top-ten hits, and earned 127 gold records.

Presley's phenomenal success earned him a new nickname— The King of Rock 'n' Roll. His popularity surpassed that of any other artist of the period and was unrivaled until the Beatles arrived in the United States almost a decade later.

Toward the end of his life, Presley's colossal success began to overwhelm him. Many people believe that drug use hastened his early death in 1974, although the autopsy report denied this suspicion. He was buried in Graceland, his home in Memphis, which thousands still visit every week. Presley's popularity flourishes because it is founded on rock 'n' roll, which continues to endure and to be reborn with each new generation.

CHAPTER CHECK

WORD MATCH
1. Cleveland, Ohio
2. Chuck Berry
3. the blues
4. Elvis Presley
5. Memphis, Tennessee

a. home of Elvis Presley and Sun records
b. where radio host Alan Freed broadcast first rock 'n' roll show
c. black performer called first poet of rock 'n' roll
d. type of music developed mainly by black rural musicians
e. first white performer to sing rock 'n' roll on national TV

QUICK QUIZ
1. What were the musical roots of rock 'n' roll? How was its growth influenced by racism?
2. What function did rock 'n' roll serve for American teenagers? Who was its most popular performer in the late 1950s?

THINK ABOUT IT
1. Why do you think rock 'n' roll appealed primarily to young people?
2. What connections can you make between the growing affluence and drive for conformity in America and the rise of rock 'n' roll?

POST-WAR AMERICA

History Detective

1. My reputation in the music world was phenomenal. Known as the King of Rock and Roll, I changed American music forever. Who am I?

2. After being blockaded by Soviet forces, this German city became the first confrontation of the Cold War between the U.S. and the Soviet Union. Where is it?

3. Many people say that my investigations into communism started the Red scare during the 1950s. Who am I?

4. With television's popularity, sponsors and commercials made this one of the fastest growing industries in the U.S. What is it?

5. I wanted to extend the Korean War into China, but this ambition almost risked a third world war, and eventually cost me my job. Who am I?

Voices From the Past

After World War II, Americans believed problems in Europe were behind them. But many politicians were unsettled by the presence of communism in many European countries. Some thought this could lead to another war. During his 1946 speech at Westminster College in Fulton, Missouri, Winston Churchill, prime minister of Great Britain, introduced a new concept to the American public. Here is part of what he said:

> I have a strong admiration and regard for the valiant Russian people. But it is my duty . . . to place before you certain disturbing facts about the present position in Europe. From Stetin in the Baltic to Trieste in the Adriatic, an iron curtain has descended across the Continent. Behind that line lie all the capitals of the ancient states of Central and Eastern Europe.

1. Does Churchill seem worried about the division that communism was causing in Europe?

2. How do you think the term "Iron Curtain" originated? What does it mean to you?

Hands–On History

Living in the TV Age—Television continues to change the way people relax, learn, and think. And television itself continues to change. In the early 1950s, families had only one or two channels to choose from. Today, there are many more choices, including cable TV. What other changes have come to television viewing? Are the changes good or bad? Write an essay discussing the importance of TV in American life during the 1980s and 1990s.

YESTERDAY'S NEWS

The American Adventures Newspaper

ROBINSON BREAKS INTO BIG LEAGUES

Brooklyn, N.Y., April 15, 1947—History was made today in Ebbets Field. It was not a particularly good game—the Dodgers didn't even win. But a young black man, Jackie Robinson, became the first member of his race to step on to an all-white, professional baseball field. A sell-out crowd witnessed Robinson's first game and his one hit.

Many expected great problems from fans, opponents, and maybe even the other Dodger players. Today's game had no such problems. Many people have noticed the great courage Robinson has shown. He is breaking new ground for his race. How will this effect sports, and all of American life in the future? **1.**

In his first months as president, Harry S. Truman played an important part in the peace for Europe.

2.

Washington, D.C., March 12, 1947—Today, in a bold move, President Harry Truman told Congress what has been billed as the Truman Doctrine. "We shall not realize our objectives," he told the Congressmen, ". . . unless we are willing to help free peoples to maintain their [freedom] and national integrity against aggressive movements. . . ." In this way, political observers believe America has taken the role of world leader from Great Britain. For the last 150 years, Britain has considered the condition of other nations when considering its own national security. President Truman has told the U.S. that peace and freedom in the world are now its responsibility.

3.

New Brunswick, N.J., September 19, 1952—The people living here have been subjects in a five-year study of TV's effect on a typical American city. Here are some of the findings: 86% of the sets are in use during weekday evening hours; the average number of hours of viewing per person has grown. And how has this TV viewing affected other aspects of life? Movie attendance in the area has dropped a shocking 77%. Radio listening has dropped 88% on the average weekday evening. There has been a 53% drop in the number of adults reading magazines. Entertaining guests has fallen off by 87%, and visiting friends by 74%. The time devoted to TV viewing seems to have affected nearly all social activity!

You Be the Reporter

Match each question with its news item above.
1. Finish this article with your own thoughts.
2. Write a headline for this article.
3. Write a title for this story.

COMPARING HISTORICAL CARTOONS

Sometimes cartoonists draw cartoons that are social rather than political in nature. These cartoons, like political cartoons, also have a message. They usually are trying to tell us something about the way we live, how we act, or how we think.

In the 1950s, newspapers and magazines published many cartoons that depicted life in the suburbs. As you have read, millions of

Americans moved to the suburbs hoping to find a better way of life than the cities offered—new houses, more privacy, a clean and safe atmosphere in which to raise children, and a variety of recreational activities. The cartoonists who chose the suburbs as their subject, however, were interested in some other aspects of suburban life. Two examples are shown in this lesson.

Study the first cartoon below and answer the questions that follow. Write your answers on a separate sheet of paper.

Drawing by Claude. Copyright © 1956 *The New Yorker*.

1. Read the small note under this cartoon.
   (a) What is the cartoonist's name?
   (b) When and where did this cartoon first appear?
2. Describe how the houses and people look. Why are the first five men staring at the man at the far right?
3. In this cartoon, all the men are returning home from work at the same time, and

   no women are shown at all. Based on this cartoon, what could you **infer** (assume) about how women in the suburbs spent their time?
4. What do you think this cartoonist was saying about the suburban way of life?

Now refer to the cartoon on this page to answer the following questions.

5. What is the cartoonist's name? In what magazine did the cartoon first appear?

6. Describe the differences between the two houses. Why do the owners of the house on the right have a sign that says "Unfortunately" on their front lawn?

7. What does the cartoonist seem to be saying about suburban **values** (what people think is important)?

Drawing by Kaufman. Copyright © *McCalls'*

Refer to both cartoons to answer the following questions.

8. The suburbs have sometimes been criticized for promoting an atmosphere of conformity in which people feel they need to do the same things and have the same things as their neighbors in order to be accepted. Do you think these two cartoonists agree or disagree with this view of the suburbs? Explain.

9. Could either of these cartoons still apply to some suburban communities today? Explain why or why not.

10. Why do you think people in the suburbs seemed to act and think in similar ways, while life in the cities seemed more varied? (To plan your answer, review information in Chapter 115. Think about how suburban housing developed and about the kinds of people who tended to move to the suburbs in the 1950s.)

For Extra Credit: Do you live in a city, a suburb, or a rural area? What aspects of life in your community could be subjects for a cartoonist? Draw up a list of them. Then draw your own cartoon about one idea on your list.

EQUAL JU

1950   1955   1960

1954

Brown v. Board of Education outlaws public school segregation.

1955

Montgomery, Alabama bus boycott

1956

Martin Luther King, Jr. emerges as Civil Rights Movement leader.

1957

Nine black students integrate Central High School, Little Rock, Ark.

1963

250,000 people attend March on Washington.

Betty Friedan publishes *The Feminine Mystique.*

Rosa Parks was tired. It had been a warm December day in Montgomery, Alabama. Christmas shoppers at the department store where Parks worked had kept her busy all day long. At closing time, the 42-year-old black woman headed for home. When Parks boarded the bus, she carefully chose a seat in the fifth row.

Like most Southern cities in 1955, Montgomery had laws segregating blacks and whites on city buses. Black people sat in the rear and white people sat in front. Blacks could sit in the middle if the white section was not full. This was where

During the 1950s and 1960s, more and more Americans began to stand up and demand one of their basic rights as citizens: fair and equal treatment under the law.

STICE

1965

1964
Civil
Rights Act
passes.

1965
Voting
Rights Act
becomes law.

1965
Cesar Chavez organizes
boycott in support
of farm workers.

UNIT 3

Parks sat on that December evening in 1955.

For a few blocks, the trip was quite routine. But soon all the seats in the white section were filled. Following bus company directions, the driver asked Parks to give up her seat to a white passenger. Parks said no. Her manner was quiet, but her voice was as solid as steel.

The driver pulled the emergency brake and went to get the police. Minutes later, he was back with two policemen. They ordered Parks off the bus. They brought her to the city police station, took her fingerprints, and put her in jail.

Parks' simple, planned protest had taken only a few minutes to make. It involved no news reporters, no popping flashbulbs, no drama of any kind. It had been a lonely act of courage. But it marked the start of a series of protests across the nation that would last more than a decade.

Segregation

This campaign was called the Civil Rights Movement. It was a movement to obtain equal rights for all Americans, both white and black.

African Americans had technically been freed from slavery for almost a hun-

Not all heroes are powerful giants. Sometimes, a simple act by an ordinary person can spark tremendous change. In 1955, Rosa Parks, an Alabama seamstress, became just such a hero in the U.S. Civil Rights Movement.

dred years. But in most places, they were still mistreated. Often they were segregated from whites. They did not have the rights and opportunities of most white people. In the North, blacks were segregated by custom. In most Northern states, laws did not require blacks to live in separate neighborhoods or attend separate schools. But custom did. Few African Americans were able to attend college. Few could get good jobs. And in hard times, blacks were the first fired from their jobs.

In much of the South, African Americans were segregated by law. Laws there required separate schools for blacks and whites. Blacks weren't allowed in white swimming pools and could drink only at separate water fountains. Voting practices, such as poll taxes, kept most blacks from voting. Some white people believed that such practices were fair.

But the times were changing. In 1952, a black writer jarred the minds of literate Americans. His name was Ralph Ellison. In his novel *Invisible Man*, he described how many whites acted as if blacks were invisible. Ellison said many whites thought they could ignore blacks altogether.

The Civil Rights Movement showed white Americans that they could not ignore black Americans. During World War II, many African Americans had fought—and died—for their country. Yet black veterans came home to segregation. After fighting a war for freedom, many African Americans began demanding their own freedom.

Dr. Martin Luther King, Jr.

The spark needed to light the fires of change came in May 1954. The U.S. Supreme Court overturned the 1896 Plessy decision, and ruled that segregated schools were illegal. Segregated schools violated the Constitution, the Court said. Segregation of other kinds was soon questioned as well.

One of the most dramatic protests came in 1955, when Rosa Parks refused to give up her seat on the bus. Her arrest sparked a year-long bus-boycotting campaign to end segregation on buses in Montgomery, Alabama. By refusing to ride the buses, African Americans in Montgomery were able to force the integration of city buses.

This protest introduced a new leader of Southern blacks to the world, Dr. Martin Luther King, Jr. King was a young minister who helped organize the protest in Montgomery. He taught his followers the ways of peaceful protest. In Montgomery, and later in other Southern towns and cities, African Americans broke laws they considered unjust. They were put in jail, but they kept on with their struggle for equal rights.

Gains made in the struggle for equal rights brought many changes into the lives of millions of Americans. For many, it meant having to learn a new way of seeing oneself, and of relating to others.

Civil Rights Movement

The Civil Rights Movement began to win victories. It also began to affect people's feelings. Some people, especially in the South, became very angry. These people sometimes responded with violence towards those in the movement. But many others began to support the cause.

In the early 1960s, many young people, both black and white, flocked to the South to work in the movement. Sometimes, they participated in sit-ins. Black students would sit at a "white" lunch counter and wait patiently for service. The protesters were often arrested, but slowly public lunchrooms were opened up to African Americans. Another important tactic was **freedom rides.** Both black and white students rode on public buses across the South. They challenged segregation on buses and in other public places.

To help end segregation, the Voting Rights Act was passed in 1965. Members of the Civil Rights Movement helped sign up many people to vote. They worked to elect blacks to some local offices. These were the first African Americans to hold such offices in the South in more than 75 years.

Civil Rights for All

African Americans inspired other groups of Americans to make their own claims for equal treatment. In California, a campaign began to organize a farm work-

Voter Turnout, 1964–1986

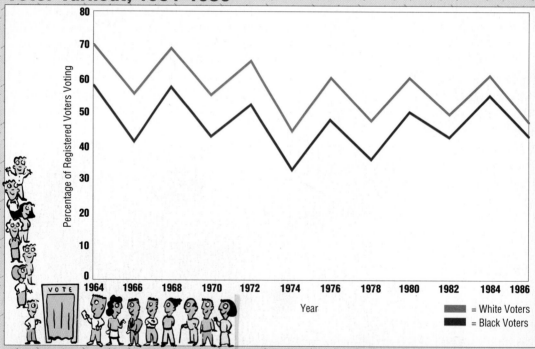

List the years in which the chart shows rises in black and white voter turnout. What recurring political event might have caused these rises? In what year did the most blacks vote? In what year(s) did fewer than 50% of blacks vote? Why do you think some ethnic groups have higher voter participation than others? What social or political factors might lead members of these groups to vote more?

AMERICAN ADVENTURES

ers' union. The workers were poorly paid. Many were Mexican Americans, just like the man who wanted a union—Cesar Chavez. His goal was to win rights for all Mexican Americans.

Native Americans also began organizing—in this case, to win back their rights. Beginning in the early 1960s, many American Indians tried to protect what was left of their tribal lands. Lawsuits were brought against the U.S. government for earlier treaty violations. In 1968, the American Indian Movement was formed to help protect Native Americans living in urban areas.

Women joined the movement for equal rights. Some called for liberation from old roles, such as housewife and mother, that they had played for so long. They named their campaign the Women's Liberation Movement. It revived issues first raised by women's rights **advocates** (people who support a cause through speaking or writing) at the turn of the century. Efforts to win equal rights for all these groups were helped by decisions made in the U.S. Supreme Court. Under the leadership of Chief Justice Earl Warren, the Court made rulings against many types of discrimination.

Homosexuals, too, organized to end discrimination. During a police raid on the Stonewall Inn, a gay bar in New York City's Greenwich Village, homosexuals fought back. This 1969 incident marked the beginning of the modern Gay Rights Movement. Soon thousands of gay women and and men were openly marching in cities across the country, declaring they were entitled to equal treatment.

The physically disabled also began to see changes during this period. The Rehabilitation Act of 1973 barred unfair treatment of disabled Americans in programs that received federal funds. Eventually, wheelchair ramps were built to provide access to public buildings.

Many national leaders gave further help in fighting discrimination. In 1965, President Lyndon B. Johnson spoke to Congress in support of the Civil Rights Movement's goals. "It is not just Negroes," he said, "but all of us, who must overcome the crippling legacy of bigotry and injustice. And we shall overcome."

Civil rights workers were thrilled to hear these words from the president. Still, few people in the movement were completely satisfied. They thought there was a long way to go before all Americans had truly equal opportunities.

Native Americans were among those groups in the U.S. fighting for more rights. Here a group of American Indians are seen at a rally in Washington, D.C.

15 "SEPARATE IS NOT EQUAL"

In 1954, Linda Brown [foreground] became one of the most famous people in the nation when the Supreme Court ruled in favor of her case. The Court's decision affected millions of Americans.

Oliver Brown, a pastor in Topeka, Kansas, had a seven-year-old daughter named Linda. Linda Brown traveled about three miles to and from elementary school every day. During winter snowstorms, she walked six blocks and then waited for a bus. Yet there was a public elementary school only four blocks from her house. Linda couldn't go to the nearby school because she was black.

One day in 1950, when Linda was seven, Brown tried to have his daughter enrolled at the nearby Sumner Elementary School. But the school's principal refused to enroll Linda. The school accepted only white students, Brown was told. Segregation was legal in Kansas and 17 other states. Brown decided to sue the Topeka Board of Education. He wanted to force the board to allow Linda to go to the school close to her home.

Brown filed his suit in the U.S. District Court of Kansas. He lost the case, but he did not give up. He took his appeal all the way to the U.S. Supreme Court. There the case was combined with four others attacking segregation in the nation's public schools.

History of Segregation

Many years earlier, the Court had given legal support to segregation. The Court had taken its stand in 1896 in the case of *Plessy v. Ferguson.* It had ruled that separate passenger cars for blacks and whites were legal on trains, so long as the cars were of equal quality. "Separate but equal" had become the law of the land.

Civil rights groups had begun challenging this decision in the courts in the 1930s. The group leading the attack was the National Association for the Advancement of Colored People (NAACP). The NAACP won several court suits. But the Court did not overturn the decision in the Plessy case.

The Brown Decision

In 1952, Oliver Brown's case opened before the highest court in the country, the Supreme Court in Washington, D.C. The case was now known as *Brown* v. *Board of Education of Topeka, Kansas.* The difficult case dragged on for more than a year. Brown's attack on segregation was argued by a skilled team of NAACP law-

yers. Heading the team was a Baltimore-born attorney named Thurgood Marshall. Marshall would later become the first black man ever to sit on the U.S. Supreme Court. Another important person in the case was Dr. Kenneth B. Clark. Clark was a black professor at the City College of New York. He supplied facts to show that schools with only black students were damaging to the children.

At 12:52 P.M. on May 17, 1954, Chief Justice Earl Warren began reading the Court's opinion in the case. It was Warren's first major opinion in his new position. He read it with a cool and steady voice. He did not give away the Court's verdict immediately. Twenty minutes went by. Still the news reporters could not be sure which way the Court had ruled.

Then they got their answer. All nine justices had agreed that segregation in the nation's public schools went against the Constitution. Separate schools for blacks and whites could never be equal, the Court said. Segregation denied black people "equal protection of the laws," a right guaranteed by the Fourteenth Amendment.

This ruling overturned the 1896 "separate but equal" decision. "Separate is not equal," the Court now said. The decision

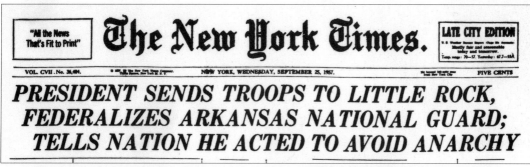

A major test of the Brown decision came in 1957. Violence threatened to erupt when black students tried to attend public schools in Little Rock, Arkansas, that had always been all white.

was limited to public education. But it challenged the basis for all forms of racial segregation in the United States.

Reaction came swiftly. In the nation's black communities, there was a sense of thanksgiving. Black people hoped that the decision would end the unfair treatment they had faced for many years. Many white people also rejoiced. One Ohio newspaper praised the Supreme Court for acting "as the conscience of a nation."

In the South, white people were mixed in their opinions. The governor of Virginia said the decision called for "cool heads, calm study, and sound judgment." But some other Southerners were furious about the Court's ruling.

Questions of public education had usually been decided by state and local government, they said. They thought the Court's opinion showed no respect for states' rights. These Southerners did not see the decision as one that touched the entire nation. Instead, they saw it as an attack on the Southern way of life.

Crisis in Little Rock

In some states, leaders took steps to fight the decision. They closed all public schools rather than bring an end to segregation. In certain areas, white people formed White Citizens' Councils. The councils often used threats to stop people from trying to make changes in the schools.

One showdown came in Little Rock, Arkansas, in 1957. Nine black students were to attend the city's all-white Central High School. To prevent this, Arkansas

Segregated Schools in Topeka, Kansas, 1958

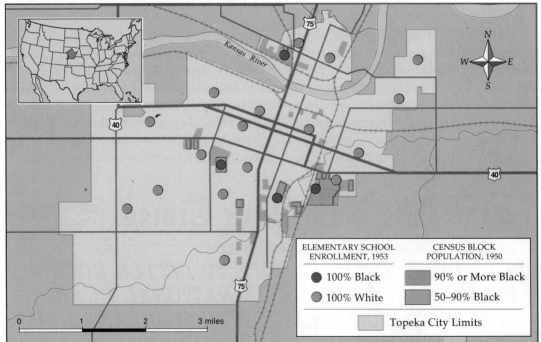

In how many schools in Topeka in 1953 was the enrollment 100% black? Did any schools in which black students were enrolled fall into areas where whites were the majority of residents?

Governor Orval Faubus called out the state's National Guard. President Dwight Eisenhower then sent federal troops into the city to enforce the law permitting black teenagers in the school. Faubus finally backed down.

Eisenhower showed that he meant to back up the Court. Many people in the South realized that a new way of life had arrived. Opposition to the Brown ruling slowly faded. In one Southern city after another, black students peacefully entered schools formerly reserved for whites.

Few issues in the history of the U.S. Supreme Court had affected so many people. Few decisions had touched more basic values. A few weeks after the Brown decision, one of the justices, Stanley Reed, commented on the case. "If it was not the most important decision in the history of the Court," he said, "it was very close."

Elizabeth Eckford was one of the students called the Little Rock Nine who integrated Central High. They all met abuse from angry whites.

CHAPTER CHECK

WORD MATCH
1. *Plessy* v. *Ferguson*
2. Topeka, Kansas
3. *Brown* v. *Board of Education*
4. Little Rock, Arkansas
5. Washington, D.C.

a. where U.S. Supreme Court is located
b. set "separate but equal" standard for black accommodations
c. where the Browns lived and fought for school desegregation
d. declared segregation of schools unconstitutional
e. where federal troops enforced school desegregation

QUICK QUIZ
1. In what ways did the Supreme Court decision in the Brown case differ from earlier decisions concerning segregation?
2. What was the reaction of most black people to the Supreme Court's decision in *Brown* v. *Board of Education of Topeka, Kansas?* What were the reactions of white people in different parts of the country?

THINK ABOUT IT
1. What do you think you would have thought of the Supreme Court decision in 1954? Why do you think much of the U.S. is still segregated by race?
2. What character traits do you think enable people like the Browns to challenge injustice?

16 "I HAVE A DREAM"

Martin Luther King, Jr.'s power as a leader came both from his ability as a gifted speaker, and from ideas he learned in church and school. His peaceful persistence and inner strength inspired others.

An angry crowd milled around the bombed-out house. Some people yelled threats at city officials checking on the damage. The house belonged to the Reverend Martin Luther King, Jr. On January 30, 1956, the Montgomery bus boycott was still underway. King had gone to a boycott meeting. While he was away, someone had planted a bomb on his porch. King's wife, Coretta, and daughter, Yolanda, who had been in the house, were unharmed. But the crowd of angry blacks was in no mood to listen to pleas for calm.

Martin Luther King, Jr. came out on the porch. He looked at the angry people on his front lawn. He knew some were ready to tear the city apart. But his face showed sadness, not anger or fear.

"We are not advocating violence," he said. "We want to love our enemies. . . . If I am stopped, our work will not stop, for what we are doing is right. What we are doing is just and God is with us."

The crowd grew silent. King's house had been damaged. His family could have been killed. Yet he stood there talking of love and forgiveness. A man's voice broke the silence: "God bless you," he cried. "Amen!" said the others.

King proved his leadership during the year-long bus boycott in Montgomery. The boycott was the start of the Civil Rights Movement of the 1950s and 1960s. That January night, King gave the movement one of its most basic ideas.

Putting Ideas Into Action

King believed that black and white people should resist laws that they thought unjust. If necessary, he thought, they should disobey such laws. But King also said that they should be ready to accept punishment for breaking such laws. In some cases, they should even go to jail.

King called for **nonviolent resistance** (defying a law peacefully). He did not believe in angry threats. He did not believe in fighting back when attacked. King thought the Civil Rights Movement should try to end injustice by appealing to the conscience of the nation.

King drew his ideas from several sources. He learned love for one's enemies from his religious heritage. King learned about **civil disobedience** (opposition to a law through refusal to obey) from the writings of a 19th-century American, Henry David Thoreau (tho-ROH). Thoreau had written about resistance to laws dealing with slavery. Now King used Thoreau's ideas to fight racial injustice.

The life of Mohandas Gandhi (mo-HAHN-dus GON-dee) inspired King. Gandhi had led India's struggle for independence from Great Britain in the 1930s and 1940s. Under Gandhi's leadership, millions of Indians had refused to buy British goods. Many had refused to pay British taxes. These were forms of nonviolent protest. From Gandhi, King had learned how to build a movement based on such ideas.

King's political and religious training began in his youth. His father was the minister of a leading black church in Atlanta, Georgia. Young Martin did not know poverty as a boy. But he did know the meaning of segregation firsthand.

Putting Faith to a Test

At Morehouse College in Atlanta, King received training to become a minister. After graduating from Morehouse, he continued his studies in Massachusetts and Pennsylvania. But he wanted to do more than care for souls. He felt it was his duty to do something to end segregation, and poverty too.

King used the fame he won during the bus boycott to wage a vigorous campaign against segregation. From 1956 to 1964, King was arrested 29 times for protesting the unfair treatment of black people.

The year 1963 was a special one for African Americans. It was the 100th anniversary of the Emancipation Proclamation, the first step toward ending slavery. Yet 100 years after freedom, black people still suffered from injustices. In Washington, D.C., President John F. Kennedy spoke out against unfair treatment of blacks. He sent an important civil rights bill to Congress. But Congress delayed acting on the bill. Civil rights leaders thought it was time to put pressure on Congress. They planned a big demonstration in the nation's capital.

The March on Washington took place on August 28, 1963. It was a hot, clear summer day. Marchers came in car pools, buses, trains, and planes. By noon, 250,000 people had formed around the reflecting pool in front of the Lincoln Memorial. Affluent merchants marched beside poor farmers. Northerners marched beside Southerners. Blacks marched beside whites.

Putting Hope Before Despair

Millions of people watched the march live on television. Stars of the entertainment world performed. Then, after several speeches, Martin Luther King, Jr. was introduced. He spoke of how black people hoped for full equality. Now was the time, he said, for America to fulfill its promises of democracy.

I have a dream, that one day on the red hills of Georgia the sons of former slaves and the sons of former slave-owners will be able to sit down together at the table of brotherhood. . . .

I have a dream, that my four little children will one day live in a nation where they will not be judged by the color of their skin but by the content of their character.

I have a dream. . . .

Over and over again he invoked his dream for America. The crowd listened breathlessly to the rolling words. King ended the speech with the hope that one day all Americans would know the meaning of an old black spiritual:

Free at last!
Free at last!
Thank God Almighty,
We are free at last!

For a moment there was silence. Some people wept openly. Others were too moved to respond. Then the silence was replaced by thunderous applause.

King's efforts made a powerful difference in the lives of millions of American blacks. He has been honored many times in African American art, writing, music, and dance.

The next year, King was awarded the Nobel Peace Prize for his civil rights work. He continued to lead the struggle for civil rights, but he was challenged by other black leaders. By 1965, new leaders were impatient with King's call for nonviolence. They were angry and defiant. "Black power" was their rallying cry.

But King stood behind the idea of nonviolence. In 1968, King broadened his con-

AMERICAN ADVENTURES

cerns. He organized a Poor People's Campaign to attack poverty. He went to Memphis, Tennessee, to support a sanitation workers' strike there.

On April 4, Martin Luther King, Jr. was killed by an assassin, James Earl Ray. King was 39 years old. When news of his death spread, black communities across America exploded in rage. Riots in 100 cities across America left $45 million in destroyed property, 27,000 arrested people, and 46 dead.

Many people found a bitter truth in Martin Luther King, Jr.'s murder. They believed it proved that love and forgiveness were useless against hatred. But others remembered his dream. For them, the fulfillment of that dream remained as the work for all Americans.

The March on Washington was a key event in the Civil Rights Movement. The 250,000 protesters, and King's "I Have a Dream" speech spurred Congress to pass major civil rights laws in following years.

CHAPTER CHECK

WORD MATCH

1. civil disobedience
2. nonviolent resistance
3. March on Washington
4. Mohandas Gandhi
5. Henry David Thoreau

a. led India's nonviolent struggle for independence from Great Britain
b. 1963 demonstration in support of civil rights bill
c. 19th-century writer who supported resistance to slavery
d. avoiding the use of physical force to protest injustice
e. opposition to a law through refusal to obey

QUICK QUIZ

1. Who was Dr. Martin Luther King, Jr.? How did he become the leader of the U.S. Civil Rights Movement in the 1950s?
2. Why was 1963 a special year for black Americans? How did civil rights leaders mark the occasion?
3. Describe the various influences that led King to his philosophy.

THINK ABOUT IT

1. Do you think that nonviolence made the Civil Rights Movement more or less effective? Explain.
2. How did King expand the range of his activities? Why do you think he did this? Why do you think some people objected?

Through the work of people like Cesar Chavez, founder of the United Farm Workers, the new California farm laborers union won their first contract with the growers in 1966.

"**V**iva la causa!" (Long live the cause!)

The cries in Spanish filled the hot, dusty hall. Mexican American farm workers in Delano (deh-LAY-no), California, were voting to strike against the large grape growers. Cesar Chavez called for order.

For three years, Chavez had tried to get people to join his National Farm Workers Association. To do so, he had traveled up and down California's Central Valley. Wherever he had gone, he had asked the mostly Mexican American farm workers if they liked their working conditions. Their answer had been, "No!" Now, in 1965, the time had come for action.

Dusty Harvest

Chavez had grown up on a small farm near Yuma (YOO-muh), Arizona. As a boy, he had worked in the fields with his family. But when he was 10, the Chavez family lost their farm in the Depression. They packed up and headed for California.

The family soon learned the hard and uncertain life of farm laborers. They traveled around the fertile California valleys looking for work. They lived in shacks or sometimes in their car. When he was 15, Chavez left school to work in the fields. He was then living in a run-down slum in northern California.

Chavez joined the Navy during World War II, and returned to California when he got out. In 1950, he met a man there named Fred Ross. Ross worked for the Community Services Organization (CSO). The CSO was a private agency that tried to help farm workers and other poor people. Ross was looking for someone to help him organize farm workers to fight for their rights. Chavez took a job with the CSO. Over the next 10 years, he learned what it took to be a union organizer.

Many of the larger farms in California's Central Valley were owned by wealthy people. They used Mexican American workers to harvest the crops they grew. When the harvest was over on one farm, these migrant workers would move on to another.

Bitter Fruits

These workers almost always received low pay. Yet there was little they could do to improve this. They were specifically left out of federal laws giving workers the right to form unions. So most attempts by farm

Because of harsh working conditions, members of the United Farm Workers participated in protest marches such as this one held in 1968.

workers to improve their lives had been wasted effort.

Chavez believed that the only way for farm workers to help themselves was to form a union. In 1962, he moved with his wife and eight children to Delano. With a few trusted friends, he began to build the National Farm Workers Association.

Chavez continued his organizing for three years. Then, in 1965, came the strike known as La Causa against the large grape growers. Chavez set down only one absolute rule. The strikers had to be nonviolent. As he put it, "No union movement is worth the life of a single grower or his child or a single worker or his child."

The strike started slowly. The growers argued that if farm workers went into the union, prices would be pushed so high that they could not make a profit. The growers had many people on their side. Among them were most of the leaders of local government. The union, on the other hand, had little money and even less power.

But this was La Causa. It was the struggle for self-respect of an entire people. It was led by a man who seemed able to persuade his followers to do almost anything. Chavez' power came from his being a part of the community.

The farm workers organized committees to run the strike. A community kitchen made sure that no one went hungry. Other labor unions and community groups pledged support for La Causa. College students, housewives, and clergymen came to Delano to help with the strike.

Fertile Soil

But the strike could not be won with such support alone. At one point, Chavez led a group of farm workers on a 300-mile march to Sacramento, the state capital. His key tactic in the strike—and the most controversial one—was a boycott. Strike leaders fanned out across the country, urging people not to buy wine or grapes. More than one of Chavez' opponents termed this tactic illegal. Still the farm workers kept up the plea for a boycott. Slowly, wine and grape sales began to fall.

At first, the growers had thought of Chavez as a mere troublemaker. Now some of them began to take a more serious second look. Chavez was accused of being power-hungry. His critics claimed

he would destroy the very workers he was trying to save.

Yet some growers feared that their business would suffer badly if the boycott continued. One by one, they began talks with the union. In 1966, the United Farm Workers, as the union was now called, signed its first contract with growers.

Cooler Climate

Other growers kept refusing to talk with Chavez. Tension grew. For a time, it seemed that violence might flare up. Chavez believed that time was on the side of the farm workers. What they needed was courage and an example to follow. Chavez gave them both.

As a devout Roman Catholic, Chavez took up an old religious practice. He fasted for 25 days. During this time, he ate nothing and drank only water. Union members came to visit him from all over the state. "I guess one time I thought about becoming a priest," Chavez said later. "But I did this instead, and I'm

Working as migrant farmhands, these men and women harvest a lettuce crop in the San Joaquin Valley in California.

happy to [have been] a part of it." At the end of the fast, a thanksgiving feast was held. The farm workers cheered their leader. La Causa had gained publicity and continued.

The major breakthrough came in July 1970. The largest grape growers in the Central Valley agreed to a contract with the union. One grower spoke for the others. "We are happy that peace has come to this valley."

The contract was a real victory for Cesar Chavez. But

peace did not last for the United Farm Workers. By the mid-1970s, grape growers were awarding contracts to the giant Teamsters Union (organized to protect truckers) instead of to the United Farm Workers. As membership in the United Farm Workers fell, Chavez tried to organize vegetable and citrus fruit pickers, but he had difficulty getting contracts. In fact, the United Farm Workers' contracts dwindled from a high point of 100 when they first started to less than 30 by the mid-1980s.

Despite these setbacks, Chavez remained a national figure, directing several lettuce boycotts in the late 1970s. But the growers were getting more sophisticated, hiring special attorneys to think of legal ways to delay making contracts with farm workers. Harvesting machines were also replacing many workers in the fields.

Chavez' work continued through the next decade. He remains a symbol of the farm labor movement for millions. Said Chavez, "I think we've raised the consciousness level of the American public and the consumer about the problems the workers are faced with."

Many migrant workers and their families were forced to live in poorly-built housing.

CHAPTER CHECK

WORD MATCH
1. Cesar Chavez
2. Teamsters Union
3. Community Services Organization
4. United Farm Workers
5. Fred Ross

a. worked for agency that helped farm workers and poor people
b. private agency that protected rights of farm workers and the poor
c. union created by Chavez, followed nonviolent principles
d. head of the movement to organize farm workers
e. organized to protect the rights of truckers

QUICK QUIZ
1. What tactics did the United Farm Workers use to build their influence? Were they successful?
2. Why had previous efforts to help farm workers been unsuccessful?

THINK ABOUT IT
1. What characteristics made Cesar Chavez a successful leader? Why is such leadership so important in a political or social movement?
2. Would you be willing to pay more for food if it helped to improve the lives of workers? What responsibility do consumers have if workers are unfairly treated?

18 WOMEN ON THE MARCH

In the 1950s, career opportunities for young women were limited. Girls were expected to become housewives and mothers—and little else. By the mid–1960s, women demanded broader options.

In the spring of 1972, a seven-year-old girl wrote a letter, in crayon, to *Ms.* magazine. "We girls are angry as turnips," she said. She went on to explain how the boys always got the big part of the playground at her school. The girls were forced into a small corner where they played with marbles or dolls.

The girl was expressing a problem that existed throughout the United States. For example, in 1969 it was found that a Syracuse, New York school board had budgeted $90,000 for boys' sports. The girls were allotted only $200. Such inequities persisted in every facet of American life. Little girls and grown women were denied opportunities given to their male counterparts.

For many women of the 1950s, marriage and motherhood was considered the only acceptable career. From childhood on, women were trained to accept marriage and motherhood as their only roles. It was considered impolite—even offensive—for a woman to demand rights that most men took for granted.

Many women worked outside the home as an economic necessity or because they enjoyed it. Because of **discrimination** (showing favor toward or prejudice against) in the workplace, the majority of these women remained in factory and office jobs. They received substantially lower pay than men for the same type of work.

An Unspoken Problem

Some housewives were dissatisfied with the role that was thrust upon them: "As she made the beds, shopped for groceries . . . [and] ate peanut butter sandwiches, with her children," wrote feminist Betty Friedan, "she was afraid to ask even of herself the silent question—'Is this all?' "

Friedan, a New York City magazine editor, began to examine the feelings and dissatisfactions of suburban housewives in the 1950s. A wife and mother herself, she drew from her own experiences to explain how women felt about their lives.

Her book, *The Feminine Mystique,* appeared in 1963, and soon became a bestseller. Friedan found that many women in the United States were suffering from "a problem that lay buried, unspoken, for many years in the minds of American women." Many women were prevented from using their talents to the fullest, said Friedan. They were

"Women's liberation!" became a common cry. These demonstrators' signs combine a fist raised in protest with the symbols for woman and equal.

frustrated and unhappy.

Friedan demonstrated how television commercials and magazine advertisements depicted glamorous, smiling housewives. Many of the advertisers were men who regarded housework as low-level drudgery. They created a "feminine mystique" to sell products. Total fulfillment would come, it was promised, with the purchase of a new refrigerator—or a box of detergent.

Friedan's book exposed the ways women were kept in a subservient (less important) role in American society. *The Feminine Mystique* helped start a movement in the United States that dramatically altered the way that both women and men thought about women's lives.

Working for Women's Rights

In the 1960s, some women who worked in the Civil Rights Movement found that they were not treated fairly by men. Many were asked to type letters and answer phones, but little else. Many women became so disillusioned that they left the so-called reform organizations to work for women's rights. These women became known as **feminists** (people who believe women deserve the same rights as men). *Ms.* magazine, taking its title from the alternative word for Miss or Mrs., became the voice of the movement.

The roots of the problem, they said, lay in childhood. They called for an end to sexual **stereotyping** (assuming all people conform to the roles society gives them). They pointed out that girls were trained to be submissive, while boys were encouraged to be strong and domineering. Children's books, they said, almost always showed men as doctors and women as nurses. Such portraits were **sexist,** the feminists said, because they favored one sex over the other. Men and women should be allowed to develop as individuals, feminists argued. Stereotypes were negative and damaging for both sexes.

Women were protesting together, trying to enact legislation that would help end stereotyping and sexism.

Laws to Prevent Sexism

Feminists also fought for laws against discrimination based on sex. One such law was made part of the Civil Rights Act of 1964. The amendment allowed some women to sue their employers to obtain equal working conditions and higher pay.

But feminists believed that such laws were not enough, so they called for an Equal Rights Amendment (ERA) to the Constitution. The ERA had a simple goal—to guarantee equal rights for all women. It had first been proposed in 1923, but Congress had struck it down. In 1972, the amendment was finally passed. But to become law, an amendment has to be ratified by three fourths (or 38) of the state legislatures within seven years.

The ERA caused great controversy. It was brought up in one state legislature after another. Some states passed the ERA at first, only to reverse their decision later. The deadline was extended by three years.

But by 1982, only 35 of the necessary 38 states had ratified the amendment. As a result, the ERA failed to become law.

Feminists argued that women, although they outnumbered men, made up the largest "minority group" in the United States. Only the ERA would give women full equality with men.

But others believed that the ERA would do more harm than good. Many opponents of the amendment were women. They feared women might lose "special protections" that they had under the law. For example, women might be drafted into the military. But some feminists believed that women could achieve full equality with men only by being subjected to the same duties, like being drafted.

Opponents of the ERA feared that feminists wanted women to be just like men. They firmly believed that a woman's place was in the home.

The ideas that grew out of the Women's Movement were as complex and diverse as the women who called for them. While many women continued to lead traditional lives, others took on new roles in society. Women were accepted to medical and law schools in record numbers. They were treated with more respect in the business world, and achieved acclaim on the playing fields. In schools, girls began to be offered the same opportunities and challenges as boys.

Although women faced many fights, they finally proved women could handle "men's work" with equal skill.

CHAPTER CHECK

WORD MATCH
1. discrimination	**a.** less important
2. sexist	**b.** favoring one sex over the other
3. feminists	**c.** people who believe women deserve the same rights as men
4. stereotyping	**d.** showing favor toward or prejudice against
5. subservient	**e.** assuming all people conform to the roles society gives them

QUICK QUIZ
1. What did Betty Friedan mean by her book title, *The Feminine Mystique*?
2. What were the benefits to women of The Civil Rights Act of 1964?
3. What objections did opponents of the Women's Rights Movement have to the ERA?

THINK ABOUT IT
1. Numerically, women are a majority in the United States. Yet they share many characteristics with minority groups. Name some of them.
2. What other books can you name like *The Feminine Mystique* that influenced social movements?

19 UNDOING DISCRIMINATION

This Austin, Texas city bus, equipped with a hydraulic lift, is one reflection of the way discrimination against the disabled has been lessened as a result of political activism.

Their movement had no one leader—no Martin Luther King, Jr., or Betty Friedan. They were a minority that anyone might join—women, men, blacks, whites, and Native Americans. They represented every race, creed, and nationality.

Through legislation and political activism in the 1970s, the physically and mentally disabled began to achieve rights they had long been denied.

Battles were often difficult, and were won only after much heartache and persistence.

Accepting Differences

An unsuccessful operation at age five had left Colleen Stewart of Atlanta, Georgia, paralyzed below the waist. She was confined to a wheelchair. In the 1960s, most disabled children were educated in special, often poorly equipped, schools, and isolated from able-bodied children. Colleen's mother decided to enroll her daughter in the local public school instead.

"My mother had to fight to get me admitted," Colleen said. "The Parent-Teacher Association was against the idea. I'm not sure why. Perhaps they were afraid that disabled children had a contagious [catching] disease."

Colleen loved school and soon made lots of friends. At an early age, she was drawn to acting. "I loved to perform," she said. "I was a real ham."

When Colleen was in first grade, her class prepared to put on a performance of Mary Poppins. "My teacher asked me if I would like to be the narrator," Colleen said. "I told her no. I wanted to be Mary Poppins, and she agreed. So I had my first start in theater. I loved it, and pursued acting through high school and college."

Colleen encountered few difficulties in her first years of school. School maintenance personnel helped her up and down the stairs each day. She participated in all classroom activities, and went on field trips.

"Everybody helped out," she remembered. "But one thing that troubled me was others' excessive attention to my needs.

As awareness of the problems of the handicapped grew, steps were taken such as creating special parking, allowing the handicapped greater self-sufficiency.

'Are you cold?' they would ask. 'Are you okay?' It was like I was a china doll.

"One teacher insisted that I wrap an old blanket around my legs during recess. While the other kids ran and played, I sat with an ugly ragged blanket covering me. One day I threw it off and the teacher never bothered me again."

When Colleen entered fifth grade, she began to feel **alienated** (detached) from her classmates. "Kids turned away from me in junior high. At that time, anyone different from oneself is a threat," she said. "But eventually we begin to understand and accept others' differences."

Barriers Begin to Fall

While Stewart was in high school, the Rehabilitation Act of 1973 became law. It barred unfair treatment of disabled individuals in programs that received federal funds. But it was not immediately enforced.

In the spring of 1977, more than 100 protesters, some hearing **impaired** (diminished in strength), others visually impaired or wheelchair-bound, gathered at the U.S. Health, Education, and Welfare (HEW) offices in San Francisco. They wanted to spur the federal government to action.

HEW Secretary Joseph Califano at last promised "a national

commitment to end discrimination on the basis of handicap." Slowly barriers began to fall. Ramps were built to provide wheelchair access to public buildings. Braille elevator buttons were installed to assist the visually impaired. Television programs offered closed-captioned viewing for the hearing impaired.

The disabled were hired in greater numbers. They were seen less and less as objects of others' assistance and more as contributing members of society.

Similar Feelings and Needs

For both mentally and physically disabled individuals, the greatest obstacles often came from the outside, not from their actual handicaps. "A person may have a lot of talent and pride," said one disabled activist, "but the disability [in the eyes of others] overrides everything else."

A bill called the Americans with Disabilities Act, introduced in Congress in the late 1980s, promised an end to job discrimination for 43 million disabled Americans. It also called for more access to public facilities such as restaurants, buses, and stores.

All the while, disabled Americans worked to prove—to themselves and others—that they could lead productive, relatively independent lives. Like Colleen Stewart, they struggled to undo the pain of past discrimination. Upon graduation from high school, Stewart went to Emory University in Atlanta. She was the only disabled student in the school at the time. Upon graduation, Stewart moved to New York City and began a career in marketing and public relations. She left behind her specially equipped

Opportunities for the disabled have increased due to political activism and legislation. Here, in North Carolina, a man competes in a wheelchair tennis tournament.

AMERICAN ADVENTURES

car, and learned to navigate by taxi.

"New York City buses, even though they have wheelchair access, are not the easiest way to get around," Stewart said. "And the sidewalks are also very difficult. I never take my wheelchair out alone. But then, I'm lucky. I have lots of friends to help me."

This disabled woman holds a press conference to criticize recently passed legislation concerning the handicapped.

CHAPTER CHECK

WORD MATCH
1. alienated
2. Americans with Disabilities Act
3. Rehabilitation Act of 1973
4. impaired
5. Braille

a. diminished in strength
b. system of writing and printing for the visually impaired
c. detached
d. bill to eliminate job discrimination
e. barred unfair treatment of the disabled in federally funded programs

QUICK QUIZ
1. What examples of stereotyping did Colleen Stewart experience? What other stereotypes are sometimes associated with disabled people?
2. In what ways was the movement to give equal rights to disabled people like other social movements of the time? How was it different?

THINK ABOUT IT
1. Why do you think parents of able-bodied children resisted allowing disabled students to attend the same schools?
2. What attitudes and assistance might help disabled people function better in America?

EQUAL JUSTICE

History Detective

1. My peaceful revolution in India served as a model for many of the beliefs practiced by Martin Luther King, Jr. Who am I?

2. I used pickets, boycotts, and fasts to help American farm workers. Who am I?

3. I was home to a year-long bus boycott that started with one black woman, Rosa Parks, who was too tired to move to the back of the bus. Where am I?

4. This was the phrase that summed up the Supreme Court's decision in *Brown* v. *Board of Education of Topeka, Kansas.* What is it?

5. We women made America aware of gender stereotyping. We organized, demonstrated, and wrote books to help women get equal rights. What were we called?

Voices From the Past

The Civil Rights Act of 1964 had a major impact on America. Many of its effects can be seen today. Here is part of Title VII, Section 703:

It shall be an unlawful employment practice for an employer: (1) to fail or refuse to hire or to discharge any individual, or otherwise to discriminate against any individual with respect to . . . race, color, religion, sex, or national origin; or to limit . . . employees in any way which would deprive . . . [them] of employment opportunities. . . ."

1. What does this passage require of all employers?

2. What are some examples from history of instances when employers didn't follow such ideas?

3. What things in today's society would have been impossible without this law?

Hands–On History

Writing an Editorial—If you are a girl, pretend you have been denied the opportunity to play on the boy's basketball team. There is no girl's team. If you are a boy, pretend you are a member of this team. Write an editorial to the school newspaper stating your feelings about this issue. Should a girl be made a member of the team? Is it fair to deny girls the right to participate in the sports program?

NO LONGER JUST AN ISLAND

San Francisco, Calif., December 16, 1969—On November 20, a group of 78 Indians calling themselves Indians of All Tribes landed on Alcatraz Island in San Francisco Bay. In the past month, this action has been arousing national interest for Indian freedom. Alcatraz, taken originally from the Indians, has been used in recent times by the federal government as a prison site. The prison has been abandoned for a few years. The Indians moved onto the island under an old law that permitted certain tribes to reclaim land taken from them by the government when it was no longer needed. They proclaimed Alcatraz to be Indian land. Though suffering hardships because of lack of water, food, and electricity, they set about making their stay permanent. Native Americans from all over the country have reacted with great interest. **1.**

Here, Jessie Lopez de la Cruz, 2.

An Interview with Jessie Lopez de la Cruz

San Jose, Calif., November 24, 1968—When people talk about the organizing efforts of the fruit pickers here, they usually discuss Cesar Chavez. But one of the people who helped La Causa and Mr. Chavez more than any other, is a woman named Jessie Lopez de la Cruz. Recently, *Yesterday's News* was able to talk with Ms. Lopez de la Cruz about her life.

Y N: What was the first type of work you performed?
JC: I did the same thing my mother, my grandfather, and my uncles did. We picked prunes off the ground . . . We were paid $4 a ton.

I was 13, and I use to lift and carry a 12-foot sack of cotton. I guess I was lifting 104 and 112 pounds. And I only weighed 97 pounds!
Y N: What was the hardest type of field work?
JC: . . . thinning beets. You were required to use a short-handled hoe. The cutting edge is about seven to eight inches wide and the handle is about a foot long. Then you have to be bent over with the hoe in one hand. You walk down the rows stooped over. You have to work hard, fast, as fast as you can because you are paid by the row, not by the hour. . . .
Y N: How did you first get involved with La Causa?
JC: I guess when the union found out how I was able to talk to people, I was called . . . to one of the meetings, and they gave me my card as an organizer. I am very proud to say I was the first woman organizer out in the fields organizing the people.

3.

You Be the Reporter

Match each question with its news item above.

1. Use library resources to tell how the government resolved this problem.
2. Write a caption that gives information about Jessie Lopez de la Cruz.
3. Write two or more questions for Jessie Lopez de la Cruz. Then write the answers to those questions as she might answer them.

UNDERSTANDING PARALLEL TIME

The three decades between 1950 and 1980 saw many groups in America struggling for equal rights. First, African Americans campaigned to end white racism and discrimination. They were soon followed by women, migrant farm workers, and other groups who demanded the fair and equal treatment and protection guaranteed by the U. S. Constitution. How were these movements related?

The timelines on the opposite page show how these struggles for equal justice were parallel in time. Notice how the decades after 1950 are marked off along the dark band. What group(s) in American society does each timeline represent?

Refer to the timelines to answer these questions on a separate sheet of paper.

1. The U.S. Supreme Court decided, in the case of *Brown* v. *Board of Education of Topeka*, that segregation of races in public schools was illegal. **(a)** In what year did the Supreme Court hand down this decision? **(b)** How many years later did the federal government send troops to Little Rock, Arkansas, to end segregation in schools there?

2. The Civil Rights Movement began in 1955. **(a)** What event occurred in that year in the struggle of African Americans for equal justice? **(b)** How many years later was the March on Washington? the assassination of Martin Luther King, Jr.?

3. In 1965, the federal government passed the Voting Rights Act to assure that every American citizen's right to vote was protected. What else became law a year earlier, and made voting easier for everyone?

4. In 1962, Cesar Chavez began organizing a union of migrant farm workers. **(a)** In what year did he begin La Causa, the strike against the grape growers? **(b)** What happened that same year in the movement of black people for civil rights? **(c)** How many years later did the United Farm Workers win their first contract from a California grape grower?

5. The struggle of American women for full rights has been a long one. **(a)** In what year did this most recent push for women's rights begin? **(b)** What event set off this struggle? **(c)** What other event in that year was important in the struggle of African Americans for equal justice?

6. Many women worked for a constitutional amendment to assure their equal rights. **(a)** What was this amendment called? **(b)** When did Congress pass the amendment? **(c)** Was the amendment ever ratified by the individual states and made into federal law?

7. In 1968, the American Indian Movement was formed. **(a)** What other event happened in the same year? **(b)** For how many years had the Civil Rights Movement been going on (it began in 1955)?

8. In the thirty-year period from 1950 to 1980, many gains were made in the struggle for equal rights. In which decades were the most gains made **(a)** by blacks? **(b)** by migrant farm workers? **(c)** by other groups?

9. Compare this timeline with other timelines in your textbook on pages 632–633 (Unit 20) and pages 696–697 (Unit 22). What other events in American history **paralleled** (took place at the same time as) these struggles for equal justice?

10. Do you think the different struggles for equal justice could have influenced each other? Explain why or why not. Refer to specific dates and events from this timeline.

Struggles for Equal Justice

African Americans

1952
Ralph Ellison publishes *Invisible Man.*

1954
Supreme Court outlaws school segregation.

1955
Montgomery, Alabama, bus boycott

1957
Federal troops in Little Rock, Arkansas

1961
Sit-in demonstrations

1963
March on Washington

1964
24th Amendment outlaws poll taxes.

1965
Voting Rights Act

1968
Martin Luther King, Jr. assassinated.

Migrant Farm Workers

1965
La Causa strike against grape growers.

1966
United Farm Workers gets its first contract.

1970
Grape growers in Central Valley sign contract with UFW.

Women

1963
Betty Friedan publishes *The Feminine Mystique.*

1964
Civil Rights Act of 1964

1972
Congress passes Equal Rights Amendment (ERA).

1982
ERA fails ratification.

Native Americans, Homosexuals, the Disabled

1968
American Indian Movement begins.

1969
Gay Rights Movement begins.

1973
The Rehabilitation Act

1977
Disabled protest in San Francisco.

A TIME FOR

1960
JFK is elected president.

1961
Bay of Pigs invasion

1961
JFK sends military advisors to Vietnam.

1962
Cuban Missile Crisis

1962
Rachel Carson publishes *Silent Spring*.

1963
President Kennedy assassinated.

1964
President Lyndon B. Johnson sends U.S. troops to Vietman.

In 1963, a young folk singer named Bob Dylan wrote a song that made him a hero. The song described how many young people in the 1960s felt about America. The song was called "The Times They Are A-Changin'."

The 1960s began with the election of a new president. His name was John F. Kennedy. Kennedy was different from the other presidents before him. He was the youngest person at age 43—and the first Roman Catholic—to be elected president. Likeable, charming, and intelligent, JFK, as he later was called, had confidence in his own abilities.

Woodstock, a musical festival held for three days in August 1969, was attended by more than 300,000 young people. Originally meant to be just a concert, Woodstock represented the ultimate coming together of music and people of the sixties.

CHANGE

1970

1968
Martin Luther King, Jr., and Robert Kennedy assassinated.

1969
Largest antiwar protest against Vietnam war

First humans walk on the moon.

UNIT 4

The New Frontier

When Kennedy took office, he announced that a "new generation of Americans" had now come to power. Kennedy seemed to promise a new beginning for the United States. He called his program the New Frontier.

The young president brought to the White House a team of people to help him much like himself. These cabinet members, department heads, and aides had new ideas about running the government.

JFK believed there were many young people with energy like his own. Thinking on a world-wide scale, Kennedy believed talented Americans could share their skills with people in foreign countries. Kennedy wanted Americans to become volunteers in the cause of peace. So, in 1961, he proposed that Congress create the Peace Corps, a government organization of volunteers who would work in foreign countries. That same year, however, he sent military advisors to Vietnam. This began the U.S. involvement in the tragedy of Vietnam.

Kennedy also worked hard to bring improvements to American life. His programs showed concern for the poor and elderly. JFK pushed for the beginning of a program to explore outer space.

Cuban Missile Crisis

The New Frontier promised great changes for America. But in some areas

The 1960s were a time of many social and political changes—not always just or peaceful ones. During the summer of 1967, riots set aflame the ghettos of Detroit, Michigan [above], and other urban centers.

Kennedy did not differ that much from the presidents before him. One such area was in political foreign affairs.

Relations with the Soviet Union were tense during the Kennedy Administration. He strongly supported the policy of containing communism. As a result, during Kennedy's term as president, the Cold War almost became "hot."

His first major decision involved Cuba. By 1959, Fidel Castro had overthrown the government in Cuba. One of Castro's first acts was to take over American-owned companies in Cuba. This angered the United States into placing certain economic penalties on Cuba. The Castro government gradually allied itself with the Soviet Union. Kennedy became concerned about the threat to the United States because Cuba is only 90 miles off the Florida coast.

Later Kennedy supported a plan to send a band of Cuban exiles to overthrow Castro's government. The operation was a disaster. The 1400 invaders were quickly surrounded by Castro's army. Many were killed on a beach in Cuba's Bay of Pigs. Many Americans were frightened by Kennedy's military response to the communist threat.

The next year, the Soviet Union began building sites for launching atomic missiles in Cuba. Soviet ships then sailed toward Cuba, carrying the missiles themselves. Kennedy ordered a naval blockade of the island nation. The Soviet Union and the United States were on the brink of nuclear war. Finally, an agreement was worked out, and the danger passed.

The Johnson Years

In November 1963, President Kennedy was killed by an assassin's bullet.

As the Vietnam war escalated, more and more Americans called for an end to it. This is one of the most popular protest posters of the time.

The nation went numb with shock. Vice-President Lyndon B. Johnson became the new president.

Johnson said he wanted to carry out Kennedy's plans. He supported passage of a new civil rights bill. It was a law that Kennedy had proposed to Congress shortly before he was killed. The new law made discrimination against blacks illegal in every state.

Johnson also declared a "war on poverty." He got Congress to enact laws in order to help the millions of poor people in the United States.

The President, however, was not satisfied. Much more could be done to make

Robert F. Kennedy, popular candidate in the 1968 presidential race, was one of two national leaders shot that year—murders that shocked the nation.

America a better place for everyone. Johnson wanted to create what he called the Great Society. In such a society, there would be no poverty, no injustice, no ugliness.

In 1965, Johnson asked Congress to pass one law after another. Among the many new programs that he was able to persuade Congress to create were medical insurance for the elderly and aid to education. Johnson also further protected voting rights for blacks.

Lyndon B. Johnson signed into law a total of 89 major acts in 1965. He brought more changes to government than any president had since Franklin D. Roosevelt. Yet his Great Society came apart, primarily because of a civil war being fought halfway around the world.

The War in Vietnam

Few Americans knew when the fighting really began. President Eisenhower had given military aid to South Vietnam's government. President Kennedy gave more. President Johnson gave a lot more.

At first, most Americans supported the U.S. role in Vietnam. American intervention was necessary, they thought, to prevent the spread of communism in Asia. Before long critics began speaking out. It seemed as if the U.S. Constitution were being ignored because Congress had not declared war against South Vietnam's enemy, North Vietnam. Under the Constitution, Congress—not the president—declares war.

By the beginning of 1968, growing numbers of Americans wanted an end to the war. More than 29,000 U.S. troops had been killed, but the U.S. government said America was winning the war. Then during the Vietnamese New Year called Tet, the rebels launched a successful major offensive. Many Americans believed their government wasn't telling the truth.

The Turmoil of 1968

One writer called 1968 "the year that everything went wrong." First there was the Tet Offensive. Then, in April, Martin Luther King, Jr. was assassinated. In June, shots rang out again. This time the victim was Robert Kennedy, one of John F. Kennedy's younger brothers. He had just won California's Democratic primary. It looked as if he might win the Democratic nomination for president.

Next came the Democratic convention in Chicago. Inside the convention hall, there were battles between those who supported the war, and those who opposed it. Outside, on Chicago's streets, there were violent battles between antiwar demonstrators and police.

Changes in America

Many Americans wondered what was happening to their country. They felt as if they were living in a revolution. Violence appeared to be everywhere. In the South in the early 1960s, black and white civil rights workers were killed and beaten. Civil rights leaders were assassinated. Every summer from 1964 to 1967, riots broke out in black neighborhoods in cities across the country. Rioters looted stores and set buildings on fire.

Besides the political changes, many social changes began to occur in American society. Many people, especially the young, began to question the conformity and acceptance of values that had been part of life in the 1950s. Some began experimenting with new lifestyles.

Americans grew more aware of the problems in the environment. In 1962, Rachel Carson wrote a book called *Silent Spring*. In it she warned how the future of life depends on how we take care of our planet. Many people became concerned that human actions were damaging the environment.

Older Americans worried about what was happening to young people. Youths wondered what was wrong with adults. Many young men let their hair grow long. Large numbers of students on college campuses protested against the U.S. involvement in the Vietnam war. The two generations seemed to be drifting farther apart. People called this the **generation gap**.

By the end of the 1960s, the decade had made people aware of major issues such as war, peace, space, the environment, and poverty. The 1960s broke up the conformity of the 1950s, and unleashed new debates about which direction the United States would head.

The Southeast Asian nation of Vietnam had been ravaged by war long before the United States entered the fight. In less than 10 years, however, U.S. military might devastated the countryside.

CHAPTER 20 THE KENNEDY YEARS

John Fitzgerald Kennedy (1917–1963) set a new tone of activism for the nation. He told Americans, "Ask not what your country can do for you—ask what you can do for your country."

He was the youngest man ever to be elected president of the United States. He was also the first Catholic to be elected president. Tall, slim and boyish, John F. Kennedy looked even younger than his 43 years. When he took the oath of office, January 20, 1961, he told the nation that "a new generation of Americans" had come to power. Clearly he meant a younger generation, one that was not afraid to face challenges.

Kennedy also stated his determination to defend freedom by stopping communist **guerrilla** (operating outside the military establishment) movements in countries around the world. "Let every nation know . . . that we shall pay any price, bear any burden, meet any hardship, support any friend, oppose any foe to assure the survival and success of liberty," JFK announced. He also promised to seek peaceful solutions to the Cold War, the hostility between the United States and the Soviet Union. "Let us never negotiate out of fear," he said, "but let us never fear to negotiate."

Kennedy's youth and vigor inspired many Americans with hope for a better world. Under his leadership, the White

114

AMERICAN ADVENTURES

House took on a new tone. He and his wife Jacqueline were an elegant and attractive couple. Their two little children, Caroline and John, charmed the public. The first lady was devoted to the arts. Artists, writers and musicians were often invited to the White House.

Some people compared the Kennedy White House to Camelot, the legendary palace where King Arthur, his queen Guinevere, and many brave knights gathered. Kennedy himself was very fond of a musical play about King Arthur called *Camelot*.

The dream of Camelot lasted only about 1000 days. On November 22, 1963, in Dallas, Texas, an assassin's bullet shattered it. Americans were stunned by the murder of their young president whose spirit had already made its mark on American society.

Growing Up a Kennedy

John Fitzgerald Kennedy was born May 29, 1917, in a suburb of Boston, Massachusetts. His father Joseph Kennedy was a millionaire businessman.

Jack, as he was nicknamed, had his share of problems while growing up. He

John F. Kennedy [upper left] grew up in a privileged family, but his wealth did not blind him to the pain of the less fortunate.

was a frail, skinny kid, plagued with a bad back and numerous illnesses. He lived in the shadow of his older brother Joseph, Jr., who was both a skilled athlete and a good student.

John Kennedy received recognition during his senior year at Harvard University. He wrote a long essay on why England was unprepared when World War II broke out in 1939. The paper was so good that it was published as a book after his graduation in 1940. Called *Why England Slept*, it quickly became a bestseller.

During World War II, Kennedy had been the commander of a Navy PT (patrol torpedo) boat in the South Pacific. One night a Japanese destroyer cut his boat, PT 109, in two. Kennedy's back was hurt, but he swam with his men to an island three and one-half miles away. He towed an injured crewman the entire distance, then spent most of the next four days in the water, trying to to get help. Finally, on the fifth day, Kennedy and his men were rescued. Kennedy won two medals for heroism, and the Purple Heart, awarded to soldiers wounded in action.

World War II was a turning point in Kennedy's life. His father had always hoped that one day Joe, Jr. would become president. But in 1944, Joe, a Navy pilot, was killed while on a secret bombing mission. Now Jack would take his older brother's place, and enter politics.

Kennedy Enters Politics

After the war, Kennedy ran for the House of Representatives. His mother Rose, and his brothers and sisters campaigned enthusiastically. His father spared no expense to help his campaign. Kennedy, a Democrat, easily beat his Republican opponent.

In 1952, John Kennedy ran for the U.S. Senate. His campaign was managed by his younger brother Robert. Many Republicans were voted into office with the new Republican president, Dwight D. Eisenhower. But John Kennedy won his election. The following year, he married Jacqueline Bouvier, a stylish, well-educated, and wealthy young woman.

Shortly after election to the Senate, he had back surgery. His back problems had worsened since his war injury, but he chose a dangerous operation rather than a life on crutches. While recovering from surgery, Kennedy wrote a book called *Profiles in Courage* that later won a Pulitzer Prize. The book told the stories of eight American politicians who risked their careers by bravely supporting unpopular causes.

Kennedy Becomes President

In 1960, Kennedy fought hard to win the Democratic nomination for president. Some Democrats feared that his religion would turn people against him, but Kennedy persuaded many voters that prejudice should have no place in the election. "If this election is decided on the basis that 40 million [Catholic] Americans lost their chance of becoming president on the day they were baptized," he said, "then it is the whole nation that will be the loser in the eyes of history, and in the eyes of our own people."

In a very close race, Kennedy defeated the

Republican candidate, Richard M. Nixon, who had been vice-president under Eisenhower. Kennedy set out to do many things in three years as president. His programs became known as the New Frontier. He established the Peace Corps, pushed for putting an American on the moon before the end of the decade, and worked on a new civil rights law.

The Peace Corps

In 1961, President Kennedy started the Peace Corps, using American volunteers to teach skills to people in developing countries. In the 1950s, many people in developing countries could not grow enough food and often starved. They had few schools, and many could not read or write. Often their homes had no running water or electricity. They needed hospitals, schools, roads, and bridges.

The Peace Corps sent nurses, doctors, teachers, engineers, and farmers to these countries. These volunteers started health clinics and schools, increased food production, and improved the water supply. Five thousand young Americans joined the Peace Corps in its first year.

The Peace Corps was great public relations for the United States. It aided people in developing countries, but few of the changes improved their way of life permanently.

On November 22, 1963, President and Mrs. Kennedy arrived in Dallas, Texas. The young president was slain only hours later.

The Space Program

In 1957, the Soviet Union had amazed the

world by launching the first satellite, *Sputnik,* into outer space. Later, Yuri Gagarin, a Soviet astronaut, became the first human to circle the earth in a satellite.

President Kennedy worried that the United States was lagging behind. In September 1962, he promised the nation that the United States would put an American on the moon by 1970. Congress approved billions of dollars for his goal, although many people questioned whether this was the best use for so much money. However, on July 20, 1969, U.S. astronaut Neil Armstrong became the first human to set foot on the moon. Unfortunately, JFK did not live to see this spectacular success.

Civil Rights

In the 1950s, blacks increasingly demanded an end to segregation and discrimination. After initially hesitating, JFK spoke to the nation about the need for civil rights legislation on June 11, 1963. "Are we," he asked, "to say to the world . . . that this is a land of the free except for Negroes? That we have no second class citizens except Negroes?"

A week later, Kennedy sent a new civil rights bill to Congress. This bill outlawed discrimination in public places, and offered some protection for the rights of blacks to vote and to work.

Most of the bill was passed by Congress on July 2, 1964, eight months after President Kennedy's death. His successor, Lyndon B. Johnson, signed it into law the same day. Earlier Johnson had said, "No memorial oration . . . could more eloquently honor President Kennedy's memory than the passage of the civil rights bill for which he fought so long."

CHAPTER CHECK

WORD MATCH
1. guerrilla
2. Yuri Gagarin
3. Peace Corps
4. Neil Armstrong
5. New Frontier

a. Soviet astronaut and first person to circle the earth
b. operating outside the military establishment
c. U.S. agency composed of volunteers who teach and work in less-developed countries
d. Kennedy's program for a new and better America
e. U.S. astronaut and first person to set foot on the moon

QUICK QUIZ
1. In what two ways was the Kennedy presidency a first?
2. Name at least three programs of the New Frontier.

THINK ABOUT IT
1. What large groups of Americans have never been represented in the presidency? Do you think any one of them is likely to have a member elected in your lifetime? If so, which one or ones?
2. How did the Cold War affect U.S. foreign policy during the Kennedy presidency?

21 CRISIS IN CUBA

A fiery orator and persuasive leader, Fidel Castro [above] led a successful rebellion against Cuba's dictator. His growing power and his alliance with the communist Soviet Union worried U.S. leaders.

The year was 1962. Eighteen Soviet ships steamed toward Cuba. Six Soviet submarines sailed with them. U.S. Navy ships rushed to stop them from reaching Cuba. Soviet Premier Nikita Khrushchev (kroosh-CHAWF) warned that Soviet submarines would sink any U.S. ship that tried to stop his ships. The United States, however, was ready to sink the Soviet submarines, if necessary.

This showdown took place between the United States and the Soviet Union. In many ways, it was the most frightening confrontation of the Cold War. If shooting started, it could lead to the use of nuclear weapons. People everywhere were afraid that this would happen.

Why was this showdown taking place? What was so vital about the island of Cuba that it brought the world to the edge of nuclear war? The story had begun in the late 1950s. At that time, Cuba was controlled by the dictator, Fulgencio Batista (ful-HEN-see-oh bah-TEE-stuh) who had been supported by the U.S. government for years. A Cuban named Fidel Castro (fee-DELL KASS-troh) led a revolt against Batista. The U.S. government recognized that Batista would lose. So at first, Castro and his rebel force had some support from the United States.

In 1959, Castro came to power. Soon after, he began to place communists in positions of power. When the U.S. withdrew support from him, Castro began to ally Cuba with the Soviet Union. His moves alarmed many people in the United States. Unlike Korea, Cuba is not a distant land. It is a Caribbean island, only 90 miles off the Florida coast.

At first, the United States did not take direct military action against Castro. However, the United States did put a temporary embargo on the purchase of Cuban sugar. The U.S. government also gave aid to a group of anti-Castro Cubans who had fled their country. These Cubans organized into a military force to overthrow the Castro government.

Flawed Invasion

President Kennedy learned about this force in January 1961. He agreed to go ahead with a plan developed during the Eisenhower Administration that would allow these Cubans to invade their own country. The invaders planned to join with other anti-Castro Cubans at home, and drive Castro from power.

The invasion took place on April 17, 1961. The invaders landed on a Cuban beach at the Bay of Pigs. The plan failed completely. Most of

A spy plane flying over Cuba in 1962 took this photo. The evidence of a military buildup so near U.S. shores worried American leaders.

the invaders were killed or captured. President Kennedy later maintained that the invasion had failed because of poor planning. He took the blame himself for what had happened at the Bay of Pigs.

A few months later, Fidel Castro announced that he was a communist, and would be one "until the day I die." As the United States increased its opposition to him, Castro relied more and more on the Soviet Union.

Missile Buildup

In 1962, the Soviets began to send many missiles and planes to Cuba. The Soviet Union also sent technicians to show the Cubans how to use this military equipment. Khrushchev said that the missiles and planes were meant only to protect Cuba. He insisted that the missiles were the kind that could only shoot down planes flying overhead.

U.S. spy planes flying over Cuba had not spotted any nuclear missiles. Even so, President Kennedy was taking no chances. He ordered the spy flights to continue. In October 1962, photographs made by a U.S. spy plane clearly showed nuclear missiles being set up by soldiers. These offensive missiles would be able to reach as far into the United States as Dallas or St. Louis. The atomic warheads they could carry were much more powerful than the atomic bomb dropped on Hiroshima in 1945.

President Kennedy believed he had to act fast. In a few days, the missiles would be set up completely. He asked his advisers for suggestions. There were several different ideas. The United States could: (1) do nothing—after all, the U.S. had missiles set up in Turkey and in Europe near the Soviet Union; (2) meet with Soviet leaders and hold diplomatic talks; (3) blow up the missiles with air attacks; (4) invade Cuba, and drive out Castro; (5) blockade Cuba by sending the U.S. Navy to stop any ships from reaching it.

JFK believed that decisive action was needed. On the one hand, there was no time to meet with Soviet leaders. On the other hand, air attacks or an invasion of Cuba might lead to nuclear war. A blockade was dangerous too, but not as dangerous as other actions. A blockade would give both sides time to cool off. Finally, President Kennedy decided to blockade Cuba.

Solemn Suspense

On October 22, 1962, JFK told the American people about the Soviet missiles. He said he was sending U.S. Navy ships to blockade Cuba until the missiles were taken away. He warned this action could lead to nuclear war. However, Kennedy said he was sure the American people would rather take that chance than do nothing about the arming of Cuba.

In the Soviet Union, Khrushchev made warlike statements. He threatened that he would not let U.S. ships stop Soviet ships. Soviet submarines were ready for action. Now the question became clear. Would

The Cuban Missile Crisis, 1962

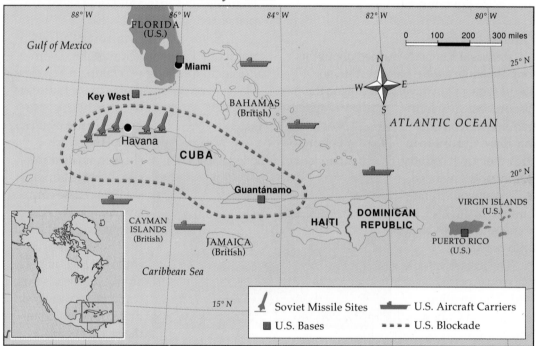

How far is Cuba from the United States? What U.S. territory is near Cuba? Where were U.S. bases located during the Cuban Missile Crisis?

Soviet ships try to force their way through a U.S. Naval blockade? The whole world waited nervously.

People anxiously watched TV news reports. Schools even held air raid drills in case the Soviets attacked. Finally good news came. Soviet ships heading for Cuba had stopped, then turned back. People breathed a little easier. Yet there was still the danger of the missiles already in Cuba. The United States was ready to invade Cuba, if necessary, to get the missiles out of Cuban hands.

Then Khrushchev sent Kennedy a letter. It said that the Soviet Union would take back its missiles if the United States promised not to invade Cuba. Kennedy agreed. The Soviets took their missiles out of Cuba. Kennedy called off the blockade. It was a great moment for both Kennedy and Khrushchev—they had avoided war.

The awful danger of a nuclear war

These protesters against U.S. intervention in Cuba demonstrated across the street from the United Nations in New York City.

was over. Afterward, the United States and the Soviet Union put aside some of their differences. A treaty was signed between them that stopped the above-ground testing of nuclear weapons. Many other nations later signed this treaty. President Kennedy called it an important "first step" toward world peace.

CHAPTER CHECK

WORD MATCH
1. Fidel Castro
2. Nikita Khrushchev
3. Fulgencio Batista
4. Bay of Pigs
5. Turkey

a. Cuban dictator supported by U.S. Government
b. Soviet premier during late 1950s and early 1960s
c. Cuban leader who led communist revolt in late 1950s
d. country near Soviet Union where U.S. had set up missiles
e. where Cuban rebels were killed in a U.S.-backed attempt to remove Castro

QUICK QUIZ
1. What set off the crisis in Cuba in 1962? How was the Soviet Union involved in it?
2. How did the Soviet Union react to the actions of the U.S. Navy in the Caribbean—initially and finally?

THINK ABOUT IT
1. What might be the situation today if the Bay of Pigs invasion had succeeded? Do you think it was a good idea?
2. How do you think the following people felt about the Monroe Doctrine: John F. Kennedy; Fidel Castro; Nikita Khrushchev?

22 CRUSADER FOR THE ENVIRONMENT

Rachel Carson (1907–1964) was a talented writer as well as a marine biologist. Her book *Silent Spring* vividly described how humans were destroying the planet and sparked an ecology movement.

T here once was a town in the heart of America where flowers bloomed in the Spring . . . and the countryside was famous for its variety of birds. . . . Then a strange blight crept over the area and everything began to change. . . . Cattle and sheep sickened and died. . . . Farmers spoke of much illness among their families. . . . There was a strange stillness. The birds, for example, where had they gone? What has happened to silence the voices of Spring?

This description was written in 1962 by a scientist named Rachel Carson. She warned about the dangers of **pesticides** (poisons that are used to kill insects.) Her book *Silent Spring* caused a sensation because it alerted people for the first time that the future of the human race was dependent on the health of the environment.

Carson's Childhood

Rachel Louise Carson was raised on a farm in Pennsylvania. There were no other children nearby, and her brother and sister were much older. Rachel spent a great deal of time with her mother who taught her to love the outdoors and respect nature. Often they took walks in the woods to look at plants and small creatures.

Rachel was a good student. She wanted to be a writer, and published her first story when she was ten years old. When Carson attended college, she changed her focus from writing to science. "Scientists are never bored," she wrote. "We can't be. There is always something new."

A Writer-Scientist

As an adult, Carson combined both of her interests and became a writer-scientist. She spent summers at the famous ocean research center in Woods Hole, Massachusetts, where she studied tidal pools and ocean currents. After attending graduate school, she worked for the U.S. Fish and Wildlife Service. Then she wrote two books about the wonders of the the sea.

Carson's research for the government during World War II made her aware of the dangers of the many new **toxic** (poisonous, destructive) chemicals. In the 1950s, chemical companies started selling these new chemicals to kill weeds and bugs. Carson became concerned. Her concern deepened when a friend told her an alarming story about a pesticide called DDT. The friend had sprayed DDT to kill mosquitoes and gypsy moths that were eating her plants. The DDT had also killed 14 robins. Carson decided to gather research, and write a book about these new pesti-

Today's demand for clean air and water, and for conservation of natural resources, can be traced to Carson's efforts.

cides. She worked on the book, *Silent Spring*, for five years.

Dangers of Pesticides

Silent Spring alerted people to the dangers of pesticides. "Sprays, dusts, and aerosols applied to farms, gardens, forests and homes have the power to kill every insect, 'the good' and 'the bad'," Carson wrote. She explained that this mass killing throws off nature's balance. One form of life is dependent on another, and the environment needs varied forms of life to stay healthy, Carson said. For example, ladybugs and birds control undesirable insects. Bees and other insects help crops to grow.

Carson also pointed out that a poison like DDT does not just disappear. It remains in the soil and in the cells of animals. When a bird eats a poisoned insect, some of the original chemical stays in the bird's body. If it eats enough DDT, the bird might die, or be unable to produce offspring. Human beings also become endangered by this poison when they eat animals poisoned by this chemical.

Chemical pesticides should only be used by people who understand their effect on "soil, water, wildlife and man himself," argued Carson. She ended her book by stressing that there was "the other road" to consider—one without such pesticides.

Controversy Over Silent Spring

Silent Spring was widely read and was translated into 15 languages. It caused a great deal of controversy. Heads of chemical industries argued that pesticides provide many benefits, and that banning them would cause the return of terrible diseases such as malaria, which is spread by insects. The U.S. Department of Agriculture also attacked *Silent Spring*. Government officials argued that pesticides helped farmers grow more crops, and that big harvests kept the cost of food down. One critic said that Carson "would rather let people starve than harm an insect." Another said that "her book was even more poisonous than the pesticides."

Many respected scientists, however, praised *Silent Spring* for creating a new awareness about the planet. After months of study, President John F. Kennedy's Science Advisory Committee published a formal report that supported Carson's theories. The report emphasized that pesticides killed many forms of life. It recommended that people dramatically change their treatment of the environment.

Carson's Legacy

Rachel Carson died in 1964, only two years after *Silent Spring* was published. But her influence lived on. She made **ecology** (the science of relationships between living things and their environment) a household word. More important, Carson was responsible for the emergence of the environmental movement. People became aware of pollution in the water and air, and of the danger in dumping nuclear wastes.

By 1970, the federal government had begun to take action. Congress passed new laws to stop pollution. One was the

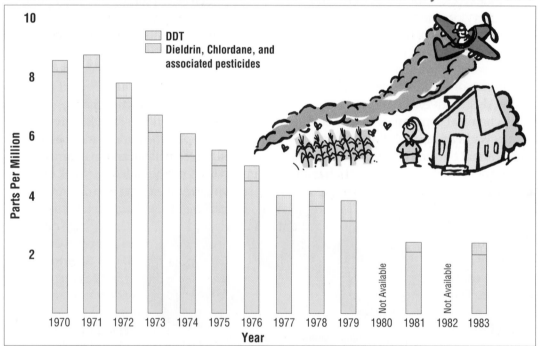

Rachel Carson's book *Silent Spring* led to the creation of the Environmental Protection Agency (EPA) in 1970. Her warnings about the dangers of pesticides led many to be banned. Do you think the EPA's bans made a difference? How?

AMERICAN ADVENTURES

Clean Air Act (1970 and 1977) which required manufacturers to produce cars that give off less poisonous exhaust fumes. The government also created the Environmental Protection Agency (EPA). The EPA ordered a ban on nearly all use of DDT, and established stricter government regulations of pesticides.

Our earth became safer because of the laws passed by the government after *Silent Spring* was published. But controversy continued. These new laws came under attack by businesspeople and farmers who feared that these restrictions would hurt their businesses. Often the laws were difficult to enforce. Particularly in poor countries, chemicals are still used in agriculture, and their use is growing.

More Americans became aware that their future was linked to the fate of the earth because of Rachel Carson's work. People are a part of nature, Carson said, and the war against nature is a war against themselves.

Thousands of volunteers joined the movement to clean up the environment in the 1970s. These young volunteers with the Central Park Conservancy care for a New York City park.

CHAPTER CHECK

WORD MATCH

1. pesticides
2. toxic
3. ecology
4. Environmental Protection Agency
5. Clean Air Act

a. law requiring reduction in poisonous car exhaust
b. created to develop laws to limit damage to the earth
c. poisonous, destructive
d. chemicals used for killing weeds and insects
e. the science of the relationship between living things and their environment

QUICK QUIZ

1. Why do people use chemical pesticides? What are their undesirable side effects?
2. What movement did Rachel Carson inspire? Name at least two of its successes, and two of its shortcomings.

THINK ABOUT IT

1. How was Rachel Carson ideally qualified for her life's work?
2. What did Carson mean by a "silent spring"? Do you think response to her concerns has been too much, not active enough, or about right? Explain.

23 LBJ'S GREAT SOCIETY

CHAPTER

Lyndon B. Johnson took office after a national tragedy—the murder of John F. Kennedy. Despite Johnson's work on behalf of minorities and the poor, his presidency was marred by another tragedy—the Vietnam war.

Vice-President Lyndon Baines Johnson was in shock. Only two and one-half hours before, he had been riding behind President John F. Kennedy's car in Dallas, Texas. Cheering crowds lined the roadway. Now, in the president's plane, *Air Force One,* Johnson was being sworn in as Kennedy's successor. Next to him stood Jacqueline Kennedy, her face filled with grief, her pink suit stained with the blood of her dead husband.

Johnson called on Americans to put aside their differences, and honor President Kennedy by supporting his programs. "Let

us put an end to the teaching and preaching of violence," he pleaded in a television speech. Then President Johnson used his well-known powers of persuasion to get Congress to pass President Kennedy's historic civil rights bill.

A few years earlier, when Johnson was Senate **majority leader,** senators had called his technique "the treatment." As a leader of the dominant party, the majority leader's job is to push bills through Congress. Johnson, a Texan who stood six feet, three inches tall, would put his arm around the shoulder of a senator whose vote he needed. Speaking in a soft drawl and using colorful slang, he would flatter the senator. If that didn't work, he would complain, accuse, or persuade until the senator gave in.

A Political Upbringing

Lyndon Johnson learned early about politics and persuasion. He was born August 27, 1908, near Stonewall, Texas, in a small house that had no electricity, hot water, or indoor toilet. His mother, Rebekah Baines Johnson, cooked on a wood-burning stove. His father, Sam Ealy Johnson, Jr., had served in the Texas House of Representatives in Austin since 1904.

In time, the Johnsons' fortunes improved. A few years after Lyndon was born, the family bought a nice house in Johnson City, where Sam often entertained visiting Texas politicians. When Lyndon was older, he began to accompany his father on trips. Lyndon recalled, "I loved going with my father to the legislature. . . . The only thing I loved more was going with him on the trail during his campaigns for re-election."

To raise money for college, Lyndon took a year off to teach at a grade school. His students were mostly poor Mexican Americans. The experience made a strong impression on Johnson. "Somehow you never forget what poverty and hatred can do when you see its scars on the hopeful face of a young child."

Entering Politics

Lyndon Johnson's rise in politics was tied to President Franklin D. Roosevelt's New Deal. As Texas director of the National Youth Administration (NYA), he put 20,000 high school and college students to work. In 1937, Johnson ran for Congress with a single message: "A vote for Johnson is a vote for Roosevelt's program." He won the election, and helped pass legislation that brought electric power, housing, and jobs to the people of his district.

After the war, in 1948, Johnson was elected to the U.S. Senate. When the Democrats won a majority of seats in the Senate in 1955, Johnson was chosen majority leader. In this position, he decided what bills would be voted on, and often controlled the outcome. He pushed through two civil rights bills designed to protect the voting rights of blacks, especially in the South. It was the first civil rights legislation passed by the Senate in 87 years.

Johnson was aiming for the presidency. In 1960, he battled John F. Kennedy for the Democratic nomination and lost. When Kennedy asked Johnson to run as his vice-president, Johnson surprised everyone by accepting.

The job of vice-president gave Johnson much less power than he had as Senate majority leader. Then, on

LBJ (1908–1973) was known for his dry wit, sharp tongue, and boundless energy. Yet even these assets could not help him soothe a nation torn by a war overseas.

November 22, 1963, fate thrust Johnson into the role he most wanted. Kennedy's death allowed him to become the nation's 36th president.

In May 1964, when he spoke to the nation about his dream for America, Johnson had begun to create his own program called the Great Society. In this society, there would be no poverty or racial injustice. Johnson declared a "war on poverty." The United States would be a place where every child would get a good education. It would be a land of beautiful cities and countryside.

On November 5, 1964, President Johnson defeated his Republican opponent, Arizona Senator Barry Goldwater, in the greatest landslide in U.S. history up to that time. His popular vote was 43 million to Goldwater's 27 million.

Second Term

Now Johnson pushed through Congress a flood of bills to carry out his dream. The first was Medicare, a health insurance plan for people 65 years old and over. Medicare would pay the hospital bills and most of the doctors' bills for elderly Americans.

Next was a bill for federal aid to education. It provided $1.5 billion to improve public schools, particularly in areas where there were many poor families. No schools could receive aid unless they obeyed laws prohibiting segregation and admitted both black and white students.

Despite some progress, most blacks in the South were still denied their right to vote by unfair state laws. In March 1964, Johnson asked Congress for a law that would permit the federal government to supervise state elections in any county where black citizens were prevented from voting. One year later, the Voting Rights Act was passed. Black officials began to be elected in many communities throughout the South. Black voting dramatically increased throughout the country.

Many other laws were passed to help create the Great Society. There were laws to improve the nation's highways, and to clean up air pollution. Other laws helped poor people in the Appalachian Mountain region, cleaned up city slums, and provided low-rent public housing. A total of 89 laws were passed that were designed, in Johnson's words, "to advance the quality of our American civilization."

Vietnam War

But President Johnson's War on Poverty was soon crippled by another war—the military war in Vietnam. After August 1964, the United States became more and more involved in the struggle in this East Asian country between communist and anti-communist forces. Many Americans originally supported the war. However, as the war dragged on, and thousands of American soldiers died, more people wanted the United States to get out of Vietnam. President Johnson's popularity fell sharply. In March 1968, he told the nation that he would not run again for president. He wanted to devote all his time to trying to end the war.

On January 20, 1969, Richard M. Nixon took office after winning the 1968 presidential election against Vice-President Hubert Humphrey. Johnson became a private citizen without a government job for the first time in 34 years. Many Americans would remember him as a man who tried to end poverty and injustice in the United States. Others would remember him as a man who bogged the United States down in a hopeless war fought halfway around the world.

This 8-foot by 11-foot wooden construction, *Patriots Parade*, shows anti-Johnson sentiment due to President Johnson's intervention in Cambodia.

CHAPTER CHECK

WORD MATCH
1. Voting Rights Act
2. majority leader
3. Medicare
4. Great Society
5. War on Poverty

a. Johnson's program to eliminate economic suffering
b. health insurance plan for elderly Americans
c. Johnson's plan to improve the quality of life for all Americans
d. senator chosen by dominant party to push bills through Senate and House
e. allowed government supervision of elections where blacks were prevented from voting

QUICK QUIZ
1. How did Lyndon Johnson learn about politics? What was his political style?
2. What two "wars" were fought during the Johnson administration? Which was the more successful?

THINK ABOUT IT
1. How did Johnson's knowledge of Congress help him as president?
2. Johnson's War on Poverty was successful in raising the income of the poorest Americans. However, it was not popular with many people. Who do you think might have opposed it, and what interests would they represent?

24 THE TRAGEDY OF VIETNAM

U.S. troops jump from helicopters into tall elephant grass as the enemy fire on them in a South Vietnamese jungle north of the Dong Dai River in 1965.

M*other*
I am cursed.
I was . . . trained to kill
asked to die
I could not vote
I can't ask why

Mother
I am cursed
spit on
and shunned
by long-haired doves

Sergeant Thomas Oathout wrote the lines above while serving in the Vietnam war. Like thousands of American soldiers he eventually came home to "furled [rolled up] flags and silent drums."

In the early 1960s, few Americans could locate Vietnam on a map. But by the beginning of 1968, the Vietnam war had cost Lyndon B. Johnson the presidency. How could a civil war, begun in a small far-away country, cause such turmoil in the United States?

History of U.S. Involvement

Before World War II, Vietnam was a French colony. During the war, it was occupied by the Japanese. Then, in 1946, the French returned. They began fighting Ho Chi Minh, a Vietnamese nationalist communist leader, for control of the country. Truman and other government officials feared the spread of communism.

President Eisenhower also supported the French, who were eventually defeated by the Vietnamese. In the spring of 1954, France and the Vietnamese rebels agreed to divide Vietnam into two parts—a communist North, headed by Ho Chi Minh, and a non-communist South, headed by Ngo Dinh Diem (no din ZEE-em). This arrangement was supposed to be temporary, until elections could be held in 1956 to unify the country.

When elections were scheduled for later that year, the South, with Eisenhower's blessing, refused to hold them. They feared that the communists would win and take control of all Vietnam. Eisenhower sent military advisors to train a South Vietnamese army.

After Kennedy became president, he sent additional aid and military personnel in 1961. The number of Americans in Vietnam increased to at least 15,000 by the fall of 1963.

In the meantime, Diem's popularity waned. In November 1963, after a Buddhist rebellion, he was killed. Three weeks later, President Kennedy was gunned down. Kennedy's intentions for future U.S. involvement in Vietnam would remain a mystery.

Johnson's War

When Lyndon B. Johnson became president, he continued support for South Vietnam, where the Vietcong (South Vietnamese communists) were fighting the government. South Vietnamese leaders were corrupt and unstable. Johnson became increasingly concerned that they were vulnerable to a communist takeover.

Johnson decided to take action in August 1964. He claimed that American ships were attacked in the Gulf of Tonkin, off the coast of North Vietnam. Others, including the captain of one ship, were not so sure. Johnson did not wait to learn the truth. He saw the supposed incident as a way to enter the war. He asked Congress to give him support for any measures he might take against the Vietnamese communists.

Congress agreed and passed the Gulf of Tonkin Resolution that granted Johnson "all necessary measures to repel any armed attack against the forces of the United States and to prevent further aggression." Johnson then sent the first U.S. combat troops to South Vietnam. He also decided to bomb North Vietnam. The bombing continued for three years, and proved to be a failure. Many Vietnamese civilians were killed, yet the capacity of the Vietcong to fight grew.

The Tet Offensive

The United States continued sending troops to Vietnam. By the end of 1968, there were almost 500,000 American soldiers in South Vietnam. At that point, North Vietnamese troops were aiding the Vietcong. On January 31, 1968, the communists launched their most dramatic attack of the war. Tet, a week-long celebration of the Vietnamese New Year, had just begun, and the Americans and the South Vietnamese were off-guard. Their opponents seized the opportunity to attack cities. Fighting was especially intense in Saigon, the capital of South Vietnam.

One American soldier who had arrived in Vietnam the day before the offen-

The War in Vietnam

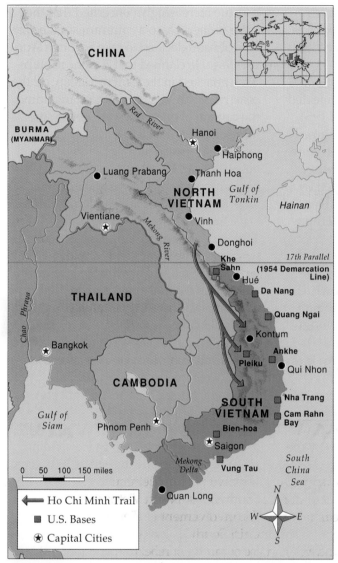

What countries border on Vietnam? What was the capital of South Vietnam during the war in Vietnam? How long was the Ho Chi Minh Trail?

sive began was immediately sent to Saigon. He described the fighting:

We fought from house to house and street to street. We'd just shoot inside [a house] with our rifles and then the M-60 [a machine gun]. Then we had to go up into the house and make sure they were dead. We didn't have any flamethrowers. I didn't see any tanks in Saigon. They didn't have things like you see in the movies on TV about World War II. It surprised me.

The War at Home

Despite the counterattack, the Tet Offensive marked the beginning of American resolve to get out of Vietnam. Film clips of the brutality were broadcast into millions of American living rooms.

College students gained support in their protest of the war, which began as early as 1965 and the first big draft. Many people thought that Johnson should withdraw all American troops. These people, known as **doves,** thought the Vietnamese should be allowed to settle their own problems. Others, known as **hawks,** felt America should take an active role in stopping the spread of communism.

Johnson knew he was in serious trouble. Eugene McCarthy, a Democratic senator from Minnesota, campaigned against Johnson for the presidency. McCarthy said that American involvement in the war was wrong and immoral.

Government officials were reporting that America was winning the war. Television images gave a different story. After the Tet Offensive, Johnson realized that the war could not be won. The South Vietnamese government could not gain enough support among its people. But if America withdrew from Vietnam, Johnson and others feared that America would be disgraced and that communism would spread.

McCarthy made a strong showing in the New Hampshire Democratic presidential primary. Other critics of the war then entered the race. One was Robert F. Kennedy, a Democratic senator from New York.

On March 31, 1968, Johnson stunned the nation. At the end of a televised speech about new peace plans and military strategies, he announced that he would not run again for president.

America at War With Itself

That summer, the violence continued. Crowds of antiwar protestors gathered at the National Democratic Convention in Chicago. The police grew enraged at the demonstrations. They swung billy clubs, injuring many protestors.

Inside the convention hall, Hubert Humphrey, Johnson's vice-president, won his party's presidential nomination. But Democrats remained divided over American participation in the war. Many associated Humphrey with Johnson's war policies.

Richard Nixon, the Republican candidate, was able to take advantage of Democratic division. He announced a plan for "peace with honor." Nixon wouldn't disclose the details of this plan, but it helped him win the election.

Americans continued to be haunted by TV images of the war. In the steamy jungles of Vietnam, young American soldiers continued to be killed. Many of them were poor, and members of minority groups. They fought the war while affluent young men studied in universities. The voices coming from those universities grew louder and louder: "The senseless carnage must stop."

CHAPTER CHECK

WORD MATCH
1. Vietcong
2. doves
3. Ho Chi Minh
4. hawks
5. Ngo Dinh Diem

a. people against U.S. involvement in Vietnam
b. leader of nationalist communist North Vietnam
c. people in favor of U.S. involvement in Vietnam
d. head of anti-communist South Vietnam
e. the South Vietnamese communist rebels

QUICK QUIZ
1. Describe American involvement in Vietnam under Presidents Eisenhower, Kennedy, and Johnson.
2. What was the Tet Offensive, and why was it important?

THINK ABOUT IT
1. Do you think television shortened or prolonged the Vietnam war? Explain your reason.
2. Until Vietnam, the United States had never lost a war. What weight might this fact have on decision makers in Washington?

25 THE PEACE MOVEMENT

More and more Americans, seeing death nightly on TV news, came to oppose the Vietnam war. This photo of a young person placing a flower in a soldier's rifle became one of the most famous images of the peace movement.

On April 17, 1965, twenty thousand people, mostly college students, marched through the nation's capital in protest of the Vietnam war. The protesters, almost all white, middle-class, and neatly dressed, paraded through the streets with signs and banners proclaiming their urgent message: "Stop the War!"

Students had traveled from 50 colleges across the country to take part in the first national antiwar protest. In part, the march was a reaction to President Lyndon Johnson's recent order to bomb North Vietnam.

Traditionally, American college stu-dents were more interested in daily cam-pus life—studying, enjoying friends, or dating—than in national political issues. Unlike their counterparts in Europe and South America, and those in the Civil Rights Movement, they had no tradition as **political activists** (people who work to change governmental policies). This changed by the mid–1960s, as the war in Vietnam began to wrench apart American public opinion.

Some Americans argued that U.S. support for South Vietnam was vital to prevent all of Vietnam from coming under communist control. They insisted that the United States was obligated to stand behind South Vietnam under the terms of the South East Asia Treaty Organization (SEATO). SEATO was an alliance of eight nations (Australia, France, Great Britain, New Zealand, Pakistan, the Philippines, Thailand, and the United States) created to prevent the expansion of communism in Southeast Asia. President Lyndon Johnson later said, "If I left that war, and let the communists take over Vietnam, then I would be seen as a coward and my nation as an appeaser. . . ."

Critics said that America's involvement in Vietnam was a disastrous mistake in foreign policy. They pointed out that the United States had gripping problems at home—poverty, rising crime, segregation, and inflation. In addition, the South Vietnamese leadership was notoriously corrupt. Finally, Americans asked, what business did the U.S. have interfering in another country's internal affairs, especially one so far away as Vietnam?

The War at Home

As American involvement in the war in Vietnam **escalated** (increased), many young people enlisted in the armed services. Others were drafted into service. By the end of 1965, a total of 250,000 American troops had been sent to Vietnam, by the end of 1967, as many as 450,000.

At home, influenced by the dramatic, media-covered civil rights protests of the early 1960s, many college students turned their energies to Vietnam.

In the spring of 1965, "teach-ins" began at universities around the country. Professors and students debated the causes and effects of the war. One student group, Students for a Democratic Society (SDS), organized demonstrations, or protest marches, such as the one in Washington, D.C. As the war dragged on, opposition took many forms—from highly dramatic to horrifying.

In Oakland, California, protesters blocked army trains carrying Vietnam-bound soldiers. In October 1967, thousands marched to the Pentagon, the nation's military defense headquarters, and confronted the armed National Guard.

Thousands of antiwar protesters in Washington, D.C., hold lighted candles at a rally.

As the war escalated overseas, images of peace, such as doves and flowers, became more common at home. This poster illustrates a popular question of the day.

As the peace movement grew, it became an uneasy **coalition** (union of different groups with common objectives). Many people opposed U.S. involvement in other countries' wars. Others did not support the war because they felt it could not be won. Some felt that the global spread of communism was not a threat. Some radical groups insisted that the war was a sign that American society needed to be transformed through revolution. Radicals—such as one group called the Weathermen—captured worldwide attention when they bombed public buildings.

Not all the protestors were young. Some were older, more conservative people in influential positions. But public opinion polls throughout the 1960s showed the majority of Americans, young and old, supported U.S. involvement in Vietnam.

Resisting the Draft

The draft system angered many Americans, especially young people. Critics pointed out that most of the people drafted into the armed forces were poor or black, sometimes both. Initially, young men who had the grades and money to be enrolled in college were not drafted.

But in 1966, the draft system ended automatic student **deferments** (temporary delays of military service). College students were outraged. As the numbers drafted into the armed forces soared, students across the country bitterly resisted the draft. Many burned draft cards and went to jail. Some fled to Canada, Sweden, and other countries.

Nixon's War

In 1968, Richard M. Nixon defeated the Democratic candidate, Hubert H. Humphrey, to become president. In his campaign Nixon promised to bring the war to an "honorable end." The president announced he would turn over the defense of South Vietnam to its government and army. Meanwhile, he would slowly pull U.S. troops out of Vietnam.

But many Americans couldn't wait as hundreds were still being killed each week. The continued to march, resist the draft, and plaster their message on car bumpers: "Peace now!" More than a million people took part in the largest

AMERICAN ADVENTURES

demonstration of the decade on October 15, 1969, in Washington, D.C. They lit candles, wore black armbands in mourning, and listened to speeches, and songs such as Bob Dylan's:

> *How many times must the*
> *cannonballs fly*
> *before they're forever banned?*
> *The answer, my friend, is blowing*
> *in the wind. . . .*
> *The answer is blowing in*
> *the wind.*

The peace movement gained new strength when some soldiers returning home joined the protest against the war. Vietnam veterans led this 1972 antiwar march in San Francisco.

CHAPTER CHECK

WORD MATCH

1. political activists
2. escalated
3. deferments
4. SDS
5. coalition

a. union of different groups with common objectives
b. temporary delays of military service
c. people who work to change governmental policies
d. increased, particularly in relation to war
e. group of students who organized demonstrations against U.S. fighting in Vietnam

QUICK QUIZ

1. What points of view were represented in the peace movement during the Vietnam war?
2. What was the reasoning behind the position of those who supported American involvement in Vietnam?

THINK ABOUT IT

1. Why do you think college students were given the draft deferments? Do you think this policy was fair?
2. Would you say that those who protested the war were successful? Give reasons for your answer.

26 THE NOW GENERATION

Many hippies lived in communes like this one in Martha's Vineyard, Massachusetts.

In the summer of 1967, Janet, a runaway from the Midwest, sat on the curb of a street in Haight-Ashbury, a section of San Francisco. She watched a parade of **hippies** stream by. Hippies were young people who were rebelling against traditional values. Many wore wire-rimmed glasses, denim jackets, bell-bottom jeans, tie-dyed shirts, sandals, beads, and headbands. As one popular song of the time said: "If you're going to San Francisco, be sure to wear some flowers in your hair. . . . "

Who were these young people? How had they so quickly become a **counterculture** (a group with values markedly different from those of the mainstream)? After all, Janet had been raised in middle-class comfort. Why had she run away from home?

Social Discontent

"I couldn't put my finger on it, but I knew there was something wrong with the society I lived in," Janet said. Many young people agreed. As part of the first generation to grow up with television, she witnessed American society becoming more and more **materialistic** (concerned with money and possessions). At the same time, she observed glaring social inequalities between whites and blacks, and rich and poor. Hippies didn't have patience with those who said that correction of these problems had to wait. They demanded justice—now.

Janet wasn't interested in party politics. But she found herself affected by the turmoil of the political events of her times. In a few short years, there was the war in Vietnam, then civil rights demonstrations, and the assassinations of President John F. Kennedy, later his brother, Senator Robert Kennedy, and Dr. Martin Luther King, Jr.

Janet wasn't alone. Many people in her generation felt frustrated with American society. While Janet headed for San Francisco, Tim, another discontented young person, quit his New England college and hitchhiked to New York City's Greenwich Village, another hippie center. As one college teacher wrote, students had come to see American universities as "factories" that treated all students the same. Students were expected to get unimaginative corporate jobs after graduation.

Tim agreed. He didn't want to finish college simply to join a mass work force. Instead, he resisted middle-class society's pressure, so strong in the 1950s, to conform.

Janet and Tim rejected the world of their parents, and wanted to separate themselves from the **Establishment.** This word was used to describe prominent figures of American culture and politics. Social scientists began to use the term generation gap to refer to the difference in values between baby boomers and their parents. Long hair and frayed clothing symbolized these differences.

"Here and Now"

By the late 1960s, Greenwich Village, Haight-Ashbury, and other urban areas around the country— and the world— became havens for hippies and others drawn to the growing counterculture.

Some hippies turned to campus rebellion, some to cultural rebellion. Clothing and long hair was only one mark of the group's defiance. Another was an outlook that stressed living in the "here and now" rather than for future goals such as careers, marriage, or material success. Many hippies moved into **communes** (group living situations in which members share money and chores).

Sharon, who made her way to Venice, California, in 1967, said, "I .was a groupie.

Peter Max, a famous artist of the 1960s, captured the imagination of an entire generation with his images of peace and global awareness.

I lived for music, and for the next rock concert." Some hippies lived for, danced to, and took drugs to their music—rock 'n' roll, folk, or rhythm and blues. Angry, brash, often with a powerful dance beat, the music of the 1960s caught the world's attention. Music by the Beatles, the Rolling Stones, Bob Dylan, Joan Baez, Otis Redding, Aretha Franklin, the Doors, Jefferson Airplane, and the Grateful Dead was popular among the young.

Some young people experimented with drugs. Sharon became heavily involved in the drug scene. She turned to a free clinic for help. These makeshift health centers spread as fast as the hippie communities. Free clinics tackled drug abuse for the first time, as well as the soaring increase in sexually transmitted diseases.

In their heyday, Haight-Ashbury, Venice, Greenwich Village, and other communities housed thousands of hippies. In rural areas, hippie groups founded communal ranches and farms.

The counterculture was largely a movement of affluent white youth. The majority of young Americans didn't define themselves as hippies, even if some boys wore long hair or girls wore jeans instead of dresses. They never completely rejected the adult world. Yet many young people were influenced by the hippies and the student peace movement. They became actively involved in social change. Some took part in social work and education projects in city slums. Others worked to alert the American public about growing environmental problems. Still others worked at overcoming rigid sex roles. Young men sometimes stayed home with the children while their wives went to work.

Generation Gap

What brought about the counterculture? Some Americans said the cause was parents who had given their children too much, and raised them too permissively. But social scientist Margaret Mead had another explanation. In her 1970 book, *Culture and Commitment,* she wrote that young people were growing up in a world totally different from that of their parents. In the past, parents had been able to teach children how to cope with daily life. They taught children how to raise crops, build homes, and rear children. But now the world was changing too fast. Old skills and values often didn't work or fit.

Several forces seem to have brought about the decline of the counterculture. One was

The Beatles [left to right: John Lennon, Paul McCartney, George Harrison, Ringo Starr] were one of the most popular groups in rock music history. They exploded onto the American pop music scene in the 1960s, and rapidly became an indistinguishable part of the culture.

AMERICAN ADVENTURES

the end of American involvement in the Vietnam war. This made a military draft no longer necessary and short-circuited some of the anger that young people had toward the Establishment. Another was a down- turn in the economy in the 1970s that made it harder to survive without full-time work. Yet another was the growing realization that drugs could seriously damage one's health and life.

Music, whether it was folk, rock 'n' roll, or rhythm and blues, was the voice of the Sixties, and echoed the feeling of that generation.

Chapter Check

WORD MATCH
1. counterculture
2. materialistic
3. hippies
4. Establishment
5. communes

a. concerned with money and possessions
b. 1960s young people who rebelled against traditional values
c. the prominent figures of American culture and politics
d. group living situations in which money and chores are shared
e. group with values markedly different from those of the mainstream

QUICK QUIZ
1. What were the main moral values of hippies?
2. What effect did hippies have on more ordinary people?

THINK ABOUT IT
1. What do young people today have in common with hippies? How are they different?
2. Do you think the generation gap was a particular problem in the 1960s? Or will there always be one?

A TIME OF CHANGE

History Detective

1. When U.S. forces invaded this area in Cuba on April 17, 1961, it became a source of U.S. embarassment. What am I?

2. College students were outraged with me when, as president, I ordered the draft to also include them. Who was I?

3. The appeal and charm of President and Mrs. Kennedy caused many to compare the White House with this magical kingdom. What was it?

4. Although our long hair, denim jackets, tie-dyed shirts, and sandals caused anger and confusion, our protests were for peace. We became some of the most memorable participants of the 1960s. Who are we?

5. Rachel Carson informed an entire generation of the problems that were caused by this method of controlling pests. What am I?

Voices From the Past

An important radical student group during the 1960s was Students for a Democratic Society (SDS). The group stated its purpose in the Port Huron Statement. Here is part of it:

When we were kids the United States was the wealthiest and strongest country in the world . . . As we grew, however, our comfort has changed. The Cold War, with the presence of the Bomb, has brought an awareness that we might die. Also, the declaration "all men are created equal . . ." has rung hollow before the fact of Negro life in the south and the big cities of the north . . . {But} the search for truly democratic alternatives to the present . . . , is a worthy and fulfilling human enterprise, one which moves us and, we hope, others today.

1. What situations in the U.S. were the students unhappy with?

2. What were the students suggesting?

Hands–On History

Writing a Letter—It is March of 1968. Your older brother chose to enlist in the U.S. Army a year ago. Now he has been sent to fight in Vietnam. How do you feel about the war? About his decision? About the possibility of him dying in the war? Write him a letter telling him why you do or do not support his decision to fight.

YESTERDAY'S NEWS

The American Adventures Newspaper

1.

Accra, Ghana, August 23, 1961—The much talked about Peace Corps is now a reality. After two months of training, the first recruits arrived here to teach in the secondary schools of Ghana. In March, President Kennedy signed the order creating the Corps on a pilot basis. He did so with the words: "Our Peace Corps is . . . designed to . . . permit people to exercise . . . their responsibilties in the great common cause of world development." Over 20 thousand Americans have applied to participate in the program. By 1964, Peace Corps director Sargent Shriver expects the Corps to reach about 50 different countries.

Peace Corps workers teach these children at the Ebenezer Secondary School in Accra, Ghana.

Pesticide Pollution in the Mississippi River

Memphis, Tenn., April 14, 1964—The Public Health Service (PHS) today released reports of massive pollution problems in the Mississippi River. This pollution is not garbage floating on top of the water, it is pesticides and other chemicals that can only be detected through chemical testing. The PHS investigated the waters after Louisiana's Division of Water Pollution Control reported a massive fish kill in the Mississippi River in November 1963. An estimated five million dead fish were floating, belly up, in this great river. These sort of fish kills were said to have become an annual event here since the 1950s. The PHS has been under public pressure to conduct a thorough investigation because of the recent publication of Rachel Carson's *Silent Spring*. Many experts believe this is just the beginning of the effect that this popular book will have on people's concern for the environment.

2.

Official Report on the Tet Offensive

Washington, D.C., February 27, 1968—General Earle G. Wheeler, chairman of the joint chiefs of staff, today reported the gruesome results of January's Tet Offensive. After signing a peace treaty to last through the Tet holidays, the communist forces broke the treaty by unleashing their most awesome attack in late January. It was some of the first fighting to kill villagers and destroy major cities in the region. General Wheeler reported that the offensive was fought by 84,000 communist troops—40,000 of whom were killed. It also claimed many American lives. The worst fact, reports General Wheeler, is that the offensive has given the enemy forces new life, which will mean the fighting will go on. Groups throughout the U.S. have responded in different ways to this new development in the war. **3.**

> ### *You Be the Reporter*
> Match each question with its news item above.
> **1.** Write a title for this story that reflects the excitement over the Peace Corps.
> **2.** Finish this article by discussing the ways that *Silent Spring* will effect public concerns.
> **3.** Finish this story with your ideas on the different ways Americans might feel about the Tet Offensive. How would it change their feelings about Vietnam?

CONTRASTING VIEWPOINTS

Why was there so much controversy about the Vietnam war? People in all segments of American society had different opinions and views on the war. People in the military disagreed about **tactics** (how the war should be fought). American foreign policy officials could not agree on the purpose of United States involvement in the war. Some Americans believed that the U.S. had to help stop North Vietnamese communists from taking over South Vietnam. Others protested that U.S. forces had no business being in Vietnam.

Where a person stood on the Vietnam issue had a lot to do with his or her own particular experiences or **viewpoints.** From the readings below, you can compare the viewpoints of three people—two servicemen and a reporter—who had different experiences in Vietnam.

The first account is by Admiral William Lawrence, a U.S. Navy pilot and prisoner of war in Vietnam. The second account is by Robert Rawls, a rifleman in the First Cavalry Division. Read their recollections and answer the questions that follow.

Admiral William Lawrence: *I was shot down on the twenty-eighth of June, 1967, and I was released on the third of March, 1973. . . . I was the commanding officer of the squadron [when] I was shot down. All of our missions were up in the northern part of North Vietnam. . . .*

I was shot down over the Red River Delta . . . . Our particular camp was all pilots, officers. I was never with enlisted personnel until they moved us into Hoa Lo, Christmas 1970. . . .

I'm sure that there are POWs [prisoners of war] that came out of the experience devastated, and that's very unfortunate. But I think the people who were basically pretty solid individuals and were stable and had the wherewithal to cope in there, they came out even better people. I see so much of value that I derived from the experience, and it's a wonderful thing to be at that point in your life where you know that there's nothing that could happen that you couldn't handle. . . . I was thirty-seven when I was captured and fortunate enough to have that amount of life experience and responsibility at that point. There's no question about it, if you had to be shot down and become a prisoner, if you were over thirty you were far better off.[1]

Robert Rawls: *On Ho Chi Minh's birthday, May 19, 1969, I got wounded in an ambush. . . . They just patched me up. Then as the stitches got well, they cut 'em out and sent me back to the unit. . . .*

I got married a couple of months before I got drafted, and they said they couldn't catch up with the paperwork to keep me out of the draft. . . .When I got back everything was changed. The way I feel about life now . . . it's just a bum trip. I have flashbacks and people can't understand me sometimes. I sit by myself and I just think. . . .

Where we were it was jungle. Completely jungle. And the company commanders and all of them was like gung-ho-type guys. They were lifers, and I just couldn't cope with the service and what they stood for.

Thinking back on the training, all they told us to do was kill. "KILL! KILL!" "What is the spirit of the bayonet?" "To KILL!" It was just a bummed-out trip. And I just didn't go for it, you know.[1]

[1] From *Everything We Had* by Al Santoli, Copyright © 1981 by Albert Santoli and Vietnam Veterans of America. Reprinted by permission of Random House, Inc.

1. Refer to Admiral Lawrence's account. **(a)** For how many years was he a prisoner of war in Vietnam? **(b)** What was his rank when he was shot down?

2. How does Lawrence feel about his experience in Vietnam? How do you know?

3. Refer to the account of Robert Rawls. **(a)** How did Rawls become a serviceman? **(b)** Why does Rawls refer to company commanders as "lifers"?

4. How does Rawls feel about his Vietnam experience? How do you know? Explain how his feelings differ from those of William Lawrence.

5. Now **contrast** (explain the differences between) the rank and experiences of these two men. How do you think these differences might account for their different viewpoints on the Vietnam war?

Were military operations the only targets of U.S. bombing in Vietnam or were civilians hit as well? Read the following two accounts. The first is by Admiral Lawrence. The second is a report by Harrison Salisbury in December, 1967, for The New York Times.

> ***Admiral William Lawrence:*** *I had no bad feelings toward the Vietnamese people. I was doing my job as a military man. I would very meticulously [carefully] try to plan my bombing missions to avoid any impact on civilian population. I briefed and planned my flight to insure that we hit only military targets, because I knew we were at war with a country that was largely rural and that the people were not well-off, and we really worked hard at hitting only military targets and avoiding any unnecessary injuries or death to the civilian populace.[1]*

> ***Harrison Salisbury:*** *Whatever the explanation, one can see that United States planes are dropping an enormous weight of explosives on purely civilian targets. Whatever else there may be or might have been in Nam Dinh [a North Vietnamese city], it is the civilians who have taken punishment.*
>
> *. . . the city's population of 90,000 has been reduced to less than 20,000 because of the evacuation; 13 percent of the city's housing, including the homes of 12,464 people, have been destroyed; 89 people have been killed and 405 wounded.[2]*

6. What did Admiral Lawrence try to do as a pilot flying bombing missions over North Vietnam?

7. What did Harrison Salisbury report about the effects of United States bombing missions?

8. What conclusions can you draw from these two accounts about the impact of the war on civilians? Why didn't bombing crews always avoid hitting towns and villages?

9. Why do you think the two accounts are so different? What experiences did each person lack when reporting on similar events?

10. How do you think Americans reacted when they read reports like Salisbury's? Do you think reports like this should have been permitted during the war? Explain why or why not.

[2] From *Vietnam: the Valor and the Sorrow* by Thomas D. Boettcher, Copyright © 1985 by Thomas D. Boettcher. Reprinted by permission of Little, Brown, and Co.

JOHN D CAYCE
GARY E HARDY · PETER A HENSLEY
ABRAHAM HARDY · ROBERT C MELENDREZ
DANIEL J KLOS Jr · WILLIAM E NULPH Jr · JOHN
FORREST A McKINNEY · BILLY GENE SMITH
ELZIE SANDERS Jr · RICHARD J WARREN · GOLER J WILL
LEONARD A THOMAS · DAVID E BUNKER · NATHANIEL CHATMAN
JAMES C BERRY · DAVID E BUNKER · NATHANIEL CHATMAN
GLENN R EISENHOUR · LAMONT G EPPS · ROBERT
ALPHONSO L HARMON · ZAN HESS · VANESTER L HE
RAY M K JONES · LAWRENCE A LETTERMAN · FRANCIS L MAPLES
RICHARD V MYERS · WILLIAM O McKOY · JAMES E RAFFENSF
RICHARD A SCHEIBER · EDWARD A SCULLY · WILLIE I SIMMONS
LARRY K WILLIAMS · FRANCIS L BRYANT · RICHARD KOVA
JAMES P CRYSTER III · ROBERT E DOUGLAS Jr · JOSEF HEME
PAUL E JOHNSON · MILTON G KELSEY · ROBERT G K
THOMAS A CARTER · RICHARD KROLIKOWSKI · FRANK A
RONALD I PHELPS · LARUS W ROLAND · JOHN C R
STEPHEN H THORNTON · GERARD M WYNN · JOHN C R
HENRY G CRIGGER · GERARD M WYNN · ROBERT P CA
JOHN S GORDON · DONALD C DAVES · BRYANT D FANN
DAVID I HARNER · HENRY B HAWKINS Jr
JOSEPH P MAREK · JIMMIE LUE McMORRIS · WILLIAM
JOHNNY A SIGURDSON · OTIS T SMITH · WILLIAM
WAYNE R ADAMS · RALPH E BYRD · WALTER A
ROBERT W BREDE · ROBERT AUSTIN
BOBBY RAY ALEXANDER · LEWIS C

SEARCHING
FOR NEW

1965	1970					
1969		**1970**	**Nixon**	**Watergate**	**1972**	**1973**	**1974**

1969
Neil Armstrong
is first person
on moon.

U.S.
invades
Cambodia.

1970
National Guard kills four
Kent State students at
campus antiwar protest.

Nixon
visits
China.

Watergate
break-in

1972
U.S. and Soviet Union ratify
Strategic Arms Limitation
Treaties (SALT).

1973
Vietnam
war
cease-fire.

1974
Oil Crisis—
severe fuel
shortage

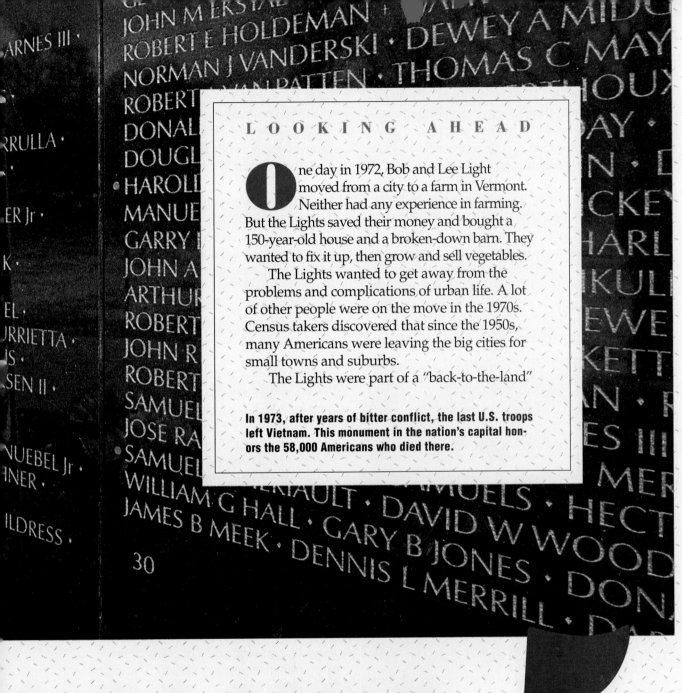

LOOKING AHEAD

One day in 1972, Bob and Lee Light moved from a city to a farm in Vermont. Neither had any experience in farming. But the Lights saved their money and bought a 150-year-old house and a broken-down barn. They wanted to fix it up, then grow and sell vegetables.

The Lights wanted to get away from the problems and complications of urban life. A lot of other people were on the move in the 1970s. Census takers discovered that since the 1950s, many Americans were leaving the big cities for small towns and suburbs.

The Lights were part of a "back-to-the-land"

In 1973, after years of bitter conflict, the last U.S. troops left Vietnam. This monument in the nation's capital honors the 58,000 Americans who died there.

30

VALUES

UNIT 5

1975		1980
1975	**1977**	**1979**
North and South Vietnam are reunited.	Jimmy Carter becomes president.	Iranian terrorists take 68 Americans hostage.

movement. They joined many city-bred men and women who wanted to grow their own food, breathe cleaner air, get more exercise, and be more self-sufficient.

In the 1970s, Americans became more preoccupied with personal issues such as health and fitness than they had been in the 1960s. Political rights, such as equal opportunities in the workplace, also became more important. Millions gave up smoking and took up jogging. People became more aware of additives in foods, and began reading labels more carefully. Women's liberation led to greater job opportunities for women than ever before.

In the 1970s, Americans became concerned about such personal issues as improving physical fitness. Millions in the "me generation" took up jogging and other types of exercise.

New Technology

The 1960s had ended with a spectacular display of American technology and determination. On July 20, 1969, the United States thrilled the world by fulfilling the late President Kennedy's pledge to put an astronaut on the moon before the end of the 1960s.

Most people called this a great achievement. But during the 1970s, more and more people became critical of the space program. They wanted to know why billions of dollars were being spent on space programs when there were so many problems on Earth.

The War in Vietnam

When Richard Nixon became president in 1969, he promised "to bring Americans together again." Nixon hoped to put "an honorable end" to the war in Vietnam. He said that he would pull U.S. troops out of Vietnam slowly. Many Americans did not want to wait. They wanted peace now, and wore black armbands symbolizing death and mourning in protest. Special days were set aside for demonstrating against the war. Sometimes more than a million people took part.

Occasionally, antiwar demonstrations ended in violence. In May 1970, soldiers from the Ohio National Guard fired into a crowd of students at Kent State University. Four students were killed. The news shocked the nation. Angry protests swept other campuses. A few days later, two students at Jackson State University in Mississippi protesting against Kent State deaths were killed by police gunfire.

Finally, in January 1973, a cease-fire was signed by the United States and North Vietnam, and U.S. forces left

Vietnam, Two years later, the communists defeated the South Vietnamese army, and took over South Vietnam.

The war was over. But both the United States and Vietnam had paid a heavy price. America never accomplished its military objectives. Many people thought the war was just one ghastly mistake. Others felt America had gone "soft" and failed to use enough military power to win in Vietnam. Politicians, however, had to recognize that, for the time being, many Americans remained cautious. After Vietnam, the American people were less willing to see U.S. troops fight in foreign countries.

Foreign Relations

During the 1970s, Americans tried to ease the tensions of the Cold War in other ways. Many people had lived most of their lives in the Nuclear Age. They could not remember a time when the atomic bomb did not exist.

During much of this time, the United States and the Soviet Union had maintained a "balance of terror." Each was so powerful that it could completely destroy the other. According to the leaders of the two nations, neither country would voluntarily start a war that would inevitably destroy both sides. This threat was supposed to make all-out war impossible. Many people, however, began to worry that the impossible might happen.

Nixon tried to ease world tensions by improving relations with the People's

The war in Vietnam caused enourmous destruction and death. Peasants worked in the Me Kong Delta rice fields while bombs fell behind them.

Republic of China. He also worked at improving relations with the Soviet Union. The United States and Soviet Union signed a treaty in 1972 that was aimed at slowing the nuclear arms race.

Politics at Home

During the 1970s, many Americans had doubts about the ability of their political leaders. A bungled burglary at the Watergate offices of the Democratic

National Committee in Washington, D.C., grew into an enormous scandal. Many members of the Nixon administration were involved. Watergate cast a shadow over the government. It preoccupied President Nixon and the nation for more than two years. It seemed that each day brought new stories of government wrongdoing or misuse of power. In the end, the Watergate scandal led to President Nixon's resignation—the first presidential resignation in American history. Vice-President Gerald Ford became president.

In 1976, Jimmy Carter defeated Ford and was elected president. He promised the American people that he would never lie to them. Many people found this appealing. One of Carter's greatest accomplishments was bringing peace between Egypt and Israel.

But by the end of Carter's presidency, Americans had lost confidence in his ability to lead the nation. They were frustrated by his failure to rescue American citizens held **hostage** (prisoner) in Iran. They especially disliked Carter telling the American people that they would have to expect less for themselves and their nation. While many Americans did not like what their president was telling them, much of what Carter said was true. American society was changing and people were altering their expectations.

In the 1970s, the U.S. economy changed. In the winter of 1974, an oil shortage made a big impact on American society. There was a sharp drop in the economy. Service stations, factories, and offices closed. Prices soared, and Americans were forced to survive on less than they had in the past. Though wages rose to record heights, they could not keep up with escalating prices. For the first time since the Great Depression of the 1930s, many middle-class Americans had a hard time earning enough to support a family. While married working-class women had often worked, for the first time, many married middle-class women had to work to supplement the family income. People found they had to earn more money, or lower their standards of living.

Many Americans also became more concerned about pollution. As their health

This cartoonist saw the 1973 oil embargo as robbery. The cartoon shows the Arab nations (represented by the Arab) holding up the U.S. (represented by U.S. Secretary of State Henry Kissinger), using a gas-station pump as a weapon.

was threatened by polluted air and water, people began to feel that for too long American society had developed with little or no concern for its impact on the environment. Factories provided goods cheaply, but they also polluted the air and water with industrial wastes. Cars improved transportation, but they also contributed to air pollution and used a lot of oil. Nuclear power plants promised an alternate source of electricity. Yet they produced hazardous wastes for which no one could find a safe disposal method or politically acceptable plan. Many Americans liked the idea of nuclear power. But none of them wanted nuclear waste dumped near them.

Environmentalists (people working to solve problems affecting the earth and its resources) believed that pollution needed to be stopped at its source. In the 1970s, new laws set up strict rules against what could be dumped into the land, air, and water. Americans were looking for ways of balancing the benefits and costs of industrial growth.

In the 1970s, Americans were searching for ways to deal with some very complicated problems. They wanted to preserve old-fashioned values while adopting a more realistic view of their society and its place in the world.

In the 1950s and 1960s, demonstrators cried "Ban the Bomb." In the 1970s, a new call was raised—"No Nukes." Demonstrators demanded an end to nuclear weapons and nuclear power.

27 KENT STATE AND THE END OF WAR

In one of the most famous photos of the 1970s, a young woman kneels in anguish beside the body of a classmate slain by National Guardsmen at a college protest against the U.S. bombing of Cambodia.

Tom Grace, a Kent State University student, had just taken a history exam on the morning of Monday, May 4, 1970. He was a history buff and loved reading about the battles of Antietam and Gettysburg in the Civil War. As he walked across campus at noon, he found himself in the latest skirmish of American resistance to another civil war. Although that civil war was thousands of miles away in Vietnam, it was dividing Americans as no war

had since the Civil War.

At Kent State, in Ohio, an antiwar rally was planned for that afternoon. Many students were protesting the recent U.S. bombing of Vietnam's neighbor, Cambodia. A few nights before, students had set fire to an empty campus building in which military recruits were once trained. The building had burned to the ground.

Governor James A. Rhodes ordered the National Guard to the campus to stop the student protests. About 3000 National Guard entered the town of Kent. They made their way slowly in jeeps and trucks to the campus.

Rally Leads to Bloodshed

As Grace arrived at the student activity center, he located his roommates among several hundred students already assembled. The students began to yell at the guardsmen, "Pigs off campus! We don't want your war." Some students threw stones and rocks. Others threw bottles. No guardsmen were hurt, but they began to panic. They pointed their guns and shot tear gas into the crowd.

A few students threw more rocks. Others picked up the tear-gas canisters and threw them back at the guards. Most of the students fled. They were frightened and their eyes were burning from the tear gas.

The guardsmen moved to the top of a hill on campus. Then, "all of a sudden there was . . . a flurry of activity, and then a crack, or two cracks, of rifle fire," Grace remembered. "I just hugged the ground so as to expose as little of my body as possible to the gunfire. It seemed like the bullets were going by within inches of my head."

Grace was hit in the heel by a bullet. Eight others were also shot. Four students were killed, and their bodies lay in fresh pools of blood. Two of the students killed had not even been involved in the protest. They had just been walking across campus.

One guardsman was horrified by what he had done. He fell to the ground and cried, "I just shot two teenagers!" The rest of the guardsmen marched off the hill, leaving the dead and wounded behind.

Cambodian Invasion

What was behind the tragedy at Kent State? Students there and across America were becoming increasingly frustrated that U.S. participation in the Vietnam war was dragging on. An announcement by President Nixon on April 30, 1970, enraged the war's opponents even more. Nixon revealed that he had ordered American troops to invade Cambodia, a neutral country bordering Vietnam. He said that the Vietcong and their North Vietnamese supporters had military supplies hidden in Cambodia. Nixon planned to get rid of these hideouts by sending in U.S. troops.

Students at Kent State and at thousands of other college campuses responded to seeing the war expanded by protesting. Nixon claimed that he had not previously invaded Cambodia because he "did not wish to violate the territory of a neutral nation." Foreign news correspondents reported, however, that he had already

At first, President Nixon claimed that U.S. troops had not invaded Cambodia. But when U.S. actions there were revealed later, Americans' bitterness over the Vietnam war deepened.

authorized over 3000 secret bombing missions over Cambodia.

Americans in Vietnam

The bombings indicated that the United States was losing the guerrilla war on the ground. U.S. soldiers often complained that they were fighting an enemy they couldn't see. They also said that they couldn't determine which civilians were cooperating with their enemies, the Vietcong.

Many U.S. soldiers fought bravely and honorably. Some soldiers panicked and lashed out at innocent civilians in frustration. Others were ordered by their officers to commit brutal acts. In the village of My Lai, for example, U.S. soldiers, under orders to search out and kill enemy troops, massacred 350 unarmed civilians.

Drug abuse among U.S. soldiers was common. Many of the soldiers were still teenagers. They were less able to cope with the constant violence, danger and death than older soldiers. They were unsure of why they were fighting in Vietnam.

On April 9, 1975, hundreds of South Vietnamese crowd the deck of a ship as they evacuate one of their cities.

Making friends was also difficult because individuals were routinely transferred from one unit to another. Many soldiers were lonely and afraid.

Withdrawal of U.S. Troops

Nixon had been elected in 1968 largely because he had said that he had a secret plan to bring America "peace with honor." He had no specific plan, but peace talks did begin in Paris that year.

Nixon continued President Johnson's program of **Vietnamization.** American troops were gradually brought home, and the burden of fighting shifted to South Vietnamese forces.

Nixon, however, remained reluctant to withdraw all U.S. forces from South Vietnam. President Nguyen Van Thieu (WIN vahn TEE-ow), brought to power by the United States in a corrupt election in 1967, was a weak leader. He did not command the loyalty of his people. If the United States left South Vietnam, Thieu's government would surely fall. Nixon believed that such a defeat would mean disgrace and humiliation for America.

Peace Talks Resume

In March 1972, North Vietnam, in support of the Vietcong, began a major invasion of the South. In response, American planes dropped more bombs on North Vietnam. Both the North and South suffered heavy losses during the invasion. Ultimately, this devastation led to more peace talks. U.S. diplomats, led by Henry Kissinger, met secretly with North Vietnamese diplomats, led by Le Duc Tho (LAY duck TOE). On January 27, 1973, the United States, South Vietnam, North Vietnam, and the Vietcong signed a cease-fire and peace agreement. Two months later, the last U.S. combat troops left Vietnam. The peace agreement soon broke down, but Congress voted to oppose further U.S. involvement in Vietnam. The U.S. did not send troops.

In April 1975, South Vietnam's army fell apart. The South Vietnamese leadership conceded defeat, and a communist government took over the country. Vietnam became one nation again.

About 2,700,000 American men and women served in Vietnam. Some 58,000 died there. Another 365,000 were wounded. For many Vietnam veterans the war left deep emotional scars. For some, it led to such problems as unemployment, divorce, and drug and alcohol abuse.

The Vietnamese people suffered far greater losses. In North Vietnam, 500,000 to 1 million died. In South Vietnam, 1 million were killed. As a result of the war's devastation, almost 10 million South Vietnamese—one half of the population—lost their homes and became refugees.

Saigon and much of South Vietnam was destroyed by the war. Here, South Vietnamese look through the rubble of destroyed buildings.

CHAPTER CHECK

WORD MATCH

1. Vietnamization
2. My Lai
3. Henry Kissinger
4. Le Duc Tho
5. Nguyen Van Thieu

a. where U.S. soldiers massacred 350 unarmed Vietnamese civilians
b. president of South Vietnam, brought to power in 1967 by U.S.
c. North Vietnamese diplomat involved in U.S.–Vietnam peace talks
d. U.S. diplomat involved in U.S.–Vietnamese peace talks
e. U.S. policy giving South Vietnam responsibility for carrying out the war, while removing U.S. troops

QUICK QUIZ

1. What action by President Nixon triggered demonstrations at Kent State and elsewhere in May 1970? What were the president's goals?
2. Why was the war in Vietnam particularly frustrating for American troops?

THINK ABOUT IT

1. How else might the National Guard have been directed to handle the demonstration at Kent State?
2. Before the war in Vietnam, U.S. troops had never taken part in a war that they lost. How do you think this affected American policy there?

28 ONE GIANT LEAP

The 1969 moon landing was a major milestone in the U.S. space program. NASA had achieved President Kennedy's goal to get Americans on the moon by 1970. During Edwin "Buzz" Aldrin's historic walk on the moon [above], his helmet visor reflected the Lunar Module.

It was an early Sunday evening on the West Coast of the United States on July 20, 1969. In Europe, stars shone in the early morning sky. In Asia, the sun was already up. Wherever they were, nearly 500 million people were all doing the same thing at that moment. They were watching the most spectacular TV show in history.

The image on TV sets was ghost-like. There was U.S. Astronaut Neil Armstrong coming out of his spaceship. Slowly, he lowered himself down the nine-step ladder. As his foot touched ground, Armstrong's voice buzzed across 240,000 miles of space. "That's one small step for a man, one giant leap for mankind," Armstrong proclaimed. Humans had landed on the moon.

For thousands of years, people had dreamed of exploring beyond Earth. Until human beings learned to fly, these dreams had always seemed fanciful. Then scientists began to invent new ways of flying farther and faster. In 1957, the Soviet Union sent the first artificial satellite, called *Sputnik*, into orbit around Earth. The Space Age had begun.

President Dwight D. Eisenhower started a program to catch up with the Soviets in space exploration. President John F. Kennedy decided to try to beat them to be the first on the moon. In May 1961, in a speech to Congress, Kennedy challenged the United States to put an astronaut on the moon before 1970. That was only nine years away.

Congress liked Kennedy's idea. The race to the moon was on. A total of about 400,000 Americans worked in the space program. Its cost was more than $24 billion.

Around the Earth

Many space flights were made, some with astronauts, some without. In 1962, John Glenn became the first U.S. astronaut to orbit Earth in space. In the United States, astronauts such as Glenn were heroes. Television brought the spaceflights into American living rooms. Gradually, the United States caught up with the Soviet Union.

The last moon practice flight, Apollo 10, took place in May of 1969. Two astronauts flew to within nine miles of the moon. Everything went well. The stage was set for Apollo 11—the moon landing.

Apollo 11 was set to blast off from Cape Kennedy, now Cape Canaveral, Florida, on Wednesday, July 16, 1969. Nearly a million people crowded nearby beaches to see it. On the launching pad,

The U.S.–Soviet race to conquer outer space led to the creation of NASA, the National Aeronautics and Space Administration, in 1958.

the huge rocket and spaceship looked like a tall white candle. It was as high as a 36-story building.

At 6:45 A.M., the three astronauts—Neil Armstrong, Edwin Aldrin, and Michael Collins—stepped into the spaceship. The door was shut and sealed behind them. During the long countdown, ground crews checked all equipment. Then a worker pressed a button in the control room. Orange flames and dark smoke shot out from under the rocket. A roar filled the air. Apollo 11 lifted off. Within minutes it was out of sight.

To the Moon

On Saturday, July 19, Apollo 11 neared the moon and went into orbit. The next day, Armstrong and Aldrin entered the machine that would take them to the moon's surface. It was called a **Lunar Module** (LM). The LM looked like a big bug with four legs. Collins remained in the command ship *Columbia* in orbit around the moon.

The actual landing on the moon was the most dangerous part of the trip. The moon's surface has many large **craters** (bowl-shaped cavities) and rocks. If the LM had struck a rock or fallen into a crater, it could have been the end for the astronauts. On the way down, they saw that they were headed for a crater. Armstrong took over the controls from the automatic pilot. He steered the LM to a safe landing. At 4:17 P.M., on July 20, Armstrong radioed a message back to Earth: "The *Eagle* has landed."

On Earth, millions of people shouted with joy.

Six hours later, Armstrong and Aldrin stepped on the moon. They set up a U.S. flag. They picked up rocks and sand to take back to Earth for study by scientists. The astronauts spent 21 hours on the moon. Their spacesuits protected them from the extreme heat and cold. It was 234 degrees Fahrenheit in the sunlight, and 279 degrees below zero in the shade. The spacesuits also provided oxygen and water.

The next day, Armstrong and Aldrin climbed back into the LM and took off from the moon's surface. They rejoined the *Columbia* and headed home. From 175,000 miles out in space, the astronauts sent back a television picture of Earth. On Thursday, July 24, they splashed down safely in the Pacific Ocean.

Far Into Space

Five more flights went to the moon. Then the space program began exploring farther reaches of space with riderless rockets.

In the 1970s, more people became criti-

The U.S. space program had made its mark, as this footprint on the moon's surface shows. But many Americans wondered how to justify the program's huge expense in the face of pressing needs at home.

cal of the space program. They said it was wrong for the United States to spend so much money exploring space. Some argued that the United States should take care of its problems on Earth. Poverty, disease, and injustice were the problems that needed attention, not outer space. Others felt that government costs should be reduced, and indicated that the space program was one expense that could be cut.

The space program's defenders pointed out its benefits. Humankind gained knowledge about the universe and the creation of Earth. Much of the research done for the space program helped improve life on Earth. Out of this research came devices such as pocket calculators and tiny cells that produce energy from the sun.

Just about everyone agreed that the moon landings were a great achievement.

Scuba divers at the Space Flight Center in Huntsville, Alabama, practice working on a space station component underwater.

CHAPTER CHECK

WORD MATCH
1. Lunar Module
2. craters
3. Apollo 11
4. Apollo 10
5. Cape Kennedy

a. name for space center in Florida
b. spaceflight that orbited very near the moon in May 1969
c. bowl-shaped cavities on the moon's surface
d. portion of the Apollo spaceship in which astronauts landed on the moon
e. spaceflight that landed on the moon in July 1969

QUICK QUIZ
1. What was the purpose of the Apollo program? Which presidents were first to see the need for such a program?
2. What were the benefits of the space program?

THINK ABOUT IT
1. Some critics have said that money spent on the Apollo program should have been used to end poverty, disease, and injustice. Do you agree? Do you think it was a good idea or a bad idea to use so much money for the Apollo program?
2. Do you think that competition with the Soviet Union was useful in developing the space program? Why or why not?

29 TIME FOR A THAW

In 1971, U.S. Secretary of State Henry Kissinger took off on a top-secret mission. His goal: to try to forge a new alliance with an old enemy, communist China.

enry Kissinger was sick in bed. At least that is what reporters traveling with President Nixon's top foreign policy adviser were told. No news today, they thought, but they were wrong. Kissinger was not in bed at all.

Pretending he was ill allowed Kissinger to slip away from the press. He was supposed to be meeting with the leaders of Pakistan, an ally of the United States. In fact, on that July morning in 1971, he was in a plane flying over the Himalaya (him-uh-LAY-uh) Mountains. For the first time in 22 years, a high-ranking official of the U.S. government headed to China.

The United States and China had not had diplomatic relations since 1949. That was the year the Chinese civil war ended with the communist forces of Mao Zedong (MAH-oh dzay-DOONG) firmly in power. One year later, United States and Chinese troops were shooting at each other in Korea. After the war in Korea, the United States and China exchanged little but threats.

Several things combined to reduce hostilities in the early 1970s. The United States needed help in putting pressure on North Vietnam to sign a peace agreement. The U.S. also needed a counterbalance to Soviet power. Finally, President Nixon, through his top foreign policy advisor, Kissinger, needed a major political success to counteract American opposition to the Vietnam war, and to help win the upcoming presidential election.

Now was the time, Kissinger and Nixon felt, for the United States to recognize China, and to open relations between the two countries. The Chinese could help persuade the North Vietnamese to consider peace plans, and they could keep the Soviet Union occupied with concerns about its borders with China. China desired economic and technical aid from the United States, and wanted allies against its old enemy, the Soviet Union.

Easing Tensions

In 1969, the United States, China, and the Soviet Union all had nuclear weapons. If fighting broke out between any of these countries, thought Nixon, it might grow into a nuclear war.

Nixon's plan to change this situation came to be called **détente** (a French word meaning relaxation). Reducing political tensions was not easy to do. Both Chinese and Soviet leaders were suspicious of the United States' motives. Many Americans, including Nixon, believed communists wanted to expand their style of government to all the countries of the world—with force, if necessary.

Disagreements between the communist nations of China and the Soviet Union gave Nixon his chance to try détente. The two countries had been close allies during the 1950s. Then, in 1960, they began to argue over their differing views of communism. They also disagreed over the location of the boundary between the two countries. By 1969, Soviet and Chinese soldiers were shooting at each other over disputed territory.

President Nixon realized that China was ready for a change. If it were handled carefully, he thought, a new relationship with China could be the first step toward global détente. Yet any change in diplomatic relations would create a lot of activity, so the planning had to be done in secret. Kissinger went quietly to China. For two days he met with Chinese Premier Zhou Enlai (jou ehn ly). The Premier gave Kissinger an invitation for President Nixon to visit China. Then Kissinger flew back to Pakistan. He had "recovered" from his illness.

Nixon in China

After Kissinger returned home, Nixon went on TV with the dramatic news about China. Nixon, Kissinger, and other officials flew to China in February 1972. With them went swarms of news reporters. Every word, every gesture was recorded for history. At home, Americans watched on TV as Nixon clinked glasses with Zhou Enlai at a glittering banquet. Glasses clinked dozens of times as the leaders exchanged toasts. Arm in arm, Nixon and Zhou marched from table to table. However, Zhou and Nixon did not iron out all the differences between their two countries.

China Joins the U.N.

For the 20 years after 1949, China had been isolated in many ways from the rest of the world. Especially after 1960, when China began quarreling with the Soviet Union, Chinese leaders did not have a single ally among the world's most powerful nations.

In 1971, shortly after Kissinger's visit, the communist government in Beijing (bay-JHING) was given China's seat in the United Nations. It had been held previously by the defeated nationalist government in Taiwan after it fled mainland China. Nixon's visit, in 1972, also paved the way for other American allies, such as Japan, to establish their own ties with China.

On January 1, 1979, the United States and China announced that they had "normalized relations" between the two countries. Nixon and Kissinger successfully planted a seed that grew into a new era with China as an active member of the world community.

U.S.–Soviet Relations

The new relationship between the United States and China worried the leaders of the Soviet Union. They didn't want China and the United States to become allies against them. They decided to seek new agreements with the United States, too.

In May 1972, President Nixon traveled to Moscow to confer with Soviet leader Leonid Brezhnev (BRESH-nyev). It was the first time a U.S. president had visited the Soviet Union in peacetime. The two leaders signed an agreement aimed

In 1972, China's Premier Zhou Enlai [center] toasted his honored guests, U.S. President and Mrs. Nixon. The banquet marked new, "normalized" relations between the two nations.

AMERICAN ADVENTURES

at slowing down the arms race. For the first time, it put limits on one category of nuclear weapons each side could have. The agreement was called the Strategic Arms Limitation Treaty (SALT).

The SALT pact did not stop the nuclear arms race. It merely slowed it down. More talks were held later in the 1970s. A second treaty, SALT II, was drawn up, but the time of détente had passed. Tensions arose in 1979, when Soviet troops moved into Afghanistan to support a communist regime. The United States Congress refused to ratify SALT II. Both the United States Congress and the Soviet Union added deadly new weapons to their arsenals.

Warmer U.S.–China relations led to warmer U.S.–Soviet relations. Above, President Carter meets Soviet leader Leonid Brezhnev.

CHAPTER CHECK

WORD MATCH
1. SALT I
2. Mao Zedong
3. Zhou Enlai
4. Leonid Brezhnev
5. détente

a. French word meaning relaxation
b. Chinese communist leader who came to power in 1949
c. Chinese premier during opening of China in 1970s
d. agreement limiting arms race between Soviet Union and United States
e. leader of Soviet Union during SALT talks

QUICK QUIZ
1. Why did Henry Kissinger go to China in secret? What did he accomplish?
2. Why did China have no diplomatic relations with the U.S. after 1949? When did China have serious problems with the Soviet Union?

THINK ABOUT IT
1. President Nixon had built much of his political career on opposing communism. Why do you think he went to China and the Soviet Union, both communist countries?
2. Why do you think communist leaders in China, and in the Soviet Union wanted to meet with President Nixon?

30 WATERGATE

President Richard M. Nixon resigned from office in August 1974, as a result of the Watergate scandal.

Late one Friday night in June 1972, in Washington, D.C., a watchman became suspicious over an unlocked door while patrolling an exclusive apartment and office complex called the Watergate. Minutes later, the police arrived, and arrested five burglars inside the Democratic National Committee headquarters. They were caught in the act of tampering with telephones—"bugging" them to secretly record conversations.

When the break-in made the news the next morning, few Americans could have dreamed that Watergate would become an infamous American political scandal, and that it would lead to the resignation of President Richard Nixon.

The burglars were prosecuted for their crimes, found guilty, and sent to jail. The media and the Democrats kept asking questions. They tried to discover who else might be behind this crime that seemed to be motivated by politics.

The 1972 Democratic candidate for president, George McGovern, blamed the Republicans. Two persistent *Washington Post* reporters, Bob Woodward and Carl Bernstein, investigated. They accused former U.S. Attorney General John Mitchell of being involved in the break-in. While Mitchell was serving as the chief law enforcement agent in the country, they said, he had planned and paid for the burglary.

Mitchell had worked closely with President Nixon. If Mitchell was involved, had Nixon himself known about the burglary? The President assured the country that nobody in the White House was involved in the Watergate burglary.

Before the 1972 election, a federal grand jury began an inquiry. Meanwhile, Nixon was re-elected by a landslide. Concern about White House involvement in the Watergate break-in, and about Republican financial improprieties and presidential campaign "dirty tricks," began to spread.

In early 1973, a special Senate committee started to investigate the Watergate break-in. The committee ordered key members of Nixon's White House staff to appear as witnesses. These hearings were broadcast daily on TV. The entire nation watched in astonishment as, piece by piece, the events of the Watergate burglary came to light.

Background to the Burglary

In January 1972, John Mitchell headed a special group called the Committee to Re-Elect the President (CREEP). Mitchell and John Dean, President Nixon's personal lawyer, met with a professional spy, G. Gordon Liddy. Liddy described a plan for spying on the Democrats in order to find out their campaign strategies. Mitchell rejected the plan as too expensive. Two

months later, Liddy proposed a less costly scheme that included the Watergate break-in. This time Mitchell approved the plan.

Liddy and another professional spy, Howard Hunt, hired two Americans and three Cuban refugees to do the "dirty work" of the actual break-in. After these burglars were caught, one of them leaked information about the roles of Liddy and Hunt, the two masterminds. Later, Liddy and Hunt were also arrested, tried, convicted, and jailed.

When John Dean testified at the Senate committee hearings in June 1973, he not only admitted his own guilt in the crime, but also connected both John Mitchell and President Nixon to the crime. While Mitchell had authorized the burglary, Nixon had helped plan a coverup

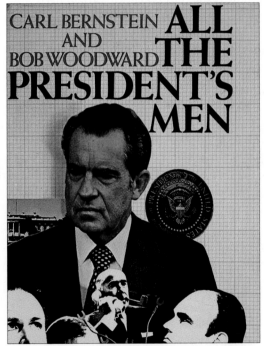

The *Washington Post* reporters who broke the Watergate story—and investigation—wide open, later wrote this best-selling book about that experience.

when the burglars were caught, he said. Nixon had arranged "hush money" to keep the burglars from talking, ordered documents destroyed, and pressured the FBI to limit the scope of its investigation.

If what Dean said were true, Nixon was guilty of trying to cover up the Watergate break-in. This was another crime—"obstructing justice." Nixon responded that he first learned about Dean's coverup a few months earlier, in March 1973. Nixon also claimed that he was trying to get all the facts about Watergate. Who was lying—Dean or the President?

Hidden Recorder

Then another bombshell rocked the Senate hearings. A witness revealed that the President had a hidden tape recorder in his White House office. Nixon had taped all of his conversations so that he could refer to them in the future. By listening to these tapes, the Senate committee might, at last, learn the whole truth.

Nixon refused to give up the tapes, and a lengthy legal battle over their control started. In January 1974, a committee of the House of Representatives met to start

Millions of Americans watched as government officials were probed in televised Senate-held hearings. The hearings, held in the wake of the Watergate scandal, uncovered information that led to President Nixon's downfall.

impeachment proceedings. According to the U.S. Constitution, a majority of the House of Representatives must vote first to impeach, or accuse, the president of "high crimes and misdemeanors." Then the Senate must vote on whether or not the president is guilty. If two thirds of the senators find him or her guilty, the president must leave office. Only one president had ever been impeached—Andrew Johnson, in 1868. But because two thirds of the senators did not find him guilty, he was acquitted.

In a national TV broadcast in April 1974, Nixon said, "I want there to be no question remaining about the fact that the President has nothing to hide." But Nixon only partly met the demands of Congress. He was prepared to release only edited transcripts of the tapes, not the tapes themselves. Finally, the Supreme Court ordered Nixon to turn over a complete set of the tapes.

The President had good reason to be worried. In a taped meeting only one week after the Watergate burglary, Nixon had told a close advisor to make sure the FBI dropped its investigation of the case. In an earlier taped conversation, Dean may have summed up both the crime and coverup. "We have a cancer within, close to the presidency, that is growing."

Congress and Nixon's own lawyers were shocked by the tapes. Many people called for Nixon's impeachment. In an effort to avoid an almost certain impeachment, and a probable Senate finding of guilty, Richard Nixon resigned on August 9, 1974.

Gerald Ford succeeded Nixon as president. Nixon had named Ford vice-president after his first vice-president, Spiro Agnew, had resigned in October 1973, having been accused of taking part in a bribery scandal. One of President Ford's first acts was to pardon Nixon for any illegal acts he might have committed as president. This meant that Nixon would not have to go on trial and face punishment for his crimes. Ford said that Nixon had suffered enough and that the nation should put Watergate behind it. Some praised Ford for his mercy, while others believed Nixon should go to trial, like any other person accused of a crime.

Nagging Questions

Historians continue to debate the questions.

When John Dean [above], President Nixon's lawyer, testified before the Senate, he admitted his own guilt—and helped reveal the President's.

Why did Watergate happen? Was it due to one man, President Nixon, and the flaws of his character? Was it due to the ruthless ambition of the politicians around him? In his testimony, Dean had said that Watergate was the outgrowth of a climate of both fear and absolute power inside the White House. Concerned that the Vietnam antiwar movement might damage Nixon's chance for re-election, Nixon's staff took the law into its own hands.

The U.S. system of government had been tested to the utmost by the Watergate scandal. It survived the test. Watergate remains a symbol of corruption and unchecked governmental abuse of power.

CHAPTER CHECK

WORD MATCH

1. prosecuted
2. bugging
3. Carl Bernstein
4. John Mitchell
5. pardon

a. conducted criminal proceedings in court
b. excuse or release a person from criminal punishment
c. secretly recording a conversation
d. former U.S. attorney general and later head of CREEP
e. *Washington Post* reporter who persisted in the Watergate investigation

QUICK QUIZ

1. Why did burglars break into the Democratic National Committee headquarters at the Watergate? Under whose instructions did they do it?
2. Why were the tape recordings in President Nixon's office so important?

THINK ABOUT IT

1. What might have happened if the Watergate investigation had not been pursued, or if Nixon's coverup had succeeded?
2. Do you think President Ford was right to pardon Nixon? Explain.

31 THE ENERGY CRISIS

Out of gas—and out of luck. The oil crisis of the 1970s threatened Americans' love affair with their cars. The fuel shortage forced drastic changes in lifestyle for millions.

The line of cars stretched for several blocks. Drivers sat behind the steering wheels reading newspapers or talking with friends. Automobile exhaust fumes formed small, white clouds in the cold air. This scene was repeated all across the United States in the winter of 1974. People were waiting to buy gasoline, but service stations often ran out. Stations posted signs: "No Gasoline Today."

Some people couldn't afford to buy oil to heat their houses. Airlines had to cancel flights because they could not get enough jet fuel. The shortage of fuel forced many factories and offices to close. Many people were laid off from their jobs. There hadn't been so many people out of work since the Great Depression.

The Energy Crisis

By 1973, the United States was the biggest user of energy in the world. This energy came from crude oil, natural gas, coal, and nuclear power. The most heavily used of these was oil. Oil was used to make thousands of products from gasoline to heating oil, to plastics, to medicines. It also was used in making electricity for power and heat in factories, schools, and homes.

The energy crisis of 1973 and 1974, experts say, was caused by many factors. Between 1950 and 1970, the demand for oil in the United States doubled. Americans were using more gasoline to run their cars. As more households used appliances such as freezers and clothes dryers, they required more electricity. This electricity was often created by burning oil. The creation of many new synthetic materials also relied on oil as a base.

The United States used so much oil that it could not produce all it needed to keep everything running. So it bought what it needed from other countries.

Most of that oil came from the Arab countries of the Middle East.

The Arab Oil Embargo

In the fall of 1973, fighting broke out in the Middle East between Israel and its Arab neighbors, Egypt and Syria. There was a short but bloody war, and the United States sent aid to its ally, Israel.

To punish the United States for supporting Israel, some Arab nations decided to stop selling crude oil to America. Some of these nations formed the Organization of Petroleum Exporting Countries (OPEC). The members of OPEC included Venezuela, Iran, and the Arab nations of Iraq, Saudi Arabia, and Kuwait. They decided to charge higher prices for oil. OPEC also reduced its oil production. Two things happened almost overnight—oil became both scarce and very expensive.

The Arab oil embargo lasted until

Trying to shorten the long lines at gas stations, government leaders set up special systems. In some places, for instance, only cars with odd-numbered license plates would be sold gas on odd-numbered days.

March 1974. In the spring, there was more gasoline available, but its price did not come down. Many laid-off workers were rehired, although the nation's economy recovered more slowly.

Conservation

Three weeks after the start of the Arab embargo, President Richard Nixon went on television to ask the American people to conserve energy in the coming winter months by stopping wasteful habits. He helped to change U.S. driving habits by cutting highway speed limits to an energy-saving 55 miles per hour. The President also ordered that the temperature in federal office buildings be lowered in order to save heating oil.

When President Jimmy Carter took office in 1976, he also stressed conservation. He called America's response to the energy crisis the "moral equivalent to war." For the first time since World War II, Americans were forced to conserve. Carter gave tax breaks to people who put more insulation in their homes. He convinced Congress to set up a Department of Energy (DOE) to study energy usage and its effects on people. Carter also supported legislation governing the price of gasoline. Gas stations would then compete against one another, Carter thought, thereby lowering the price of gasoline to the consumer.

Changing Habits

Rising prices in oil and gas forced changes in American habits. As gasoline prices rose from 30 to 60 cents a gallon, and then to well over $1, big cars became less popular. Many people switched from station wagons to compact cars that got better gas mileage. During the winter months, people looked for ways to cut home heating bills. They lowered their thermostats and wore sweaters at home. Schools even dropped their thermostats so low that students had to wear their coats and hats in the classroom. In the summer, families cut their cooling bills by using less air conditioning. Families were also concerned about usage of electricity. Low-wattage light bulbs replaced high ones. Companies also found ways to save by investing in high-tech, fuel-saving equipment.

While Americans tried to conserve ener-

In the scramble for new sources for fuel, the U.S. government built the Alaska pipeline to carry precious crude oil from oil fields in the icy north to major shipping areas nationally.

gy, oil companies looked everywhere for new supplies of oil. They built a 789-mile-long pipeline across Alaska to get the oil from northern Alaska to the West Coast cities.

Scientists found new ways to use heat and power from the sun, called solar power, and from deep in the earth, geothermal power, and from the wind. They used satellites to search for new sources of energy both on land, and under the sea.

Conservation and changing American habits both played a part in slowing the growth of demand. The shortages of the 1970s left their mark on the lifestyles of Americans. They began to economize.

Nuclear power was another energy source explored in the 1970s. However, its disadvantages often outweighed its advantages.

CHAPTER CHECK

WORD MATCH

1. conserve
2. DOE
3. OPEC
4. solar
5. geothermal

a. group of oil-rich nations that cut crude production and raised prices
b. government department formed to study energy usage
c. power from deep in the earth
d. stop wasteful habits to prevent losses
e. power from the sun

QUICK QUIZ

1. List three things that caused U.S. oil usage to double between 1950 and 1970.
2. What was OPEC? Why and how did it want to penalize the United States?

THINK ABOUT IT

1. Does the U.S. still need to conserve oil? Name some conservation measures that are in use today.
2. Besides oil, what other resources do nations regulate to affect politics?

32 THE CARTER YEARS

During his inaugural march [above], Jimmy Carter walked hand-in-hand with his wife, Rosalyn. Carter had promised a scandal-weary nation that he would bring honesty and decency back to government.

I will never lie to you," Jimmy Carter told American voters during his 1976 campaign for the presidency.

Carter's promise had great appeal. Americans were still reeling from the Watergate scandal. Many were stunned by Nixon's actions. Some were angry when President Ford pardoned Nixon.

Jimmy Carter, the 39th president, became the first Democrat to occupy the White House since Lyndon Johnson.

From the Deep South

James Earl Carter was born in the small, southern town of Plains, Georgia. Because Carter managed a family farm and peanut warehouse, he was known as a peanut farmer. But Carter was much more than a peanut farmer. After graduating from the U.S. Naval Academy, Carter served on the world's first nuclear-powered submarine.

As a young man, Carter was active in local politics and won election to the state senate. From 1971 to 1974, he served as governor of Georgia. He was a Baptist deacon in his church, and taught Sunday school even after he entered the White House.

Throughout his political career, Carter

worked to help blacks achieve equality in the South. As president, he appointed many blacks, such as Andrew Young as ambassador to the United Nations and Eleanor Holmes Norton to head the Equal Employment Opportunities Commission.

The Carter White House

Because Carter had no experience in national politics, he was viewed as an outsider by Washington politicians. He went by his nickname, Jimmy, and shunned the formalities embraced by many past presidents.

Carter believed strongly in the dignity of individuals. His commitment to human rights guided him during his presidency. He pardoned people who had evaded the Vietnam draft. He said that these "draft dodgers" had the right to stay out of a war they felt was immoral.

In the first year of Carter's presidency, the economy improved, but then inflation soared and prices rose. A new energy crisis developed. By summer 1979, many Americans were displeased with President Carter's performance.

Carter invited religious leaders, edu-

Egypt's Anwar Sadat, U.S. President Jimmy Carter, and Israel's Menachem Begin [left to right] announce the historic Camp David Accords.

cators, economists, and state governors to Camp David, the presidential retreat in Maryland. For ten days, Carter and these leaders discussed America's problems.

Carter reported his findings in a nationally televised speech. "The true problems of our nation are much deeper . . . than gasoline lines . . . , deeper even than inflation or recession," Carter said. "We've learned that piling up material goods cannot fill the emptiness of lives which have no confidence or purpose."

In foreign affairs, Carter also faced major problems. He worked for a new Panama Canal treaty. The U.S. had controlled the canal since its construction in the early 1900s. The waterway links the Atlantic and Pacific oceans and is important to the United States for both military and economic reasons.

Responding to the Panamanians' desire to control the canal, Carter negotiated two treaties. One treaty allowed for Panamanian ownership of the canal by the year 2000. The other stated that the U.S. could still use military force to defend the canal.

The Camp David Accords

In the Middle East, Carter was the force behind an agreement that promoted peace between Egypt and Israel. For almost 30 years, the two Middle Eastern nations had fought. Carter believed that Jewish survivors of the Holocaust deserved their own homeland. He also greatly respected Anwar Sadat, Egypt's president.

In September 1978, Carter met with Sadat and Israeli Prime Minister Menachem Begin (meh-NAHK-em BAY-gin) together at Camp David. They ultimately reached a peace agreement.

In March 1979, Carter, Sadat, and Begin

gathered at the White House to announce what would be known as the Camp David Accords. "We have won, at last, the first step of peace," Carter said, "a first step on a long and difficult road."

A declaration of peace did not mean an end to bitterness and hatred. Other Arab nations were angry. They said Sadat had betrayed them. In 1981, he was assassinated by Egyptian terrorists.

America Held Hostage

Throughout the world in the 1970s, Muslim **fundamentalism** (strict obedience to religious law) gained strength. Fundamentalism became especially strong in Iran.

The Middle East in Conflict, 1949–1990

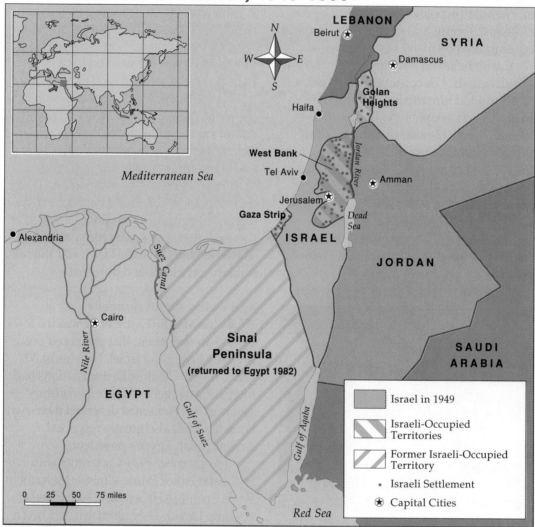

Where are Jewish settlements located? Which areas used to be occupied by Israel?

At the beginning of Carter's presidency, the leader of Iran was Shah Mohammad Reza Pahlevi (sha moo-HAM-id ri-ZA PA-la-VEE), who was not a fundamentalist. The U.S. had good relations with Iran. It had supplied the Shah with billions of dollars of aid and military equipment.

Many Iranians said that the Shah had been a cruel leader. He had pushed modernization on a people governed by traditional Muslim ways. In 1978, bloody riots swept the country. The Shah was forced to leave. The following year, he entered the U.S. for medical treatment. Iranians demanded that the U.S. return the Shah to them for punishment.

The U.S. refused. In November 1979, outraged Iranian militants seized the U.S. embassy in Tehran, the capital of Iran, and took 52 Americans as hostages. The hostage crisis dragged on for months. Carter wanted to resolve the matter peacefully. When all other measures had failed, he ordered a rescue mission in April 1980.

The rescue attempt was not completed. Eight crew members died when their helicopters collided. This catastrophe convinced many Americans that Carter was an ineffective leader. That fall, he was defeated for re-election by Ronald Reagan.

The hostages remained in Iran until January 20, 1981, the day Carter left office. Americans, dismayed over the long hostage ordeal, hoped Reagan would fulfill his promise and restore "pride and confidence" to America.

After more than a year in captivity in Iran, American hostages were freed. Their plight ultimately affected U.S. presidential elections.

CHAPTER CHECK

WORD MATCH

1. Camp David Accords
2. Anwar Sadat
3. fundamentalism
4. Mohammad Reza Pahlevi
5. Menachem Begin

a. strict obedience to religious law
b. prime minister of Israel
c. Muslim leader of Egypt
d. diplomatic talks to achieve peace in the Middle East
e. Iranian leader who pushed for modernization

QUICK QUIZ

1. What about Jimmy Carter appealed to American voters in 1976? What happened to make him unpopular?
2. What was accomplished by the Camp David Accords? What other problems did they cause?

THINK ABOUT IT

1. Do you think presidents are wise to act like ordinary citizens? Why or why not?
2. Do you think the United States should encourage fundamentalist Muslim nations to loosen their rule? Explain.

SEARCHING FOR NEW VALUES

History Detective

1. U.S. aid to Israel in 1973 made many of the other nations in this region institute the Arab Oil Embargo. Where is this region?

2. The threat of this action by Congress forced Richard Nixon to release tape recordings for the Watergate investigation and resign as president. What is this action?

3. Many TV viewers watched in horror as confused students were being shot at during a riot here. I have come to symbolize the conflict between the government and many students over the Vietnam war. Where am I?

4. I am the historic document limiting nuclear arms that was produced by the first peacetime meeting between leaders of the U.S. and U.S.S.R. What am I?

5. With inspiring ideals, I brought truth, integrity, and small town America to the White House. Who am I?

Voices From the Past

Rachel Carson's *Silent Spring* informed America of the dangerous and unfair use of pesticides to control bugs and other pests. But the book also gave Americans a new way to look at the way they lived. Here is part of what Carson wrote in *Silent Spring*.

Through all these new, imaginative, and creative approaches to the problem of sharing our earth with other creatures there runs a constant theme: the awareness that we are dealing with life—with living populations. Only by taking account of such life forces can we hope to achieve a reasonable [existence]. The "control of nature" is a phrase [which supposes] that nature exists for the convenience of man.

1. What do you think Carson means by the phrase "nature exists for the convenience of man"? Do you think she believes this?

2. Can you point out any ideas related to Carson's that you see in the world today?

Hands–On History

Writing a TV News Report—You are the first TV news reporter to set foot on the moon! What would you do? What would you say? Write the script for a news report about your accomplishment. Try to describe how you think the moon would feel to you, and tell the American public.

1.

Cape Kennedy, Fla., July 20, 1969—Man has landed on the moon! Today the U.S. became the first nation to complete a lunar landing. The world watched and listened as Buzz Aldrin and Neil Armstrong brought the *Eagle* to rest at Tranquility Base on the moon. The landing was filled with emotion. Aldrin reported the engines had been turned off. Then there was silence. Earth's only connection with the *Eagle* was the machine monitoring Armstrong's heart rate—normally it was 77 beats a minute, now it was racing at 156. Houston Communication Control broke in, "We copy you Down, *Eagle.*" Armstrong replied, "Houston." There was a brief pause as he tried to contain his emotions. "Tranquility Base here. The *Eagle* has landed!" A little later, Houston Control said, "Be advised there are lots of smiling faces in this room and all over the world." Armstrong's responded, "There are two of them up here." Perhaps the only human not watching this event was Michael Collins, who stayed above to man *Columbia*, the command module, and wait for his crew mates to return.

Astronauts Neil Armstrong and Buzz Aldrin left footprints on the moon.

Nixon Begins Meetings in China

Beijing, China, February 19, 1972—President Richard Nixon's historic visit to China officially got under way today. After meeting Chairman Mao Zedong during the day, President Nixon went to The Great Hall for a welcome banquet. There he made a toast to China's leaders and the people of the country: "We have at times in the past been enemies. We have great differences today. What brings us together is that we have common interests which [go beyond] those differences. The world watches. The world listens. The world waits to see what we will do. . . . This is the hour, this is the day for our two peoples to rise to the heights of greatness which can build a new and a better world."

The differences between China and the U.S. are great. **2.**

Carter and Human Rights

Washington, D.C., April 23, 1977—In his inaugural address last year, President Jimmy Carter declared, "our commitment to human rights must be absolute." Since then, he and his cabinet have laid ground work that would unite human-rights concerns with a formal foreign-relations policy.

Many people argue that the U.S. has no right to meddle in the way a foreign government treats the people it governs. **3.**

You Be the Reporter

Match each question with its news item above.

1. Write an inspiring or patriotic title for this article.

2. From what you learned in this chapter, finish this article with some of the differences between the U.S. and China in 1977.

3. Why do you think America's foreign policy on human rights would have upset some people? Finish the article by guessing what some people would see wrong with these actions.

COMPARING CARTOGRAMS

The population of the United States has grown enormously since its birth in 1776. This increase in population has not happened at the same rate in every part of the country. At first, all of the citizens of the United States lived in the narrow strip of seacoast which made up the original 13 states. Ever since then, the population has moved steadily westward, and continues to do so today.

This uneven growth is hard to see. If you made a list of the populations of all 50 states at different times in their history, you would probably end up with a confusing page full of numbers which could only be interpreted after hours of close examination. What if, instead of writing the totals down, you drew a map which could show state populations? Instead of showing the physical size of each state, you could draw the states in proportion to the total numbers of people living in them.

This is exactly what the two maps on the opposite page show. One map shows the different populations in 1960, the other in 1980. This kind of map is called a **cartogram.** Population, oil reserves, gross national products—anything that can be counted can be shown on a cartogram. The more a place has of something, the larger it will appear. The less it has, the smaller it will be. Although it is difficult to learn detailed information by looking at cartograms, they are excellent for making general observations and comparisons.

Study the cartograms. Then note the answers to these questions on a separate sheet of paper.

1. What do the nine colors on the map and its key stand for?

2. Compare the two cartograms. **(a)** In which cartogram does the United States appear larger? **(b)** What does this mean?

3. The population of some states is very large in both cartograms. **(a)** Which three states have the largest population? **(b)** Which three have the smallest?

4. Compare Florida on both maps. **(a)** About how many times greater was the population in 1980 than in 1960? **(b)** Name two other states that grew rapidly in the same time period.

5. Compare Kansas on both maps. **(a)** What kind of population growth did Kansas experience? **(b)** Name two other states with a growth rate similar to Kansas.

6. The population of every state grew larger between 1960 and 1980. What place (not a state) decreased in population?

7. Look at the regions on both maps. **(a)** What two regions have the highest population? **(b)** Name four regions with low populations.

8. Compare the different regions on both maps. Was the North Plains a fast- or slow-growing region?

9. The **population density** of a place is the average number of people living in each square mile of land area. Compare either cartogram with the U.S. political map, page 812. Describe the population density of **(a)** Alaska. **(b)** New York.

10. Compare either cartogram with the map on page 812. What other states besides Alaska seem very sparsely populated?

United States Population, 1960 and 1980

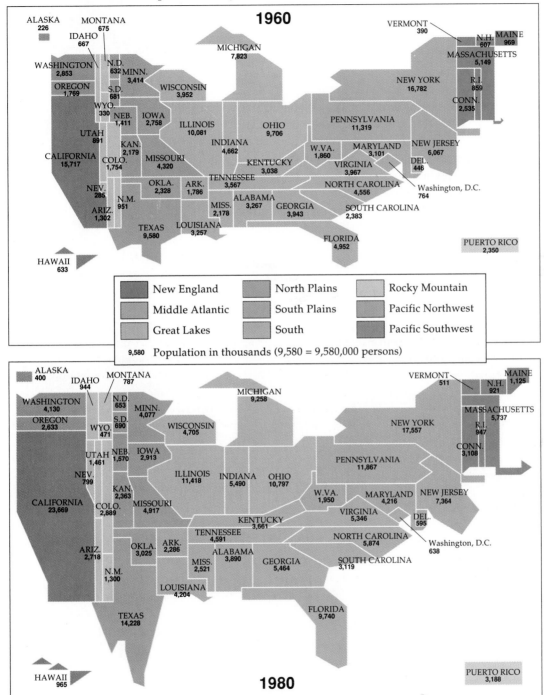

1960

ALASKA 226	
MONTANA 675	
IDAHO 667	
MICHIGAN 7,823	VERMONT 390
WASHINGTON 2,853	N.H. 607
N.D. 632	MAINE 969
MINN. 3,414	MASSACHUSETTS 5,149
OREGON 1,769	
S.D. 681	WISCONSIN 3,952
WYO. 330	NEW YORK 16,782
R.I. 859
NEB. 1,411	IOWA 2,758	CONN. 2,535
UTAH 891	ILLINOIS 10,081	OHIO 9,706	PENNSYLVANIA 11,319
CALIFORNIA 15,717	KAN. 2,179	INDIANA 4,662	W.VA. 1,860	MARYLAND 3,101	NEW JERSEY 6,067
COLO. 1,754	MISSOURI 4,320	KENTUCKY 3,038	VIRGINIA 3,967	DEL. 446
NEV. 285	OKLA. 2,328	ARK. 1,786	TENNESSEE 3,567	NORTH CAROLINA 4,556	Washington, D.C. 764
N.M. 951	MISS. 2,178	ALABAMA 3,267	GEORGIA 3,943	SOUTH CAROLINA 2,383
ARIZ. 1,302			
TEXAS 9,580	LOUISIANA 3,257	FLORIDA 4,952
HAWAII 633		PUERTO RICO 2,350

Legend:

- New England
- Middle Atlantic
- Great Lakes
- North Plains
- South Plains
- South
- Rocky Mountain
- Pacific Northwest
- Pacific Southwest

9,580 Population in thousands (9,580 = 9,580,000 persons)

1980

ALASKA 400	
IDAHO 944	MONTANA 787	MAINE 1,125
WASHINGTON 4,130	N.D. 653	MICHIGAN 9,258	VERMONT 511	N.H. 921
MINN. 4,077	MASSACHUSETTS 5,737
OREGON 2,633	S.D. 690	WISCONSIN 4,705	NEW YORK 17,557	R.I. 947
WYO. 471		CONN. 3,108
UTAH 1,461	NEB. 1,570	IOWA 2,913	PENNSYLVANIA 11,867
NEV. 799	ILLINOIS 11,418	INDIANA 5,490	OHIO 10,797
CALIFORNIA 23,669	KAN. 2,363	W.VA. 1,950	MARYLAND 4,216	NEW JERSEY 7,364
COLO. 2,889	MISSOURI 4,917	KENTUCKY 3,661	VIRGINIA 5,346	DEL. 595
ARIZ. 2,718	OKLA. 3,025	ARK. 2,286	TENNESSEE 4,591	NORTH CAROLINA 5,874	Washington, D.C. 638
N.M. 1,300	MISS. 2,521	ALABAMA 3,890	GEORGIA 5,464	SOUTH CAROLINA 3,119
LOUISIANA 4,204		
TEXAS 14,228	FLORIDA 9,740
HAWAII 965	PUERTO RICO 3,188

For almost 30 years, the Berlin Wall had been the most hated symbol of the Cold War. At midnight on November 9, 1989, thousands of people gathered as the wall was opened. People on both sides cheered and started walking through.

The Berlin Wall was not the only thing to come tumbling down in 1989. Communist governments all over Eastern Europe collapsed quickly as people began demanding more freedom. Major reforms even changed the shape of government in the Soviet Union. Under Soviet President Mikhail Gorbachev (mih-KYL gawr-buh-CHAWF), a new policy of *glasnost* (openness) has

Although Chinese students' demonstrations for freedom were crushed by their government in 1989, they marked a bold new movement toward freedom worldwide.

OUR
CHANGING

1980				1985

1981		1983	1984	1986
Ronald Reagan becomes president.	U.S. documents first case of AIDS.	U.S. adds new missiles in Europe. U.S.–Soviet relations worsen.	Geraldine Ferraro is first woman vice-presidential candidate.	Congress passes Immigration Reform and Control Acts.

WORLD

6

UNIT

1990

● **1989** ● **1990**

George Bush becomes president.

Berlin Wall opens.

Eastern bloc communist governments allow free elections.

allowed for free elections. In the past, the voters were only allowed to vote for Communist party officials. Now Soviet citizens can support other political parties.

Eastern Europeans were not alone in demanding more freedom. People from all parts of the world began to demand changes from their governments. In the spring of 1989, one million Chinese citizens gathered in Tiananmen Square in Beijing. They wanted democratic reforms, but the communist government brutally suppressed their demonstrations. Thousands of Chinese were killed.

In South Africa, blacks compose a majority of the population, but whites run

Geraldine Ferraro's campaign for the vice-presidency in the 1980s was a first for U.S. politics.

the government and control the economy. In early 1990, the white government, led by President Frederik Willem de Klerk, began to introduce reforms that could lead to black participation in the political process for the first time. As a gesture of good will, the de Klerk government released some black political prisoners. The most famous of these prisoners was Nelson Mandela, who had been in jail since 1962. His release would have been unthinkable even six months earlier.

New Freedoms at Home

The demand for more freedom rang out in the United States as well. American women reached a new milestone in 1984. For the first time, a major political party nominated a woman as its candidate for vice-president. The Democratic party chose Representative Geraldine Ferraro as the running mate of Walter Mondale.

As it turned out, Mondale and Ferraro were not elected. The door had been opened, however. People no longer doubted that women would be running for the nation's top two jobs in the coming years.

Ferraro's nomination was only one signal of the new directions in which American life was beginning to move in the 1980s. Women, African Americans, and

Here are South Africans Nelson and Winnie Mandela, leaders of the campaign against their nation's racist policies. They are celebrating his release after 27 years as a political prisoner.

AMERICAN ADVENTURES

Hispanics (people of Spanish-speaking countries) broke down a number of other barriers.

Sandra Day O'Connor became the first woman justice of the U.S. Supreme Court. Jesse Jackson, an African American, ran a strong campaign in the 1984 Democratic presidential primaries. In 1988, Jackson gained even more support, coming in second in the race for the Democratic nomination for president.

On the state and local levels, too, there were major victories for American women and minorities. The cities of New York, Los Angeles, Atlanta, San Francisco, Houston, Philadelphia, Chicago, San Antonio, New Orleans, Seattle, Washington, D.C., and Cleveland each elected an African American, Hispanic, or woman for mayor. Vermont elected a woman, Madeline M. Kunin, as governor in 1984. In 1989, L. Douglas Wilder of Virginia became the first black to be elected a state governor.

Many minority groups fought for changes in American society. Disabled people worked for laws requiring public buildings to be accessible to people with physical disabilities. Inside those buildings they demanded, and got, more jobs and public offices. With less success, they asked that public transportation be made accessible to them. In 1987, gay people marched on Washington, D.C., to protest the government's lack of support and funding for the life-threatening condition of Acquired Immune Deficiency Syndrome (AIDS). The homeless also marched in Washington, seeking governmental support of affordable housing.

In 1981, Sandra Day O'Connor [above, with Chief Justice Warren Burger] became the first woman to serve as a justice on the U.S. Supreme Court.

Population Changes

Other changes occurred in American society as well. Beginning in the 1970s, record numbers of businesses and people moved from the industrial cities of the Northeast to the booming sunbelt of the South, and to the West.

America's population also changed. It grew older. Americans were living longer and having fewer children. Many of America's elderly joined the move southward. They wanted to enjoy the freedom of their retirement years in a warmer, sunnier climate.

The thousands of new immigrants to the United States also brought great changes. In contrast to the European immigrants of the 1890s, most of the newcomers of the 1980s immigrated from troubled, sometimes war-torn lands in Asia and Latin America. They hoped that in the United States, they would find the freedom and economic opportunities that were denied them in their home countries.

New Technology

New technologies transformed daily life for many Americans. People began to use microcomputers in offices, schools, and homes across the country. Tasks that used to take hours, or even days, could now be done in seconds. Americans also enjoyed videocassette recorders (VCRs), which enabled them to watch movies of their choice in their own homes. They could also record programs for later viewing. Compact discs (CDs) threatened to make vinyl, long-playing records (LPs) obsolete almost overnight.

The U.S. Economy

The federal government changed direction, too. In 1980, Americans elected Ronald Reagan, who had campaigned on a promise to restore America's strength and pride, and to reduce the government's role in people's lives.

During his first term as president, Reagan tried to reverse the trend toward an ever-expanding federal government. He believed that the government was running too many costly social programs. He wanted states, businesses, and individuals to do more to help the poor.

Reagan gave tax breaks to both businesses and individual taxpayers, although high-income taxpayers received more advantages than middle- or low-income taxpayers. He thought this plan would put more money into circulation and create new jobs.

Reagan believed that America could seek world peace only from a position of military strength. Each year, he asked for bigger defense budgets to build up the nation's military power.

While he cut social programs and lowered some taxes, Reagan increased defense spending. Because of Reagan's policies, the economy began to turn downward. By

1982, the nation was in the grips of a severe **recession** (a temporary falling off of business activity during a time of greater activity) in which many people lost their jobs.

The country slowly recovered much of its economic strength, but the cost was high. To pay its bills, the federal government had to borrow money. This made the federal **deficit** (amount of money owed) soar. During the 1980s, under Reagan policies, the federal deficit more than doubled.

Most of the borrowed money came from foreign countries. In 1980, the U.S. was the leading **creditor nation** (lender of money to other countries). By the end of the decade, the U.S. had become the leading **debtor nation** (borrower of money from other countries).

Critics also questioned Reagan's cutbacks in social programs. They pointed to the decline of quality education, to the worsening of the environment, and to the growing number of homeless people. Some even called the 1980s the "greed decade" because it seemed as if many people were concerned only about themselves and material possessions. There were too few people like Mother Hale of Harlem, who tried to assist those less fortunate than herself.

The Iran–Contra Scandal

The biggest scandal of the Reagan administration involved foreign affairs. It was the Iran–Contra scandal. Close aides of the President, who insisted he did not know of their scheme, illegally sold American-made arms to Iran. They then used the profits from the sale to support a rebel army called the Contras, in Nicaragua. Many thought the plan reflected the President's frustration with not achieving two of his major foreign policy goals: to free the American hostages from the **terrorists** (persons who use violence or threats, often to obtain political power) in the Middle East, and to support the Contra army in Nicaragua.

The Reagan administration did not tell anyone about its activities involving arms for Iran or aid to the Contras. Neither the American public nor Congress had been informed. In fact, Congress had voted to cease military aid to the Contras. Many thought the President's aides had acted illegally. Some said that a secret government had been created that was not accountable to the American people. Congress held hearings to find who was accountable. After lengthy court trials, some Reagan aides were found guilty of some crimes.

Bush Becomes President

In 1988, George Bush was elected president. He campaigned with promises of keeping many of Ronald Reagan's policies. Bush said he would not raise taxes. He also promised to spend more on education and on the environment.

As they approached the 21st century, Americans increasingly saw themselves as citizens of the world. More and more, the American economy relied on a larger global economy. In addition, the enormous world changes resulting from the movements for freedom and equality affected Americans as well. Groups in the United States that historically had been left out of our political process continued to demand more equality.

After eight years as Ronald Reagan's vice-president, George H.W. Bush was elected the 41st U.S. president. Bush vowed to improve education, the environment, and other important aspects of life.

33 THE REAGAN YEARS

President Ronald and First Lady Nancy Reagan, former actors, enjoy time relaxing in the White House screening room.

"They say the U.S. has had its day in the sun; that our nation has passed its zenith. They expect you to tell your children . . . that the future will be one of sacrifice and few opportunities. My fellow Americans, I utterly reject that view."

It was the summer of 1980, and former California governor Ronald Reagan was running for president. At age 69, when many Americans were retired, Reagan was proposing to bring new vigor to the nation. Tired of gasoline lines, high unemployment, and high interest rates, many voters perked up. Maybe things weren't as bad as they seemed. Maybe President Jimmy Carter was on the wrong track.

Reagan campaigned on the platform that America's government was too big. With less government interference, he argued, the economy would get strong again. He said people relied too much on the government to do for them what they should do for themselves. Reagan wanted the expansion of government services and regulation that had begun with Franklin Roosevelt to be reversed.

At the same time, Reagan argued for a bolder foreign and military policy.

Many Americans were frustrated by their government's failure to rescue the 52 hostages captured and held in Iran. There was also a feeling that the Soviet Union still could not be trusted. After all, it had invaded Afghanistan in 1979. Would another country be next?

Reagan's Career

A former movie actor, Ronald Reagan had a polished charm and assured manner. In fact, it was his movie career that got him into politics. From 1947 to 1952, he had been the union leader for the Screen Actors Guild. Those were the years of the McCarthy hearings, and Reagan's politics turned from liberal to **conservative** (tending to maintain established traditions and to oppose changes). During the 1950s, he toured the country as a spokesman for the General Electric Company. He warned consumers then that the government was getting too big, and he praised **free enterprise** (policy allowing private industry to operate with a minimum of government control). Although he continued to accept acting jobs

Before entering politics, Reagan was a film actor and sportscaster. One of his most famous films, *Knute Rockne, All-American*, combined his love of sports and film.

occasionally, he became active in the Republican Party. In 1964, he gave speeches for Senator Barry Goldwater, the Republican presidential candidate running against President Lyndon Johnson.

That same year, Reagan made his first bid for governor of California. Although he lost that race, he managed to win the next one, in 1966, by almost a million votes. People who had written Reagan off as a simple-minded actor who appealed only to white, conservative businessmen, began to take notice. Much of Reagan's support began to come from blue-collar workers.

As governor, Reagan worked to reduce government spending on such programs as welfare payments and the state's vast university system. He was forced to raise taxes to cover a deficit in the state budget. But as soon as there was a surplus, he returned much of it to taxpayers. He was re-elected governor, and served until 1975. Governor Reagan gained a reputation for **delegating** (giving responsibility to others) many of the tasks of governing. Jimmy Carter had been often criticized for refusing to delegate many of his presidential chores.

Domestic Policies

In 1980, American voters turned to the cheerful optimism of Reagan. "It's morning in America," Reagan proclaimed. He would be his country's president for two full terms. No president had done this since Dwight D. Eisenhower.

As president, Reagan went right to work on his program. As a candidate, he had been critical of the growing deficit of the federal government. Reagan and his advisors argued that the way to get consumers to buy more products and services—and to cut the deficit—was to cut taxes. This theory became known as **supply-side economics.** In 1981, he signed into law a huge cut in taxes. This created a boom in consumer spending, but the federal deficit grew faster than ever. Huge military budget increases created the deficit. By the time Reagan left office in 1989, it was more than twice as high as it had been in 1980.

Still, the Reagan years were marked by middle- and upper-class optimism. Many people again bought large cars—some even rented limousines for special occasions. Multi-millionaires like Donald Trump and Malcolm Forbes were heroes or scoundrels to many. Fame and wealth also came to more African Americans than ever. Comedian Bill Cosby starred in television's number one show about a two-career black couple and their children. In the process, Cosby's wealth and popularity grew. Oprah Winfrey, a television talk-show host, also became wealthy because of her popularity.

During the Reagan years, federal funds for social services were cut back, causing homelessness and other social problems to soar.

Yet racism surfaced in new ways during the Reagan years. Many more blacks suffered its consequences. For example, there was a decline in the number of black male college students.

But what of those who didn't find financial security? For some of them, Reagan's tax plan allowed six million working poor people to stop paying any income tax. But there were still those who fell through what Reagan called the "safety net"—his phrase for government programs and supports. Almost 20 percent of American children lived in poverty. An estimated 250,000 to 3 million had no homes in 1988. The Reagan administration had called for an end to government spending on housing. Many Americans suffered from alcohol, drug, or mental problems for which there were no treatment programs. All these problems would wait for Reagan's successor.

Foreign Policy

While President Reagan delivered his first inaugural address on January 20, 1981, the Iranian hostages were on their way home. Negotiating for their release had taken 14 months of outgoing President Carter's time. The failure to get their freedom sooner was in many ways responsible for Carter's defeat. Reagan entered the White House with a promise to build the country's defenses. This, he believed, was necessary in order to stand up to anyone who might attack the United States. He asked Congress for, and got, a buildup of missiles, bombers, and other weapons.

American relations with the Soviet Union had been bad since the Soviet invasion of Afghanistan. They grew worse in 1981, when the Soviets pressured the Polish communist government into imposing **martial law** (temporary rule by military authorities over civilians). This put down unrest stirred up by the Polish union, Solidarity. After a U.S.–Soviet nuclear arms treaty fell through, Reagan sent more nuclear weapons to U.S. allies in Western Europe.

Soviet leadership changed four times during Reagan's presidency. Leonid Brezhnev (BREZH-nev), Yuri Andropov (ahn-DROH-puf), and Konstantin Chernenko (cher-NYEG-koh) all died in office. In 1985, Mikhail Gorbachev became head of the Soviet Communist party.

Gorbachev saw that one way to help the troubled Soviet economy was to ease tensions with Western nations. Another was to reduce the amount of money it spent on national defense. He introduced a program called *perestroika* (restructuring) to increase economic productivity. He wanted to change the Soviet economy by allowing the market system to determine prices (as in the United States).

Gorbachev and Reagan met several times. They started by agreeing to share information about education, science, and culture. In 1987, they agreed to destroy all ground-launched missiles within a certain range. The next year, Reagan and Gorbachev agreed to reduce their country's nuclear missile arsenals. Reagan's supporters said he had been right to take a hard line against would-be opponents. The treaties proved Reagan's policies had brought the Soviets into nuclear arms negotiations, they said.

President Reagan was the first successful two-term president in 30 years. Even in the darkest hours, his personal approval rating remained high. Said Reagan, "I'd like to be remembered as the one who gave the government back to the people."

CHAPTER CHECK

WORD MATCH

1. conservative
2. supply-side economics
3. free enterprise
4. delegating
5. martial law

a. maintaining, and opposing changes in, established traditions
b. giving responsibility to others
c. cutting taxes to increase consumer spending, intended to decrease the deficit
d. temporary rule by military authorities
e. allows private industry to operate with little government control

QUICK QUIZ

1. As a presidential candidate, what position did Ronald Reagan take on the role of government at home?
2. Besides acting, what other professional experience did Reagan bring to the presidency?

THINK ABOUT IT

1. What qualities made Reagan one of the most popular presidents in modern times?
2. Which groups of Americans benefited the most from the Reagan presidency? Which benefited the least?

CHAPTER 34 THE U.S. IN NICARAGUA

U.S. opposition to Nicaragua's government added to the many problems of that Central American nation. Sandinista President Daniel Ortega campaigned in support of his government in 1984.

The secret agents carried their fake **passports** (official government papers given for citizens to travel in other countries), a stack of small weapons, and a key-shaped chocolate cake. Their mission: to negotiate an international deal so sensitive only a handful of top White House aides knew about it.

It may sound like the far-fetched plot of a spy novel. But as the American people later learned during the summer of 1987, the inner workings of government can be as strange as fiction.

Secret Arms Deals

Government officials told Congress at least part of the story. In 1985, a small White House team had begun to secretly sell weapons to Iran. They hoped these sales would lead to the release of American hostages being held by terrorists in Lebanon. The officials then sent the profits from the arms sales to the Contras, the small army fighting to overthrow the government of Nicaragua. Publicly, President Reagan said that he would never **negotiate** (make arrangements or settle) with nations

190

AMERICAN ADVENTURES

like Iran that support terrorists. Also, Congress had voted to ban any U.S. military aid to the Contras in 1984. It had voted to send money only for food, shelter and medicine to Nicaragua. By secretly selling arms to Iran, and using the sales profits to fund the Contras in Nicaragua, the President's staff was breaking the law.

Why would the President's advisors think up such a scheme to carry out foreign policy? Reagan was frustrated by the Congress's ban on military aid to the Contras, whose cause he passionately supported. His aides insisted that the President himself was unaware of their illegal methods.

Civil War

Why was the President interested in the outcome of the Nicaraguan civil war? American politicians often refer to Latin America as the "backyard" of the United States. Over the years, the United States has feared that governments friendly with U.S. enemies in Central America pose a security risk to the United States. Those who believe this, point to the importance of the Panama Canal. Seventy percent of the trade that goes through the canal is bound for American ports.

Unlike the United States, few Central Americans are very rich, but many people are very poor. People there have often looked to their governments to control the economy. Some have favored socialism or communism, while others, such as **right-wing** (more conservative section of a political party) dictators turned to opposite ideas. Regardless of these choices, many Latin Americans think that they— not the United States—should decide what kind of government to have.

Between 1939 and 1979, Nicaragua was controlled by a family of brutal dictators. The Sandinista National Liberation Front, or Sandinistas for short, seized power in a popularly supported revolution in 1979. At first, it looked like the Sandinistas would set up a democratic government. They held fair elections and were elected by the people of Nicaragua. The United States showed its support by sending the Sandinistas $135 million in aid. The new government gave Nicaragua's poor people land, health care, and education.

Soon, however, the United States came to see the Sandinistas' reforms as threatening. They did not set up a capitalist economy, but instead modeled their economic system on the communist model. In 1981, Reagan stopped sending aid to the Sandinistas. Instead, he imposed stiff economic sanctions on Nicaragua. He convinced Congress to fund and train a guerrilla army known as the Contras which he hoped would overthrow the Sandinistas.

In response, the Sandinistas put thousands of their political opponents in jail. They shut down newspapers and radio

In Nicaragua's long and bitter civil war, children were among the many who fought—and died—on both sides. This young Contra was ready for battle.

stations. They postponed elections. They turned to the Soviet Union for help.

During the next seven years, the war between the Sandinistas and the Contras claimed almost 30,000 Nicaraguan lives. Thousands were left homeless and jobless. The economy was crippled by the high cost of war, and by the U.S. ban on trade. Even schools were unsafe. "We have guards and everyone is armed," one teacher said. "In the front yard of the school we have a large trench dug in the earth to use as a shelter if the school is attacked."

Debates in the United States

In the United States, public opinion was divided about what—if anything—the U.S. government should do in Nicaragua. President Reagan was determined to help the Contras and rid Nicaragua of commu-nism. Other Americans feared the Contras would return Nicaragua to a dictatorship.

The United States mined Nicaragua's harbors in 1984 to further disrupt trade and interfere with the Sandinista govern-ment. It trained and funded the Contras, seeking help from neighboring Central American nations.

Some Americans believed the United States should stay out of Nicaragua entire-ly. Instead of promoting stability, the Con-tra war was destroying Nicaragua.

In response to the bitter debate, Con-gress changed its policy several times. In 1984, Congress voted to stop giving money and training to the Contras. But the U.S. kept the guns and money flow-ing through its secret arms deals. In 1985, the U.S. cut off trade with Nicaragua. Then, in 1986, Congress reversed its stand

Central America

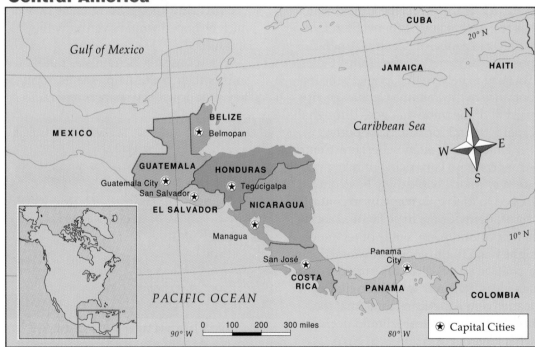

Name the seven countries of Central America. What is the capital of each?

AMERICAN ADVENTURES

and agreed to send $100 million in military aid and supplies to the Contras.

The Arias Peace Plan

In August of 1987, the leaders of all Central American nations met to discuss the problem. They agreed to a peace plan, chiefly written by Costa Rican President Oscar Arias Sanchez. Under the plan, each leader agreed to promote democracy in each country.

In 1989, President Ortega signed a pact promising free democratic elections by February 1990. In return, he and the other Central American leaders agreed that the Contras should be broken up by December 1989. In February 1990, free elections were held. A coalition of groups which opposed the Sandinistas won, and the Sandinistas agreed to give up power. President George Bush, who succeeded Reagan, was happy about the outcome.

He said that the United States would not only drop its economic sanctions against Nicaragua, but also would send aid to repair the damage done by the war.

Oliver North was one of the U.S. officials convicted of illegal actions in the Iran-Contra affair.

CHAPTER CHECK

WORD MATCH
1. right-wing **a.** official government papers given for citizens to travel in other countries
2. passports **b.** make arrangements or settle
3. negotiate **c.** small army fighting to overthrow the Nicaraguan government
4. Contras **d.** the more conservative section of a political party
5. Sandinistas **e.** members of Nicaraguan revolutionary movement that took control in 1979

QUICK QUIZ
1. Why is the United States interested in political events in Latin America?
2. How did the Sandinistas come to power in Nicaragua? Who were the Contras?
3. How was the sale of arms to Iran linked to the civil war in Nicaragua?

THINK ABOUT IT
1. Do you think the U.S. should negotiate with terrorist groups that take hostages? with countries that tolerate terrorists? Explain.
2. Why do you think President Arias was so successful in helping to negotiate peace in Nicaragua?

35 AN AMERICAN HERO

The nickname "Mother" suits Clara Hale perfectly. She has cared for hundreds of babies whose mothers were unable to do so. Hale's work is proof that one person can make a difference.

Clara "Mother" Hale stood quietly, but proudly, as senators, representatives, Supreme Court justices, and members of the president's cabinet gave her a standing ovation. President Ronald Reagan had invited her to his February 1985 State of the Union address, and in speaking, called her "an American hero."

Mother Hale's Mission

At age 80, Mother Hale was not a typical hero. What had this elderly woman from Harlem done that she would get a standing ovation from the most political-

ly powerful people in the country? She had followed her heart, and it had led her to children in need. As the founder of Hale House in New York City's Harlem, she had changed the lives of more than 600 babies and their mothers, who were all drug-**addicted** (dependent on a habit).

Hale took in her first addicted baby in 1969, and nursed the child through the terrible pain of addiction **withdrawal** (the process of giving up a substance one is dependent on). Eventually, the child was returned to her mother's care, for the mother also had kicked the drug habit.

Since then, all but a very few of the Hale House babies have been able to return to the custody of their newly drug-free mothers. While the babies are at Hale House, Hale insists that the mothers attend a rehabilitation program for 18 months and visit their babies every week.

In recent years, babies born with AIDS have become a pressing problem for inner cities. Most babies with AIDS are born to drug-addicted, AIDS-infected mothers. Hale House has been working to establish a home for AIDS infants, too.

A Love of Children

How did Mother Hale begin her work? After her husband, Thomas Hale, died of cancer, Clara, then 27 years old, worked at both day and night cleaning jobs to support herself and her three children. This work kept her away from her children, so instead, to earn a living, she began to take in other working people's children. She loved being with the children and they loved being with her—so much so that they didn't want to go home at night. Some of the children ended up spending the entire week with her and visiting their parents on weekends.

Soon, Mother Hale also began to take in foster children for New York City. She continued doing this for almost 30 years in her five-room apartment. Later, all 40 of the children went on to college— many went to graduate school, law school, or medical school.

In the case of AIDS, "Silence = Death," says this poster by artist Keith Haring. AIDS makes drug addiction more dangerous than ever— for babies as well as their addicted parents.

In 1968, at age 63 and after 40 years of raising children, Hale decided it was time to retire. Her retirement was short-lived, however. She was soon taking care of another generation of babies.

Hale House

The sight of a little baby nearly falling out of its mother's arms alarmed Clara Hale's daughter, Lorraine, as she walked through a Harlem park one day in 1969. The young mother was clearly strung out on drugs. Lorraine Hale pushed a piece of paper into the woman's hand with Clara Hale's name and address written on it. "Go there," Lorraine told the young woman. "She'll help you."

The next day, the young woman rang Clara Hale's doorbell. Lorraine had known her mother couldn't turn away a baby. "Before long, every pregnant addict in Harlem knew about the 'crazy' lady who would give her baby a home," Mother Hale told a magazine reporter. Within two months, Hale had 22 drug-addicted infants to care for.

Babies born to women addicted to heroin or cocaine become addicted in the womb. They continue to be affected after birth through the nursing mother's milk. When the first baby came to her, Mother Hale didn't know anything about treating addiction. But she knew about the healing power of love. She spent many late nights cradling the babies in her arms, and walking the floor with them. As drugs leave the babies' bodies, they suffer for weeks from stiff legs, vomiting, and diarrhea. They cry in pain and try to scratch at their skin. Mother Hale's apartment was filled with cribs. For more than a year, her own three grown children worked hard to help pay for these efforts, but they needed more money and more room.

Public and Private Funding

New York City began providing funding for Hale's work in the early 1970s. A federal **grant** (money from the government for a specific purpose) helped her to open a brownstone building called Hale House in 1975. Dr. Lorraine Hale, now an expert in child development, serves as head of the project. Hale House provides services through government funds and private donations. One of its most famous early supporters was former Beatle

John Lennon. Lennon was killed in 1980, but the John Lennon Foundation continues to donate money to Hale House.

The children who go to Hale House remain there for one to two years while their mothers get their lives straightened out. One program allows **rehabilitated** (returned to good health through medical help and counseling) mothers to live with their children at Hale House until they are capable of living independently. Mother Hale credits her own mother with teaching her to be proud, and to "always look people in the eyes." She and her staff pass those lessons on to every child who comes through the Hale House doors.

The 1980s brought a new problem to Hale House, and to others who worked with drug addicts. Crack, a particularly addictive and harmful form of cocaine, became available at low prices. It created a habit

Life in poor neighborhoods such as this one in New York City, becomes even more difficult because of crime and drug abuse.

that was harder to break than cocaine or heroin. It was even harder on babies. "Crack babies don't have a chance," Mother Hale once told a reporter.

An equally big challenge to Mother Hale was the epidemic of Acquired Immune Deficiency Syndrome (AIDS). AIDS, usually a fatal condition, is transmitted sexually, or may enter the bloodstream through contaminated needles. The AIDS virus also can be transmitted to the baby in the mother's womb. Many infected children are abandoned by their parents, and others are orphaned when their parents die of AIDS. They are left in a hospital with no place to go and no one to care for them.

Clara and Lorraine Hale could not tune out the cries of babies with AIDS. The Hales have plans to open a home for these babies. Originally scheduled to open in the late 1980s, the project has been delayed for several years. The need for such a place is critical, but until the Hales can open the home for AIDS babies, Hale House welcomes any drug-addicted baby it has room for, some of whom will also develop AIDS.

It seems there are so many overwhelming problems facing people today. What can one person do? According to Mother Hale, "Everyone comes into this world to do something." She found what she was meant to do.

CHAPTER CHECK

WORD MATCH
1. addicted
2. AIDS
3. grant
4. rehabilitated
5. withdrawal

a. returned to good health through medical help or counseling
b. the process of giving up a substance one is dependent on
c. an often fatal condition that attacks the body's immune system
d. dependent on a habit such as drugs or alcohol
e. money from the state or federal government for a specific purpose

QUICK QUIZ
1. What different kinds of services has Clara Hale offered to children during her career?
2. How do drugs enter the body of a baby? How does drug withdrawal affect a baby?
3. What new challenges did the 1980s bring to organizations like Hale House?

THINK ABOUT IT
1. Can you think of any political reasons why President Reagan would honor Clara Hale in front of a national audience?
2. Hale House insists that the mothers be treated for their addictions. Why do you think they do this?
3. What do you think is the government's best course of action to help babies with AIDS or drug addictions?

36 THE COMPUTER REVOLUTION

During the 1980s, advances in computer technology changed the lives of nearly every American. Computers made their way into homes, schools, hospitals, and offices.

One of the greatest revolutions of the 1980s was not political, but technological. It changed the world in ways that were unimaginable 10 years before. A man named Steven Paul Jobs, who brought the computer revolution of the 1980s to life, may be as important to future historians as some politicians.

Born in 1955, Jobs was an orphan who was adopted by a California machinist. According to his father, Jobs was always a little different, and was never really interested in school. "He came home from the seventh grade and said if he had to go back he just wouldn't go," his father said. "So we decided we had better move."

But Jobs did develop an interest in electronics and computers. After dropping out of college and going to India for "spiritual enlightenment," Jobs met up with Stephen "Woz" Wozniak. An electrical engineer, Woz was also a college dropout. In 1975,

Jobs joined Woz's computer club called the Homebrew Computer Club. Together, in Jobs' bedroom, the two developed a single circuit board computing device. They called it the Apple I, for a summer Jobs had spent working in an apple orchard. The computer was attractive mainly to "computer jockeys" and hobbyists, but it was the start of a company that changed the way the world saw computers. The Apple II, their next development, was the first truly "home" computer, although its memory was small by today's standards.

Computer History

The first electronic computer, the Electronic Numerical Integrator and Computer (ENIAC), had been built in 1946 by John William Mauchly and John Presper Eckert. Weighing in at 30 tons, the machine ran on 18,000 **vacuum tubes** (electron containers from which almost all air and gas has been removed) and could only compute numbers. It took up 800 square feet and got so hot that it constantly burned out tubes. Still, it was a remarkable machine. It could do 5000 additions and 300 multiplications per second and store a small amount of information.

By the late 1950s, ENIAC's huge vacuum tubes were replaced by **transistors** (electronic devices that control current flow without use of a vacuum). In addition to an electronic circuit, or pathway, transistors had a tiny piece of **silicon** (a material found in sand). Silicon speeded electricity through the transistors. The third generation of computers were developed in the 1960s, when space travel created a need for smaller computers. These computers had integrated circuits with hundreds of electronic circuits on a single piece of silicon called a **microchip.** By the 1970s, several functions could be put on a microchip. For example, one chip could both store and compute numbers. This led to the digital watch, and video games, and eventually, to the microcomputer. Until these developments, the computer was a mysterious, often intimidating machine to the average American.

During the 1970s, Apple Computers was extraordinarily successful. Started by these two self-taught college dropouts, the company earned more than $60 million by 1982, with sales up 74 percent from 1981. Jobs was considered a genius by computer and industry leaders. His critics called him a "techno-punk," but even they had to admire the company's success. The company's and Jobs' prosperity streaked upward again with the introduction of the Macintosh in 1984.

Small, portable, and "user-friendly," the

Steven Jobs [above] and Stephen Wozniak revolutionized the computer industry by building computers that were smaller, more efficient, cheaper, and much easier to us.

"Mac" was revolutionary because it truly could be used by anyone. Built-in programs "prompted" or guided the user in working with the computer. Symbols like a pointing hand, a watch, or a trash can replaced word commands. Soon millions of people were buying personal computers for use in the home, school, or office. Others began to compete with Apple for the home-computing market. International Business Machines (IBM), a manufacturing giant which had made its reputation on large mainframe computers, as well as a number of smaller companies, began to market to individuals.

The Future

Jobs' work at Apple ended abruptly however, when he was fired by the company's new Chief Executive Officer (CEO) in 1985. But Jobs was determined to develop his own style of computers, and in 1988, he launched a company to make a new computer called NeXT. Many have praised the new computer, saying it represents the future of computers in the decade of the 1990s.

In the 1980s, computers became as much a part of everyday life as telephones or radios. From doing homework, to answering the phone, to analyzing business information, computers became a part of almost every aspect of American life. In the home, computers cooked food in microwave ovens, set security systems, or entertained the children. Many automobiles had sophisticated microcomputers to help monitor gas flow or engine speed. In the future, computers may help guide cars through traffic and prevent collisions.

In schools, computers have become useful in mathematics courses and for word processing. Many educators hope that, in the future, a computer will be at every student's desk. They think computers could play a growing role in helping students learn foreign languages, history, music, and sciences.

Doctors will also use computers more and more. Computer-generated images will help them know more about the human body without using a scalpel or inserting a needle.

No doubt there are uses

Among their many uses, computers have improved the quality of life for people with disabilities. Here are blind people learning to read and write without Braille.

for the computer which no one has yet imagined. But whatever lies ahead, the foundation has been laid. As Jobs said, "Years from now we're going to look back on what's happened with computers, and I think we'll see it as one of our most enduring contributions to civilization."

Computers are also used in medicine as diagnostic tools. Doctors use computers to scan for tumors in a patient's body without using surgery.

CHAPTER CHECK

WORD MATCH

1. user-friendly
2. vacuum tubes
3. transistors
4. microchip
5. silicon

a. a tiny, square-shaped slice of material on which an entire integrated circuit is formed
b. a material found in sand, used to make microchips
c. easy to work with and understand
d. a nearly airless and gasless electron container
e. electronic device that controls current flow without use of a vacuum

QUICK QUIZ

1. When was the first electronic computer built? Who designed it?
2. What did Jobs and Wozniak do for the computer industry?
3. Name three things that are done by computer in the average American home.

THINK ABOUT IT

1. Silicon Valley is a nickname for the Santa Clara Valley in California. What do you think is the main industry there, and how did it get its name?
2. Do you agree with Jobs that the computer is one of the most important contributions to civilization? Explain.

37 THE BERLIN WALL CRUMBLES

"The Wall is gone!" was the jubilant cry on the night of November 10, 1989, when thousands of East and West Berliners celebrated the opening of the barrier that had divided them for 28 years.

It was well past midnight, but West Berlin glowed with light. The streets were packed, as thousands of East Berliners, young and old, streamed into the city. They were cheering, singing, and celebrating their new freedom. Church bells rang, car horns honked. Crowds of West Berliners joined them, shouting, "The wall is gone, the wall is gone!"

For nearly 30 years, the people of East and West Berlin had been divided by the 28-mile-long Berlin Wall. East Germany's communist government built the wall in 1961 to prevent its people from fleeing to

the West through West Berlin. The massive concrete and barbed-wire structure that cut through the city separated families and neighborhoods. Although West Berlin's streets were visible from East Berlin apartment houses, the distance created by the wall may as well have been continents. But this night, as if by magic, the Berlin Wall had crumbled.

The wall itself still stood, but it no longer symbolized division. Earlier in the day, the East German government had announced that it would lift all travel restrictions. Beginning at midnight, November 9,

1989, East Germans could freely enter democratic West Berlin and West Germany through border **checkpoints.**

"I can't believe I'm here," said one East German. "This is what we have been waiting for all these years."

East Meets West

At first, East Berliners were hesitant to test the government's new **open-border policy** (free passage between countries). After all, only the day before, a person could be shot by East German border guards for trying to escape into West Berlin. More than 70 people had died this way. Many more had been captured and dragged back to East Germany, only yards from freedom.

This night, that had changed. Cars waiting to enter West Berlin and West Germany created mile-long traffic jams. The trickle of curious East Berliners through checkpoints turned into a sea of people. Helping hands pulled people up and over the Berlin Wall. East and West Berliners stood together atop the wall. Many brought with them hammers and chisels. They chipped away at the concrete barrier long into the night.

A Wall Between Two Worlds

Nobody expected the Berlin Wall to crumble. Since its construction, the wall had divided Europe into the communist East and the democratic West. What happened to change this?

The communist world had been facing deep economic troubles. Poor planning dragged down production in factories. Food and other goods were often in short supply. When Soviet President Mikhail Gorbachev introduced social and economic reforms in the Soviet Union, people throughout Eastern Europe demanded similar changes. Free elections in Poland led to the formation of its first noncommunist government in 40 years. In Hungary, the communist government promised its people free multi-party elections. In Romania, the dictator Nicolae Ceausescu (chow-SHEHS-kyoo) was overthrown.

Now the winds of change blew through East Germany. Six weeks before the Berlin Wall fell, civil protests for political and economic reforms swept the country. Wave after wave of East Germans fled to the West by way of Hungary and Czechoslovakia. The migration of people was draining the

The Berlin Wall couldn't come down fast enough. Some people hammered holes into it, making its fall physical as well as symbolic. Others just wanted pieces to take home as mementoes of their new freedom.

country's labor force. President Gorbachev visited East Germany in the fall and warned its leaders that communism must change to fit the needs of society. "We have to react to the times, otherwise life will punish us," he said.

East Germany's leaders must have listened. Soon after his visit, their leader of 18 years, Erich Honecker, resigned. He was replaced by Egon Krenz, who opened the Berlin Wall. Krenz hoped that if East Germans were free to travel, they would choose to remain in the country.

Many East Germans who visited West Germany that first weekend agreed. "This

In January 1990, these people in Prague, Czechoslovakia, celebrated new freedoms in their government and way of life.

is what we have dreamed of since we were little children," said Knobi, a young East Berliner. "Of course we're going back home. That's where we live and we want to see what happens now. After this, there can be no turning back."

A Signal for Eastern Europe

The opening of the Berlin Wall signaled to the people of other nations in Eastern Europe that they, too, could demand democracy. In Czechoslovakia, Bulgaria, and Romania, thousands of people demonstrated for similar changes in their communist governments. They succeeded. After 40 years of communist rule, the governments of Eastern Europe promised their peoples free elections.

Yet amid the celebrations, uneasiness about the future surfaced. Democracy was new to Eastern Europe. Until now, forming any kind of political opposition to the Communist party was outlawed. Who would lead these countries, once the communists no longer held power? Would the governments keep their promises of more freedom? Even as bulldozers cleared passageways through the Berlin Wall, people waited for a crackdown that did not come.

President George Bush was just as surprised by the sudden turn of events. Nonetheless, he welcomed the changes in East Germany.

"We are encouraging the concept of a Europe whole and free," he said, but he warned the East German government against making too many changes too quickly. Now that the Berlin Wall was open, people in both East and West Germany wondered, "Why should there be two Germanys? Germany should be united." But after 40 years of a peace based on a divided Germany, it will take time to adjust to the vast changes in Europe. It will talso ake time for new relationships to develop between the United States and the new Europe.

On the chilly night of November 9, the Cold War had begun to fade. For the East Germans celebrating atop the Berlin Wall, their childhood dreams had come true.

In Romania, the fall of communism and rise of new freedom wasn't peaceful. Late in 1989, fighting broke out and Romania's dictator was killed, as were many civilians, before order was restored.

CHAPTER CHECK

WORD MATCH
1. Mikhail Gorbachev
2. open-border policy
3. checkpoints
4. Nicolae Ceausescu
5. Egon Krenz

a. free passage between countries
b. Soviet president
c. Romanian dictator
d. East German leader who opened the Berlin Wall
e. places at a border where authorities stop people for inspection

QUICK QUIZ
1. What problems plagued the communist nations of Eastern Europe in the 1980s?
2. In what countries did people demand change? In what countries were the changes most dramatic in 1989?

THINK ABOUT IT
1. What problems might a united Germany face? What advantages might it have?
2. President Gorbachev said, "We have to react to the times, otherwise life will punish us." What do you think he meant?

38 THE U.S. IN THE WORLD

Yankee know-how had kept the U.S. on top in world industries. But during the 1980s, other nations forged ahead. Americans bought more and more foreign-made products, sending their dollars overseas.

I t's 7 in the morning. In an auto factory in Normal, Illinois, music blares from a loudspeaker. Workers bend, stretch, and exercise. Why aren't they welding fenders? Why aren't they attaching mirrors? What kind of factory is this, anyway?

This is not just any American factory. It's a new auto plant, started in 1989, that is jointly owned by an American firm and a Japanese firm. Its management follows Japanese techniques such as exercising in groups, working in teams, and talking things over in "quality circles." A typical worker, Ray R., stands in the corner. As soon as exercises are over he'll join with his work team in talking over the day's plans.

It was a bit hard to get used to at first, but Ray R. and his co-workers are now into the swing of things. The exercises last only a few minutes and no one is forced to do them. Most workers seem to like the work teams. The teams allow workers to trade jobs and to do a variety of tasks. Workers don't have to repeat the same task hour after hour, day after day, as in the traditional factory.

In a Japanese-managed factory like this, supervisors and managers encourage workers to propose better ways of doing things. A worker may find a snag and correct it. "Good job," a supervisor says to the worker, who beams in the glow of the praise. Japanese-style *kaizen*, meaning "improvement suggestions," helps workers feel that they are members of one big factory family. Another way to encourage a common goal is with the use of clothing. Everyone—managers and workers—wears the plant colors of maroon work shirts and gray trousers. The factory looks like a pep rally, with everyone clad in the school colors and eager to cheer for "our side."

Workers like Ray R. feel the Japanese influence more than most Americans, but winds from across the Pacific have been felt in many other parts of America. By the mid–1980s, most Americans owned an array of Japanese products—perhaps a television set or car, perhaps a camera, walkabout radio, or VCR.

The winds of change came blowing from many directions. Americans used products from many other countries—sneakers from South Korea, shirts from China, kitchen appliances from Germany.

Every year, the economy became more global. Even American-sounding brands weren't necessarily American-made. From 10 to 50 percent of the parts in a so-called American car might be imported. In addition, some large U.S. companies weren't owned by Americans. Firms like Firestone, the large tire manufacturer, and CBS Records have been taken over in recent years by Japanese corporations, while other U.S. firms have been bought by British or Canadian corporations.

Let's Make a Deal

In a dynamic economy like that of the United States, business people are always looking for a good deal. If they can make money buying tape players in Taiwan and selling them in California, they'll do it. That's how free enterprise works. Americans have been investing in real estate and businesses overseas for years.

Business people from other countries also look for deals. Many foreign investors have been buying into just such projects. In 1989, a Japanese corporation bought New York City's famed Rockefeller Center from its American owners. Such foreign investment in the United States has made some Americans nervous. Worries grew in the 1980s when the U.S. government went on a borrowing spree.

In the eight years of the Reagan administration, the government doubled

Where do the things you use every day come from? Chances are, most were made somewhere other than the U.S.—like these cars imported from Japan.

its debt—from $1 trillion in 1981 to $2 trillion in 1989. The government borrowed money by selling bonds to all sorts of investors. Many of the investors were foreigners. Foreigners had plenty of U.S. dollars to invest in this country for a very simple reason. Dollars were pouring out of the United States to buy all those imported cars, electronic goods, and fancy sneakers. Still more dollars went to pay for shipload after shipload of imported oil to help Americans run those foreign-made automobiles and heat their homes.

Since the early 1970s, the United States had run massive deficits in its foreign trade. This means that it bought more than it sold abroad. As a result, the United States has had a negative **balance of payments** in its current accounts. The balance of payments is the difference between what a country spends for imported goods and services, and what it earns from exported goods and services. If the balance is negative, then money is flowing out of the country.

The money may flow back again in the form of investments in U.S. land and factories, and in loans to the U.S. government. But such money belongs to foreigners—not to Americans. Foreigners will receive profits on those investments. Foreigners will receive interest on those loans.

In the late 1980s, the United States officially became a **debtor nation.** That means that foreigners had more claims on the United States than the United States had on those abroad.

For Better or for Worse?

One reason foreign products were inexpensive is that both foreign companies and American companies that have factories in other countries paid lower wages to foreign workers than American workers.

During the 1970s and 1980s, hundreds of American factories had to lay off workers or close altogether. Especially hard hit were "smokestack industries" like steel and automobile plants. For every Ray R. who got a job in a new automobile factory, there were others who lost factory jobs. They found themselves standing on unemployment lines or flipping hamburgers, at a fraction of their former pay. It was hard to tell the newly unemployed not to worry. What did it matter to them if their lost jobs were balanced in the American economy by new jobs in banking or in aircraft manufacturing?

Japanese-style methods have improved some U.S. factories. Workers take a break here at a U.S.–Japanese car factory in Tennessee.

What's to Be Done?

Historically, there have been two solutions governments have adopted to correct an unfavorable balance of trade. One is to build up barriers by taxing imports and exports, and putting quotas on the kinds and amounts of products that can be imported. Policies like this are called **protectionism.**

Another way to attack the problem is to tear down barriers to trade. Many barriers have fallen since the 1940s. Trade that is carried out without significant barriers is called **free trade.** Supporters of free trade say it will create more opportunities for everyone. They say it will lead to a bigger economic pie, with bigger slices for Americans and foreigners alike.

Japan and the European Community are our most important trading partners after Canada. It is particularly important to correct our balance of trade with them. Beginning in 1992, many of the barriers to trade among the 12 nations of the European Community will fall. There has even been talk that they will adopt a single monetary system. The U.S. government

has also been trying to convince the Japanese to drop some of their barriers against American products.

Of the two policies—free trade and protectionism—which one, or which blend of the two, would be better for Americans and for the world?

These General Motors employees, like many other American factory workers of the 1980s, were laid-off because of intense foreign competition.

CHAPTER CHECK

WORD MATCH
1. debtor nation
2. balance of payments
3. protectionism
4. free trade
5. deficits

a. one that owes more money than it has loaned to other countries
b. business between nations that is carried out without major barriers
c. to place taxes and quotas on imports and exports
d. amount of money owed
e. difference between what a country spends on and earns from exported goods and services

QUICK QUIZ
1. What practices did a Japanese manufacturer introduce to an auto factory in Normal, Illinios? What were the goals of these practices?
2. Name at least three items bought by Americans that led to an unfavorable balance of trade.

THINK ABOUT IT
1. What is the purpose of the slogan, "Buy American?" Do you agree with it?
2. Do you think American workers should try to compete in the world economy by lowering their wages and standard of living, or by becoming more competitive through better education and job training? Explain.

39 THE NEW IMMIGRANTS

Asians are among the "new" immigrants who are finding new lives in the U.S. and changing the country as much as it changes them. An immigrant family poses on a rooftop in their new hometown of Houston, Texas.

In 1980, Duong Tin and his family arrived in Grand Rapids, Michigan, from Ho Chi Minh City, formerly Saigon, Vietnam. There he had been jailed several times by the new communist government.

The family had fled Vietnam by boat. They were beaten and robbed twice by intruders from another ship. For two months the boat was tossed by rough seas and storms. Duong and his brother and sister were often hungry and cold. After the family landed at a refugee camp in Indonesia, Duong's younger brother, Tam, became sick and almost died. Eventually, the family made its way to the United States.

Duong's family found life in America difficult at first. They had little furniture, but a used television set showed them images of a world where drug use was common. Although the children were often frightened by their new surroundings, they did not give up easily. They had already fought for their lives.

For the first time, Mr. Tin began to help his wife in the kitchen. He bought part ownership in a diner. There the family worked hard. They cooked, cleaned, and washed dishes. In the evenings, they gathered in a corner booth to study and read English, and learn about America.

Slowly, they began to learn English, a language that had seemed unpronounceable at first. They made new friends. Eventually, Duong became one of the best students in his class.

The Tins are typical of new immigrants to the United States. Today, about 84 percent of new immigrants come from Latin America, Mexico, the Caribbean, and Asia. They have come to be called the new immigrants because they are new and different from earlier immigrants. Most of the immigrants who arrived on American shores before 1890 were from Northern and Western Europe. Later immigrants came from Russia, Italy, Greece, China, and other nations.

At the end of the 19th century, Congress greatly limited Chinese immigration. Many Chinese had worked as laborers, but prejudice made some Americans resent their presence. In 1907, Japanese immigration was also restricted. Laws favored white Europeans over inhabitants of Asia or Latin America. Beginning in the 1960s, those restrictions began to change. Reforms in the old immigration laws enabled more Asians and Latin Americans to seek new lives in the United States.

Immigration Laws Change

One of President John F. Kennedy's goals was to change 19th-century immigration law. He said, "A nation that was built

Immigration to the United States, 1987

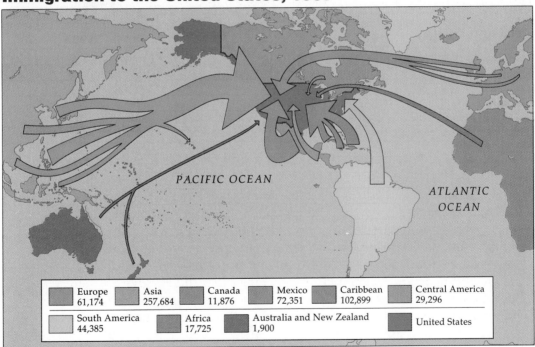

How many immigrants came to the United States from Asia in 1987? Which Asian country sent the most immigrants? How many immigrants came to the United States from the Caribbean in 1987?

by the immigrants of all lands can ask those who now seek admission, 'What can you do for your country?' But we should not be asking 'In what country were you born?' " He died before the law was changed.

In 1965, President Johnson signed a law that enabled people from all over the world to apply for U.S. **citizenship** (the right to live in and be protected by the laws of country). Individuals escaping from very poor nations or oppressive governments often sought new lives in the United States.

A **resettlement program**, begun in 1975, helped refugees, such as Duong Tin's family, to find new homes.

The Future

Although changes in immigration laws have enabled families such as the Tins to come to the United States, other obstacles remain. In 1986, Congress passed the Immigration Reform and Control Act to combat the problem of **undocumented** (without official status or legal papers) aliens living in the U.S. The act was passed in response to the fear some had that the two to four million illegal aliens in this country would take away jobs from U.S. citizens. The act offers **amnesty** (pardon for political offenses against a government) to illegal aliens who can prove that they have been living in the United States since 1982. Those who cannot, however, are sent back to their countries. Most are Central Americans seeking economic opportunity or fleeing from persecution in their own countries.

In the future, Americans will continue

Top 10 Sources of Immigrants to the United States, 1965–1985

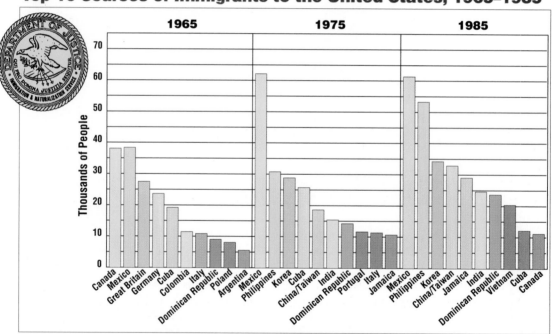

How many immigrants came to the United States from Korea in 1985? From India in 1975? From which continents did most immigrants to the U.S. come in 1965? In 1985? What does this tell you about trends in immigration? (Use the map of the world in your appendix if you need help.)

AMERICAN ADVENTURES

to try to balance the need for economic stability in the United States with their desire to offer refuge to those seeking American citizenship.

In recent years, the new immigrants have changed the face of America. Once again, Americans have heard a language other than English being spoken by their neighbors. Often this language is an Asian one. In exchange for freedom and opportunity, these new immigrants are willing to work hard to fulfill their personal ambitions. In doing so, they are becoming a part of the American tradition.

Immigrant contributions are evident everywhere in our nation. We find them in our literature, our architecture, our food, and our customs. As the novelist

Ishmael Reed says, the United States is becoming a place "where the cultures of the world crisscross."

The people in this family are just a few of the 700,000 Cuban immigrants living in Miami, Florida, today.

CHAPTER CHECK

WORD MATCH
1. undocumented
2. Immigration Reform and Control Act
3. resettlement program
4. citizenship
5. amnesty

a. finds new homes for refugees or immigrants
b. passed to control the number of illegal aliens in U.S.
c. without official status or legal papers
d. pardon for political offenses against a government
e. the right to live in and be protected by the laws of a country

QUICK QUIZ
1. From what part of the world did the first United States immigrants come? Where are the "new immigrants" coming from?
2. What groups were excluded from immigration to America in the late–19th and early–20th century?

THINK ABOUT IT
1. What do you think should be the qualifications for residency in the United States?
2. Do you think that the rise in immigrants from different nations will encourage people in the United States to study languages other than English? If so, which ones?

OUR CHANGING WORLD

History Detective

1. Tears mixed with cheers as thousands of East and West Berliners chipped away at me after 27 years of separating the two parts of their city. What am I?

2. As president of the United States, I tried to take power away from the federal government and return it to the local and state governments. Who am I?

3. I am a neighboring region of the U.S. During the 1980s, war in Nicaragua kept the U.S. involved here. Where am I?

4. In two presidential elections, I represented not just African Americans, but all those who have suffered and believe that America should offer more to all. Who am I?

5. Named after the person who created this economic policy, I led to government spending and tax cuts, and a rise in military spending in an effort to move closer to a balanced budget. What is the name of this policy?

Voices From the Past

Reverend Jesse Jackson spent many years as a leader of American civil rights. But in the 1980s, Jackson also became an important political voice. He ran two strong campaigns for president in the 1980s. Here is part of what he said at the Democratic National Convention in 1988:

> *America is not a blanket woven from one thread, one color, one cloth. When we form a great quilt of unity and common ground, we the people can win. Wherever you are tonight, you can make it. Hold your head high. It gets dark sometimes, but the morning comes. Suffering breeds character, character breeds faith. In the end, faith will not disappoint . . . Keep hope alive!*

1. What does Reverend Jackson mean when he says "America is not a blanket. . . . we form a great quilt"?

2. What message is Jackson trying to give those listening to his speech?

Hands–On History

Planting Your Family Tree—Find out about your own family's history. Were your great-grandparents, grandparents, or parents immigrants? Chart as much of the information that you can find, and then introduce it with a short essay about your family's story.

YESTERDAY'S NEWS

The American Adventures Newspaper

1.

Aledo, Ill., January 4, 1986—In recent years, farmers have found themselves in the worst crisis since the Great Depression of the 1930s. Crop prices are so low that most farmers can't pay back their debts, and many have lost their farms. Last year, Congress passed a major new farm act. It pays aid directly to farmers. But the fact is that farmers are still in great danger. Many are leaving the family business that raised them. During the 1980s, about 100,000 farmers each year left the land for good. By last year, only 2.2 million farms were left—down from 6.8 million in 1935. As the nation moves ahead, more people grow concerned that the small, private farm is becoming part of America's past.

Nelson Mandela appears with his wife, Winnie Mandela, shortly after his release from prison.

Mandela Freed

Capetown, South Africa, February, 12, 1990—Nelson Mandela was released today after spending 27 years as a political prisoner. Today, he is an old man of 71 years. But to the blacks of this country, and many people all over the world, his age means nothing. It is his long awaited freedom that means everything. Blacks, who account for nearly 75 percent of the population of this country, have suffered through years of mistreatment under a system of white domination called apartheid. With Mandela's release, many are hopeful that he will help South African President de Klerk dismantle the apartheid system. In his speech today, Mandela told the crowd:

Your tireless and heroic sacrifices have made it possible for me to be here today. I therefore place the remaining years of my life in your hands. . . . Today, the majority of South Africans, black and white, recognize that apartheid has no future. It has to be ended by our own decisive mass actions in order to build peace. . . . To relax our efforts now would be a mistake which generations to come will not be able to forgive.

Many observers find similarities between this situation and that of the U.S.'s past. **2.**

Finding the Homeless

New York, N.Y., March 20, 1990—Between 6 P.M. and midnight today, as many as 10,000 census counters hit the streets of New York and other U.S. cities. They visited shelters, park benches, and waited outside abandoned buildings for people to come out. Why? This is the first census count of the homeless population. Estimates of the homeless population run as high as 3 million, with 90,000 in New York alone. Finding out how many homeless persons live in the country will help the government figure out how to spend its money **3.**

You Be the Reporter

Match each question with its news item above.

1. Write a title for this story.

2. Finish this article with your own ideas about how the struggle of South African blacks relates to that of black Americans. What black leaders in U.S. history does Mandela remind you of? Why?

3. Finish this article with ideas on how the government can spend money to help the homeless.

UNDERSTANDING THE PACIFIC RIM: A LARGE REGION EMERGES

The Pacific Ocean covers one third of planet Earth. It reaches from the frozen north all the way to Antarctica in the south and halfway around the globe at the Equator. The ocean's rim touches five continents. Look at the map on the opposite page. Trace your finger around the ocean and read the name of each bordering country. Together, these nations form a vast region known as the Pacific Rim.

A region is a geographic area that is unified by some common or shared feature. You have located the geographic area, but what feature could be shared by such a huge region? The Pacific Rim includes very different climates, cultures, languages, and political and economic systems.

Look at the map again and you will see trade routes crisscrossing the ocean. Every kind of raw material, consumer product, and agricultural product is shipped to or from Pacific ports. This tremendous volume of trade connects these nations and makes the Pacific Rim one of the greatest economic regions in the world.

Study the map and its key. Write the answers to these questions on a separate sheet of paper.

1. With your finger, trace the nations that border the Pacific Ocean. **(a)** Which of the following nations are on this rim of the Pacific: Canada, the United States, Mexico, Colombia, Peru, Chile, New Zealand, Australia, China, South Korea, North Korea, Japan, the Soviet Union? **(b)** Which are in the Eastern Pacific? the Western Pacific?

2. Is a greater volume of trade shipped through the Northern or the Southern Pacific Ocean?

3. By the year 2000, economists predict that the total value of goods and services produced by the Western Pacific countries will be one quarter of the world's total. Referring to the map, identify eight Western Pacific nations.

4. What major trading partner does the U.S. have in the Western Pacific? **(a)** What is that nation's chief export? **(b)** What might that nation import from the U.S.?

5. Find Australia on the map. **(a)** What are Australia's chief exports? **(b)** Who are some of Australia's trading partners?

6. Most products of the Soviet Union are shipped from its European ports, but Vladivostok is its seaport on the Pacific. **(a)** What does the Soviet Union export from Vladivostok? **(b)** Who is its trading partner in the Pacific?

7. Suppose you were a manufacturer in Hong Kong. From what country might you get lumber (a raw material) to make carved boxes?

8. If you were in the food processing business located on the West Coast of the United States, from which nearby trading partners might you import food?

9. Suppose you were a U.S. importer of manufactured goods. Would most of your trading partners be Western Pacific or Eastern Pacific nations?

10. Both Hong Kong and Singapore are so small that they can not be clearly shown on your map. **(a)** What is the chief export of both nations? **(b)** Explain why both places might not be able to export other kinds of goods.

Pacific Rim Trade

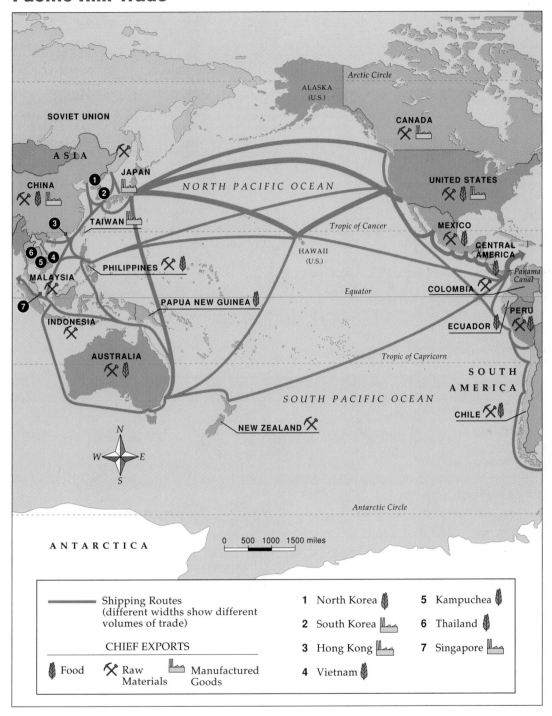

Map legend:

Shipping Routes (different widths show different volumes of trade)

CHIEF EXPORTS

- Food
- Raw Materials
- Manufactured Goods

1 North Korea (Food)
2 South Korea (Manufactured Goods)
3 Hong Kong (Manufactured Goods)
4 Vietnam (Food)
5 Kampuchea (Food)
6 Thailand (Food)
7 Singapore (Manufactured Goods)

Political Map of the U.S.

AMERICAN ADVENTURES

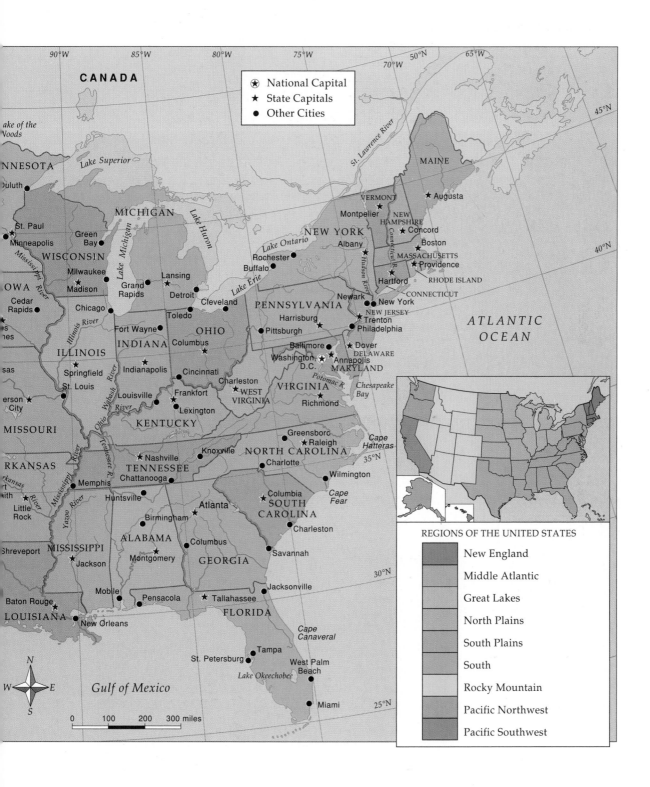

CANADA

National Capital
State Capitals
Other Cities

Lake of the Woods

Lake Superior

MINNESOTA

Duluth

St. Paul
Minneapolis

WISCONSIN

Milwaukee

MICHIGAN

Green Bay

Lake Michigan

Lake Huron

Lansing

Grand Rapids

Detroit

Lake Ontario

Rochester

Buffalo

Lake Erie

Cleveland

Toledo

NEW YORK

Albany

St. Lawrence River

MAINE

Augusta

VERMONT

Montpelier

NEW HAMPSHIRE

Concord

Boston

MASSACHUSETTS

Providence

Hartford

RHODE ISLAND

CONNECTICUT

Connecticut R.

IOWA

Cedar Rapids

Des Moines

Mississippi River

Illinois River

Chicago

Fort Wayne

INDIANA

OHIO

Columbus

PENNSYLVANIA

Harrisburg

Pittsburgh

Hudson River

Newark

New York

NEW JERSEY

Trenton

Philadelphia

ATLANTIC OCEAN

ILLINOIS

Springfield

St. Louis

Wabash River

Indianapolis

Cincinnati

Charleston

WEST VIRGINIA

Baltimore

Washington, D.C.

Annapolis

MARYLAND

Dover

DELAWARE

Kansas

Jefferson City

MISSOURI

Ohio River

Louisville

Frankfort

Lexington

KENTUCKY

Tennessee R.

VIRGINIA

Richmond

Potomac R.

Chesapeake Bay

ARKANSAS

Fort Smith

Little Rock

Arkansas River

Mississippi River

Memphis

Huntsville

Yazoo River

Nashville

Chattanooga

TENNESSEE

Knoxville

Greensboro

Raleigh

NORTH CAROLINA

Charlotte

Cape Hatteras

Wilmington

Cape Fear

MISSISSIPPI

Jackson

Birmingham

ALABAMA

Columbus

Montgomery

Atlanta

GEORGIA

Columbia

SOUTH CAROLINA

Charleston

Savannah

Shreveport

LOUISIANA

Baton Rouge

New Orleans

Mobile

Pensacola

Tallahassee

FLORIDA

Jacksonville

Gulf of Mexico

N
W   E
S

0   100   200   300 miles

St. Petersburg

Tampa

West Palm Beach

Lake Okeechobee

Cape Canaveral

Miami

90°W   85°W   80°W   75°W   70°W   65°W

50°N

45°N

40°N

35°N

30°N

25°N

REGIONS OF THE UNITED STATES

New England
Middle Atlantic
Great Lakes
North Plains
South Plains
South
Rocky Mountain
Pacific Northwest
Pacific Southwest

Political Map of the World

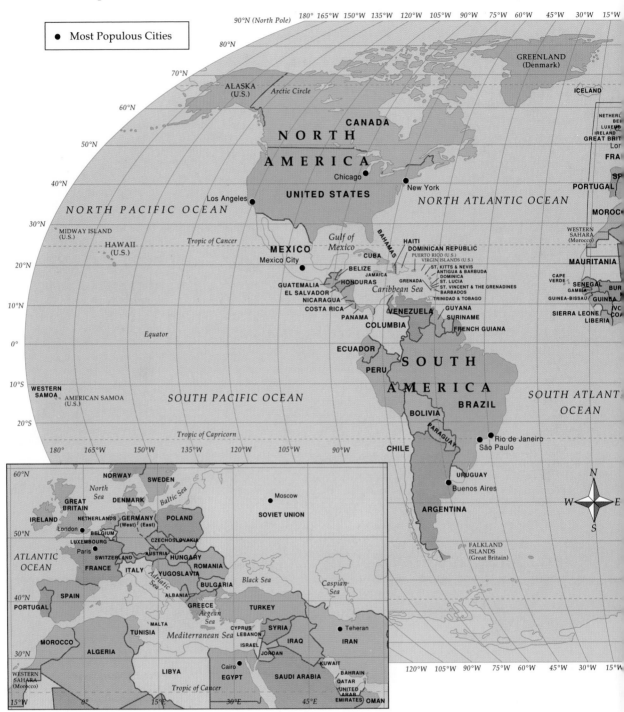

Most Populous Cities

90°N (North Pole)
180° 165°W 150°W 135°W 120°W 105°W 90°W 75°W 60°W 45°W 30°W 15°W

80°N

70°N

60°N

GREENLAND
(Denmark)

ALASKA
(U.S.)

Arctic Circle

ICELAND

NETHERL
BEI
LUXEM
IRELAND
GREAT BRIT
Lor

50°N

CANADA

NORTH

AMERICA

FRA

40°N

Chicago ●

● New York

UNITED STATES

NORTH ATLANTIC OCEAN

PORTUGAL

SP

Los Angeles ●

MOROC

30°N

NORTH PACIFIC OCEAN

MIDWAY ISLAND
(U.S.)

Tropic of Cancer

WESTERN
SAHARA
(Morocco)

HAWAII
(U.S.)

Gulf of
Mexico

BAHAMAS

HAITI
DOMINICAN REPUBLIC
PUERTO RICO (U.S.)
VIRGIN ISLANDS (U.S.)

MAURITANIA

20°N

MEXICO

Mexico City ●

CUBA

BELIZE

JAMAICA

ST. KITTS & NEVIS
ANTIGUA & BARBUDA
DOMINICA
ST. LUCIA
ST. VINCENT & THE GRENADINES
BARBADOS

GRENADA

CAPE
VERDE

SENEGAL

BUR

GUINEA-BISSAU GUINEA

GUATEMALIA
EL SALVADOR
NICARAGUA
COSTA RICA

HONDURAS

Caribbean Sea

TRINIDAD & TOBAGO

SIERRA LEONE

IVC
CO

LIBERIA

10°N

PANAMA

VENEZUELA

GUYANA
SURINAME
FRENCH GUIANA

COLUMBIA

0°

Equator

ECUADOR

PERU

SOUTH

AMERICA

10°S

WESTERN
SAMOA

AMERICAN SAMOA
(U.S.)

SOUTH PACIFIC OCEAN

BOLIVIA

BRAZIL

*SOUTH ATLANT
OCEAN*

20°S

Tropic of Capricorn

180° 165°W 150°W 135°W 120°W 105°W 90°W

PARAGUAY

CHILE

Rio de Janeiro ●
São Paulo ●

URUGUAY
Buenos Aires ●

N

ARGENTINA

W E

S

FALKLAND
ISLANDS
(Great Britain)

60°N

NORWAY
SWEDEN

*North
Sea*

Moscow ●

GREAT
BRITAIN

DENMARK

Baltic Sea

SOVIET UNION

IRELAND

NETHERLANDS
London ●

GERMANY
(West) (East)

POLAND

50°N

BELGIUM

LUXEMBOURG

CZECHOSLOVAKIA

*ATLANTIC
OCEAN*

Paris ●

SWITZERLAND
FRANCE

AUSTRIA
HUNGARY

ITALY

YUGOSLAVIA

ROMANIA

*Adriatic
Sea*

BULGARIA

Black Sea

*Caspian
Sea*

ALBANIA

40°N

SPAIN

GREECE

TURKEY

PORTUGAL

*Aegean
Sea*

MALTA

CYPRUS
LEBANON

SYRIA

Teheran ●

30°N

MOROCCO

TUNISIA

Mediterranean Sea

ISRAEL

IRAQ

IRAN

JORDAN

ALGERIA

KUWAIT

WESTERN
SAHARA
(Morocco)

LIBYA

Cairo ●
EGYPT

SAUDI ARABIA

BAHRAIN
QATAR

Tropic of Cancer

UNITED
ARAB
EMIRATES OMAN

15°W

0°

15°E

30°E

45°E

120°W 105°W 90°W 75°W 60°W 45°W 30°W 15°W

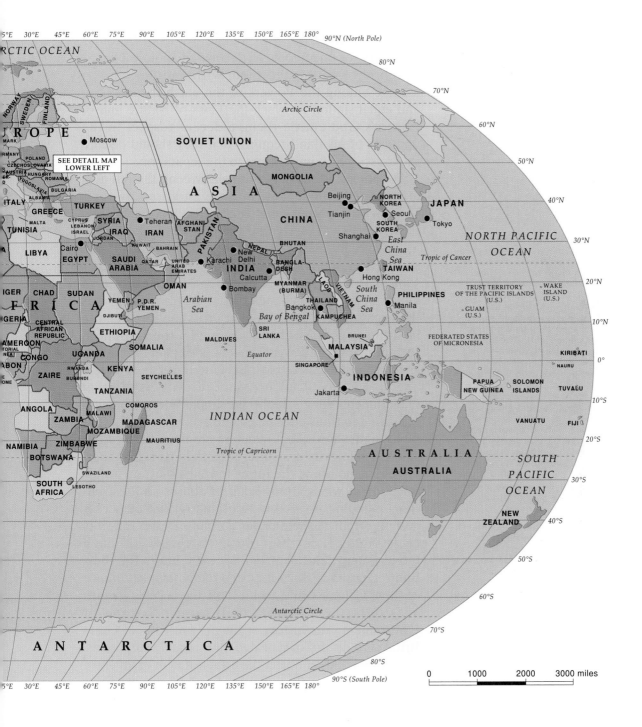

5°E 30°E 45°E 60°E 75°E 90°E 105°E 120°E 135°E 150°E 165°E 180° 90°N (North Pole)

RCTIC OCEAN

80°N

70°N

Arctic Circle

60°N

JROPE • Moscow SOVIET UNION 50°N

MARK
RMANY POLAND
CZECHOSLOVAKIA SEE DETAIL MAP A S I A MONGOLIA 40°N
ASTRIA HUNGARY LOWER LEFT
YUGOSLAVIA ROMANA Beijing NORTH
ITALY ALBANIA BULGARIA CHINA Tianjin KOREA JAPAN
GREECE Seoul
TURKEY AFGHANI- SOUTH Tokyo 30°N
SYRIA Teheran STAN KOREA NORTH PACIFIC
MALTA CYPRUS Shanghai East OCEAN
TUNISIA LEBANON IRAQ IRAN PAKISTAN NEPAL BHUTAN China
ISRAEL JORDAN New BANGLA- Sea Tropic of Cancer
LIBYA Cairo KUWAIT BAHRAIN Karachi Delhi DESH TAIWAN 20°N
EGYPT SAUDI QATAR INDIA Hong Kong
ARABIA UNITED Bombay MYANMAR LAOS South WAKE
ARAB OMAN Calcutta (BURMA) China PHILIPPINES TRUST TERRITORY ISLAND
IGER CHAD SUDAN EMIRATES Arabian THAILAND VIETNAM Sea Manila OF THE PACIFIC ISLANDS (U.S.)
FRICA YEMEN Sea Bangkok (U.S.) 10°N
GERIA CENTRAL P.D.R. Bay of Bengal KAMPUCHEA GUAM
AFRICAN DJIBOUTI YEMEN SRI (U.S.)
MEROON REPUBLIC ETHIOPIA MALDIVES LANKA BRUNEI FEDERATED STATES KIRIBATI
TORIAL SOMALIA OF MICRONESIA 0°
ABON CONGO UGANDA Equator MALAYSIA NAURU
OME ZAIRE RWANDA KENYA SINGAPORE
BURUNDI SEYCHELLES Jakarta INDONESIA PAPUA SOLOMON TUVALU 10°S
TANZANIA NEW GUINEA ISLANDS
ANGOLA COMOROS
MALAWI MADAGASCAR INDIAN OCEAN VANUATU FIJI
ZAMBIA
MOZAMBIQUE MAURITIUS 20°S
NAMIBIA ZIMBABWE Tropic of Capricorn AUSTRALIA SOUTH
BOTSWANA AUSTRALIA PACIFIC
SWAZILAND 30°S
SOUTH LESOTHO OCEAN
AFRICA

NEW 40°S
ZEALAND

50°S

60°S

Antarctic Circle 70°S

A N T A R C T I C A 80°S

0 1000 2000 3000 miles

5°E 30°E 45°E 60°E 75°E 90°E 105°E 120°E 135°E 150°E 165°E 180° 90°S (South Pole)

THE DECLARATION OF INDEPENDENCE

1. This is the preamble, or introduction, to the Declaration of Independence. Thomas Jefferson was the main author of the Declaration. Jefferson and the other American colonists believed that the time had come for them to break away from England and form their own nation. In the preamble, Jefferson writes that the colonists have a duty to state the reasons for their actions. He believes the colonists must explain to the world why they are declaring their independence from Britain.

2. In this section, Jefferson describes what he believes are the basic principles of democracy. This is perhaps the most meaningful part of the document. It is certainly the most well known. Jefferson believes that all people are born equal. That means they all have the same basic rights. The most important are "life, liberty, and the pursuit of happiness." People set up governments to protect these rights. Jefferson thought that governments should get their power by agreement of the people. This is different from previous types of government which got their authority from monarchs. Jefferson argues that when a government no longer protects the basic rights of the people, the people have a right to overthrow that government and set up a new one.

3. Jefferson adds that people do not change governments for minor reasons. In fact, they often put up with many abuses rather than change to something new and untried. But when a government grows too harsh and unjust, it becomes the people's duty to overthrow that government. The colonists believe that King George III has a long history of abusing his power. That is the reason why they are establishing a new government.

4. In the long section that follows, Jefferson lists 27 injustices committed by George III. Jefferson tries to blame the king for all the actions Britain has

1 When in the Course of human events, it becomes necessary for one people to dissolve the political bands which have connected them with another, and to assume among the Powers of the earth the separate and equal station to which the Laws of Nature and of Nature's God entitle them, a decent respect to the opinions of mankind requires that they should declare the causes which impel them to the separation.

2 We hold these truths to be self-evident, that all men are created equal, that they are endowed by their Creator with certain unalienable Rights, that among these are Life, Liberty and the pursuit of Happiness. That to secure these rights, Governments are instituted among Men, deriving their just powers from the consent of the governed. That whenever any Form of Government becomes destructive of these ends, it is the Right of the People to alter or to abolish it, and to institute new Government, laying its foundation on such principles and organizing its powers in such form, as to them shall seem most likely to effect their Safety and Happiness. Prudence, indeed, will dictate that Governments long established should not be changed for light and transient causes; and accordingly all expe- **3** rience hath shown, that mankind are more disposed to suffer, while evils are sufferable, than to right themselves by abolishing the forms to which they are accustomed. But when a long train of abuses and usurpations pursuing invariably the same Object evinces a design to reduce them under absolute Despotism, it is their right, it is their duty, to throw off such Government, and to provide new Guards for their future security. —Such has been the patient sufferance of these Colonies: and such is now the necessity which constrains them to alter their former Systems of **4** Government. The history of the present King of Great Britain is a history of repeated injuries and usurpations, all having in direct object the establishment of an absolute Tyranny over these States. To prove this, let Facts be submitted to a candid world.

5 He has refused his Assent to Laws, the most wholesome and necessary for the public good.

AMERICAN ADVENTURES

He has forbidden his Governors to pass Laws of immediate and pressing importance, unless suspended in their operation till his Assent should be obtained: and when so suspended, he has utterly neglected to attend to them.

He has refused to pass other Laws for the accommodation of large districts of people, unless those people would relinquish the right of Representation in the Legislature, a right inestimable to them and formidable to tyrants only.

He has called together legislative bodies at places unusual, uncomfortable, and distant from the depository of their Public Records, for the sole purpose of fatiguing them into compliance with his measures.

He has dissolved Representative Houses repeatedly, for opposing with manly firmness his invasions on the rights of the people.

He has refused for a long time, after such dissolutions, to cause others to be elected: whereby the Legislative Powers, incapable of Annihilation, have returned to the People at large for their exercise: the State remaining in the mean time exposed to all the dangers of invasion from without, and convulsions within.

He has endeavoured to prevent the population of these States: for that purpose obstructing the Laws for Naturalization of Foreigners: refusing to pass others to encourage their migration hither, and raising the conditions of new Appropriations of Lands.

He has obstructed the Administration of Justice, by refusing his Assent to Laws for establishing Judiciary Powers.

He has made Judges dependent on his Will alone, for the tenure of their offices, and the amount and payment of their salaries.

He has erected a multitude of New Offices, and sent hither swarms of Officers to harass our People, and eat out their substance.

He has kept among us, in times of peace, Standing Armies without the Consent of our legislatures.

He has affected to render the Military independent of and superior to the Civil Power.

5 taken against its American colonies. George III is accused of deliberately trying to destroy the colonists' rights and government.

5. Jefferson begins by describing how George III has unjustly used his power. Jefferson blames the king for trying to control the colonial legislatures. George III is accused of not approving necessary laws passed by the colonists. He has dismissed assemblies that disobeyed royal governors. He has forced the colonial legislatures to meet in unusual and distant places. And he has not called for elections to replace the colonial assemblies which he has dismissed.

6. Here Jefferson accuses the king of prohibiting the American colonists from moving west and settling the new land. Also, George III has prevented justice from being done. He has insisted that judges serve only as long as he was pleased with them. Finally, he has annoyed the colonists by keeping British troops in America after the end **6** of the French and Indian War. And he has sent large numbers of customs officials to harass them.

7. Jefferson then describes how the king has joined with others, meaning Parliament, to control the colonies. The colonists always argued that Parliament had no right to make laws for them because they were not represented in it. This argument was challenged by passage of the Declaratory Act in 1766. This act stated that the king and Parliament had total authority over the colonists. Still, many colonists continued to argue that Parliament had no right to tax them. Among the later actions of Parliament which angered the colonists was the Quebec Act, which kept French civil law in Quebec. Other unjust acts included the Quartering Act and the blockade of colonial ports.

8. In this section, Jefferson describes the warlike actions of the king. Instead of helping the colonists and protecting them, he has waged war on them. He has restricted their trade with other nations. He has hired foreign troops and sent them to America to fight against the colonists. He has encouraged the slaves in America to revolt against their masters. And he has persuaded Native Americans to attack settlers on the frontier.

7 He has combined with others to subject us to a jurisdiction foreign to our constitution, and unacknowledged by our laws: giving his Assent to their acts of pretended legislation:

For quartering large bodies of armed troops among us:

For protecting them, by mock Trial, from Punishment for any Murders which they should commit on the Inhabitants of these States:

For cutting off our Trade with all parts of the world:

For imposing taxes on us without our Consent:

For depriving us, in many cases, of the benefits of Trial by Jury:

For transporting us beyond Seas to be tried for pretended offences:

For abolishing the free System of English Laws in a neighbouring Province, establishing therein an Arbitrary government and enlarging its Boundaries so as to render it at once an example and fit instrument for introducing the same absolute rule into these Colonies:

For taking away our Charters, abolishing our most valuable Laws, and altering fundamentally the Forms of our Governments:

For suspending our own Legislatures, and declaring themselves invested with Power to legislate for us in all cases whatsoever.

8 He has abdicated Government here, by declaring us out of his Protection and waging War against us.

He has plundered our seas, ravaged our Coasts, burnt our towns, and destroyed the lives of our people.

He is at this time transporting large Armies of foreign Mercenaries to compleat the works of death, desolation and tyranny, already begun with circumstances of Cruelty & perfidy scarcely paralleled in the most barbarous ages, and totally unworthy the Head of a civilized nation.

He has constrained our fellow Citizens taken Captive on the high Seas to bear Arms against their Country, to become the executioners of their friends and Brethren, or to fall themselves by their Hands.

He has excited domestic insurrections amongst us, and has endeavoured to bring on the inhabitants of our frontiers, the merciless Indian Savages whose known rule of warfare, is an undistinguished destruction of all ages, sexes and conditions.

8

In every stage of these Oppressions We have Petitioned for Redress in the most humble terms: Our repeated Petitions have been answered only by repeated injury. A Prince, whose character is thus marked by every act which may define a Tyrant, is unfit to be the ruler of a free People.

9

Nor have We been wanting in attentions to our British brethren. We have warned them from time to time of attempts by their legislature to extend an unwarrantable jurisdiction over us. We have reminded them of the circumstances of our emigration and settlement here. We have appealed to their native justice and magnanimity, and we have conjured them by the ties of our common kindred to disavow these usurpations, which would inevitably interrupt our connections and correspondence. They too have been deaf to the voice of justice and of consanguinity. We must, therefore, acquiesce in the necessity, which denounces our Separation, and hold them, as we hold the rest of mankind, Enemies in War, in Peace Friends.

We, therefore, the Representatives of the United States of America, in General Congress, Assembled, appealing to the Supreme Judge of the world for the rectitude of our intentions, do, in the Name, and by Authority of the good People of these Colonies, solemnly publish and declare, That these United Colonies are, and of Right ought to be, Free and Independent States; that they are Absolved from all Allegiance to the British Crown, and that all political connection between them and the State of Great Britain, is and ought to be totally dissolved; and that as Free and Independent States, they have full Power to levy War, conclude Peace, contract Alliances, establish Commerce, and to do all other Acts and Things which Independent States may of right do. And for the support of this Declaration, with a firm reliance on the Protection of Divine Providence, we mutually pledge to each other our Lives, our Fortunes and our sacred Honor.

9. During this time, the colonists have peacefully tried to resolve the conflict. They have repeatedly asked for relief only to receive further suffering. They even asked the British people for help, but to no avail. Therefore, the colonists now believe that they have no choice but to separate and form their own nation.

10

10. In this final section, the colonists formally declare their independence from Britain. The signers of this document are representatives of the people of the United States and are acting with their consent. They declare that the colonies no longer have any connection to Great Britain and are totally independent states. These states can now make war and sign treaties. And the signers promise their lives, money, and honor to defend their independence.

THE CONSTITUTION OF THE UNITED STATES OF AMERICA

1. The Preamble is the opening of the Constitution. It states the purpose of the Constitution and describes the type of government to be set up. It also explains the goals to be achieved.

2. Congress has the power to make all federal laws. It is divided into a Senate and a House of Representatives.

3. Members of the House of Representatives are elected every two years. Representatives must be at least 25 years old. They also have to live in the state which they represent.

4. The number of Representatives each state receives is based on its population. Therefore a census is taken every ten years to determine each state's population. At first, each state received a Representative for every 30,000 people. Since 1929, the total number of Representatives in the House has been fixed at 435. Each state is entitled to at least one Representative. The 16th Amendment changed the collection of direct taxes. The 3/5 reference to slaves was canceled by the 13th and 14th Amendments.

5. When a House member dies or resigns, that state's governor must call a special election to fill the vacant seat. The House has the right to elect its own officers, including a Speaker, or spokesperson. The House has the power to impeach, or formally accuse, a federal official of wrongdoing.

6. Each state shall have two Senators who serve for six-year terms. The 17th Amendment changed the way that Senators are chosen. Now they are elected by the people of the state.

7. One third of the Senate is elected every two years. The 17th Amendment changed the way vacancies are filled. Today the governor of the state may choose a replacement until an election can take place. All Senators must be at least 30 years old and residents of the states they represent.

1   **Preamble.** We, the people of the United States, in order to form a more perfect Union, establish justice, insure domestic tranquility, provide for the common defense, promote the general welfare, and secure the blessings of liberty to ourselves and our posterity, do ordain and establish this Constitution for the United States of America.

2   **Article I.** Section 1. All legislative powers herein granted shall be vested in a Congress of the United States, which shall consist of a Senate and a House of Representatives.

3   **Section 2.** The House of Representatives shall be composed of members chosen every second year by the people of the several states; and the electors in each state shall have the qualifications requisite for electors of the most numerous branch of the state legislature.

No person shall be a Representative who shall not have attained the age of twenty-five years, and been seven years a citizen of the United States, and who shall not, when elected, be an inhabitant of that state in which he shall be chosen.

4   Representatives ~~and direct taxes~~ shall be apportioned among the several states which may be included within this Union, according to their respective numbers, ~~which shall be determined by adding to the whole number of free persons, including those bound to service for a term of years, and excluding Indians not taxed, three fifths of all other persons.~~ The actual enumeration shall be made within three years after the first meeting of the Congress of the United States, and within every subsequent term of ten years, in such manner as they shall by law direct. The number of Representatives shall not exceed one for every 30,000, but each State shall have at least one Representative, ~~and until such enumeration shall be made, the State of New Hampshire shall be entitled to choose three, Massachusetts eight, Rhode Island and Providence Plantations one, Connecticut five, New York six, New Jersey four, Pennsylvania eight, Delaware one, Maryland six, Virginia ten, North Carolina five, South Carolina five, and Georgia three.~~

5   When vacancies happen in the representation from any state, the executive authority thereof shall issue writs of election to fill such vacancies.

The House of Representatives shall choose their Speaker and other officers; and shall have the sole power of impeachment.

6   **Section 3.** The Senate of the United States shall be composed of two Senators from each State, chosen ~~by the legislature thereof,~~ for six years; and each Senator shall have one vote.

7   ~~Immediately after they shall be assembled, in consequence of the first election,~~ they shall be divided as equally as may be into three classes. ~~The seats of the Senators of the first class shall be vacated at the expiration of the second year, of the second class at the expiration of the fourth year, and of the third class at the expiration of the sixth year,~~ so that one third may be chosen every second year; ~~and if vacancies happen by resignation, or otherwise, during the recess of the legislature of any State, the Executive thereof may make temporary appointments until the next meeting of the legislature, which shall then fill such vacancies.~~

No person shall be a Senator who shall not have attained the age of 30 years, and been nine years a citizen of the United States, and who shall not, when elected, be an inhabitant of that state for which he shall be chosen.

8   The Vice-President of the United States shall be President of the Senate, but shall have no vote, unless they be equally divided.

---

[1] Those parts of the U.S. Constitution which are no longer applicable or have been changed by ammendments are marked through.

The Senate shall choose their other officers, and also a President *Pro Tempore*, in the absence of the Vice-President, or when he shall exercise the office of President of the United States.

The Senate shall have the sole power to try all impeachments. When sitting for that purpose, they shall be on oath or affirmation. When the President of the United States is tried, the Chief Justice shall preside: and no person shall be convicted without the concurrence of two thirds of the members present.

Judgment in cases of impeachment shall not extend further than to removal from office, and disqualification to hold and enjoy any office of honor, trust, or profit, under the United States; but the party convicted shall nevertheless be liable and subject to indictment, trial, judgment, and punishment according to law.

Section 4. The times, places and manner of holding elections for Senators and Representatives, shall be prescribed in each state by the legislature thereof; but the Congress may at any time by law make or alter such regulations, except as to the places of choosing Senators.

The Congress shall assemble at least once in every year, and such meeting shall be on the first Monday in December, unless they shall by law appoint a different day.

Section 5. Each House shall be the judge of the elections, returns, and qualifications of its own members, and a majority of each shall constitute a quorum to do business; but a smaller number may adjourn from day to day, and may be authorized to compel the attendance of absent members, in such manner, and under such penalties, as each House may provide.

Each House may determine the rules of its proceedings, punish its members for disorderly behavior, and, with the concurrence of two thirds, expel a member.

Each House shall keep a journal of its proceedings, and from time to time publish the same, excepting such parts as may, in their judgment, require secrecy; and the yeas and nays of the members of either House on any question, shall, at the desire of one fifth of those present, be entered on the journal.

Neither House, during the session of Congress, shall, without the consent of the other, adjourn for more than three days, nor to any other place than that in which the two Houses shall be sitting.

Section 6. The Senators and Representatives shall receive a compensation for their services, to be ascertained by law, and paid out of the Treasury of the United States. They shall, in all cases, except treason, felony, and breach of the peace, be privileged from arrest during their attendance at the session of their respective Houses, and in going to, and returning from, the same; and for any speech or debate in either House, they shall not be questioned in any other place.

No Senator or Representative shall, during the time for which he was elected, be appointed to any civil office under the authority of the United States, which shall have been created, or the emoluments whereof shall have been increased during such time; and no person holding any office under the United States, shall be a member of either House during his continuance in office.

Section 7. All bills for raising revenue shall originate in the House of Representatives; but the Senate may propose or concur with amendments as on other bills.

Every bill which shall have passed the House of Representatives and the Senate, shall, before it becomes a law, be presented to the President of the United States; if he approves he shall sign it, but if not he shall return

8. The Vice-President of the United States serves as President, or chairperson, of the Senate. However, he or she can only vote to break a tie. The Senate chooses all its other officers.

9. The Senate has the power to try federal officials after the House has accused them. The person on trial has the same legal rights as any person on trial. Two-thirds of the Senate must find the person guilty for conviction. Punishment is limited to removal from office. But the convicted person can then be tried in a normal court of law.

10. Each state can make its own rules about elections for Congress. But Congress has the right to change these state election laws. Congress must meet at least once each year. The 20th Amendment moved the opening date of Congress to January 3.

11. Both the House of Representatives and Senate can refuse to seat members. Neither house can conduct business unless half its members are present. Each house can make rules for the conduct of its members. Each house must keep a written record of its business. Neither house can recess for more than three days without the consent of the other.

12. Each member of Congress is paid a salary by the U.S. Treasury. Members set their own pay. No member of Congress can be arrested while serving in Congress. And no member of Congress can hold another office in the U.S. government while serving in Congress.

13. All bills, or proposed laws, for raising money through taxes must be introduced in the House of Representatives. Any bill that passes both houses of Congress is sent to the President. If the President signs the bill, it becomes law. If the President does not like the bill, the President can veto, or refuse to sign, the bill. The bill is then sent back to Congress. Congress can either drop the bill or try to pass it over the President's veto. To override the President's veto, two-thirds of both houses of Congress need to approve the bill.

13 it, with his objections, to that House in which it shall have originated, who shall enter the objections at large on their journal, and proceed to reconsider it. If after such reconsideration two thirds of that House shall agree to pass the bill, it shall be sent, together with the objections, to the other House, by which it shall likewise be reconsidered, and if approved by two thirds of that House, it shall become a law. But in all such cases the votes of both Houses shall be determined by yeas and nays, and the names of the persons voting for and against the bill shall be entered on the journal of each House respectively. If any bill shall not be returned by the President within 10 days (Sundays excepted) after it shall have been presented to him, the same shall be a law in like manner as if he had signed it, unless the Congress by their adjournment prevent its return, in which case it shall not be a law.

Every order, resolution, or vote, to which the concurrence of the Senate and House of Representatives may be necessary (except on a question of adjournment), shall be presented to the President of the United States; and before the same shall take effect, shall be approved by him, or being disapproved by him, shall be repassed by two thirds of the Senate and House of Representatives, according to the rules and limitations prescribed in the case of a bill.

14. This section states the powers granted to Congress. Congress may collect taxes to pay the nation's debt and provide for the security and welfare of the country. All federal taxes must be the same throughout the nation. Congress can borrow money. It has the right to control trade, transportation, and communication between the various states and with foreign nations. Congress can decide how immigrants become citizens. It has the power to coin money and set its value, and determine how people who make fake money shall be punished. Congress may also establish post offices, patent and copyright laws, and national courts.

14 **Section 8.** The Congress shall have power

To lay and collect taxes, duties, imposts and excises, to pay the debts, and provide for the common defense and general welfare of the United States; but all duties, imposts, and excises shall be uniform throughout the United States;

To borrow money on the credit of the United States;

To regulate commerce with foreign nations, and among the several states, and with the Indian tribes;

To establish an uniform rule of naturalization, and uniform laws on the subject of bankruptcies throughout the United States;

To coin money, regulate the value thereof, and of foreign coin, and fix the standard of weights and measures;

To provide for the punishment of counterfeiting the securities and current coin of the United States;

To establish post-offices and post-roads;

To promote the progress of science and useful arts, by securing, for limited times, to authors and inventors, the exclusive right to their respective writings and discoveries;

To constitute tribunals inferior to the Supreme Court;

15. Congress can define the punishment for people who commit crimes against ships at sea. Only Congress has the right to declare war. It has the power to determine the size of the armed forces and how much money is spent on maintaining them. Congress may call up the state militias for federal service. Today the militias are called the National Guard.

15 To define and punish piracies and felonies committed on the high seas, and offences against the law of nations;

To declare war, grant letters of marque and reprisal, and make rules concerning captures on land and water;

To raise and support armies: but no appropriation of money to that use shall be for a longer term than two years;

To provide and maintain a navy;

To make rules for the government and regulation of the land and naval forces;

To provide for calling forth the militia to execute the laws of the Union, suppress insurrections and repel invasions;

To provide for organizing, arming, and disciplining the militia, and for governing such part of them as may be employed in the service of the United States, reserving to the states respectively, the appointment of the officers, and the authority of training the militia according to the discipline prescribed by Congress;

To exercise exclusive legislation, in all cases whatsoever, over such district (not exceeding ten miles square) as may, by cession of particular states, and the acceptance of Congress, become the seat of the government of the United States, and to exercise like authority over all places purchased by the consent of the legislature of the State in which the same shall be, for the erection of forts, magazines, arsenals, dock-yards, and other needful buildings. And,

To make all laws which shall be necessary and proper for carrying into execution the foregoing powers, and all other powers vested by this Constitution in the government of the United States, or in any department or officer thereof.

Section 9. ~~The migration or importation of such persons as any of the States now existing shall think proper to admit, shall not be prohibited by the Congress prior to the year one thousand eight hundred and eight; but a tax or duty may be imposed on such importation, not exceeding ten dollars for each person.~~

The privilege of the writ of *habeas corpus* shall not be suspended, unless when in cases of rebellion or invasion the public safety may require it.

No bill of attainder or *ex post facto* law shall be passed.

~~No capitation, or other direct tax, shall be laid, unless in proportion to the census or enumeration herein before directed to be taken.~~

No tax or duty shall be laid on articles exported from any state.

No preference shall be given by any regulation of commerce or revenue to the ports of one state over those of another; nor shall vessels bound to, or from, one state be obliged to enter, clear, or pay duties in another.

No money shall be drawn from the treasury, but in consequence of appropriations made by law; and a regular statement and account of the receipts and expenditures of all public money shall be published from time to time.

No title of nobility shall be granted by the United States; and no person holding any office of profit or trust under them, shall, without the consent of the Congress, accept of any present, emolument, office, or title of any kind whatever, from any king, prince, or foreign state.

Section 10. No state shall enter into any treaty, alliance, or confederation; grant letters of marque and reprisal; coin money; emit bills of credit; make any thing but gold and silver coin a tender in payment of debts; pass any bill of attainder, *ex post facto* law, or law impairing the obligation of contracts, or grant any title of nobility.

No state shall, without the consent of the Congress, lay any imposts or duties on imports or exports, except what may be absolutely necessary for executing its inspection laws; and the net produce of all duties and imposts, laid by any state on imports or exports, shall be for the use of the treasury of the United States; and all such laws shall be subject to the revision and control of the Congress. No state shall, without the consent of Congress, lay any duty of tonnage, keep troops, or ships of war, in time of peace, enter into any agreement or compact with another state, or with a foreign power, or engage in war, unless actually invaded, or in such imminent danger as will not admit of delay.

Article II. Section 1. The executive power shall be vested in a President of the United States of America. He shall hold his office during the term of four years, and together with the Vice-President, chosen for the same term, be elected as follows:

Each state shall appoint, in such manner as the legislature thereof may direct, a number of electors equal to the whole number of Senators and

16 **16. Congress controls the District of Columbia, which includes the national capital. Congress also has the right to make all laws necessary to carry out the other powers granted to the national government by the Constitution. This clause was included to insure that Congress could adapt to the changing needs of the nation.**

17 **17. This section includes all the powers denied to Congress. This paragraph states that Congress could not outlaw the slave trade before 1808. It was abolished in that year.**

18

18. All prisoners must be told why they are being held, and no one shall be imprisoned unlawfully. No person can be punished for committing an act before that act became unlawful. The clause about direct taxes was changed by the 16th Amendment. No taxes can be placed on goods exported from any state. And no law can be passed favoring one state over another in trade. The federal government can only spend money if Congress approves it. No titles of nobility can be granted.

19 **19. This section includes all the powers denied to the states. No state can enter into a treaty with a foreign government or coin its own money. Like the federal government, no state can unlawfully imprison a person. States cannot tax imports or exports without the consent of Congress. No state can keep an army or navy without the consent of Congress or make war unless invaded.**

20 **20. The President is responsible for carrying out the laws passed by Congress. The President and Vice-President are elected every four years.**

21

21. The President and Vice-President are chosen by special electors from each state. The number of Presidential electors each state receives is equal to the number of Senators and Representatives that state has in Congress. Each state may decide how to select its electors. No federal official or member of Congress can serve as an elector. The 12th Amendment changed the way that the President and Vice-President are selected. Now each elector votes for one candidate for President and another for Vice-President. Congress has set the first Tuesday after the first Monday of November as the day each state chooses it Presidential electors.

21 Representatives to which the state may be entitled in the Congress; but no Senator or Representative, or person holding an office of trust or profit under the United States, shall be appointed an elector.

~~The electors shall meet in their respective States, and vote by ballot for two persons, of whom one at least shall not be an inhabitant of the same State with themselves. And they shall make a list of all the persons voted for, and of the number of votes for each; which list they shall sign and certify, and transmit sealed to the seat of the government of the United States, directed to the President of the Senate. The President of the Senate shall, in the presence of the Senate and House of Representatives, open all the certificates, and the votes shall then be counted. The person having the greatest number of votes shall be the President, if such number be a majority of the whole number of electors appointed; and if there be more than one who have such majority, and have an equal number of votes, then the House of Representatives shall immediately choose by ballot one of them for President; and if no person have a majority, then from the five highest on the list the said House shall in like manner choose the President. But in choosing the President, the votes shall be taken by States, the representation from each State having one vote; a quorum for this purpose shall consist of a member or members from two thirds of the States, and a majority of all the States shall be necessary to a choice. In every case, after the choice of the President, the person having the greatest number of votes of the electors shall be the Vice-President. But if there should remain two or more who have equal votes, the Senate shall choose from them by ballot the Vice-President.~~

22. The President must be a citizen of the U.S. by birth and at least 35 years old. If for some reason the Presidency becomes vacant, the Vice-President becomes President. The 25th Amendment deals with a President's inability to perform his or her duties. Presidents are paid a fixed salary for their entire term. Before taking office, the President must promise to defend the Constitution.

22 The Congress may determine the time of choosing the electors, and the day on which they shall give their votes; which day shall be the same throughout the United States.

No person except a natural-born citizen, ~~or a citizen of the United States, at the time of the adoption of this Constitution,~~ shall be eligible to the office of President; neither shall any person be eligible to that office who shall not have attained the age of thirty-five years, and been fourteen years a resident within the United States.

In case of the removal of the President from office, or of his death, resignation, or inability to discharge the powers and duties of the said office, the same shall devolve on the Vice-President, and the Congress may by law provide for the case of removal, death, resignation, or inability, both of the President and Vice-President, declaring what officer shall then act as President, and such officer shall act accordingly until the disability be removed, or a President shall be elected.

The President shall, at stated times, receive for his services, a compensation, which shall neither be increased nor diminished during the period for which he shall have been elected, and he shall not receive within that period any other emolument from the United States or any of them.

Before he enter on the execution of his office, he shall take the following oath or affirmation:

"I do solemnly swear (or affirm) that I will faithfully execute the office of President of the United States, and will, to the best of my ability, preserve, protect, and defend the Constitution of the United States."

23. This section deals with the powers of the President. The President is the Commander in Chief of the Armed Forces. The President may order written reports from Cabinet officers and pardon persons convicted

23 **Section 2.** The President shall be Commander-in-Chief of the Army and Navy of the United States, and of the militia of the several states, when called into the actual service of the United States; he may require the opinion, in writing, of the principal officer in each of the executive departments, upon any subject relating to the duties of their respective offices, and he shall have power to grant reprieves and pardons for offenses against the United States, except in cases of impeachment.

He shall have power, by and with the advice and consent of the Senate, to make treaties, provided two-thirds of the Senators present concur; and he shall nominate, and by and with the advice and consent of the Senate, shall appoint ambassadors, other public ministers and consuls, judges of the Supreme Court, and all other officers of the United States, whose appointments are not herein otherwise provided for, and which shall be established by law. But the Congress may by law vest the appointment of such inferior officers, as they think proper, in the President alone, in the courts of law, or in the heads of departments.

The President shall have power to fill up all vacancies that may happen during the recess of the Senate, by granting commissions which shall expire at the end of their next session.

Section 3. He shall, from time to time, give to the Congress information of the state of the Union, and recommend to their consideration such measures as he shall judge necessary and expedient. He may, on extraordinary occasions, convene both Houses, or either of them; and in case of disagreement between them, with respect to the time of adjournment, he may adjourn them to such time as he shall think proper. He shall receive ambassadors and other public ministers. He shall take care that the laws be faithfully executed; and shall commission all the officers of the United States.

Section 4. The President, Vice-President, and all civil officers of the United States, shall be removed from office on impeachment for, and conviction of, treason, bribery, or other high crimes and misdemeanors.

Article III. Section 1. The judicial power of the United States shall be vested in one Supreme Court, and in such inferior courts as the Congress may, from time to time, ordain and establish. The judges, both of the Supreme and inferior courts, shall hold their offices during good behavior; and shall, at stated times, receive for their services, a compensation, which shall not be diminished during their continuance in office.

Section 2. The judicial power shall extend to all cases, in law and equity, arising under this Constitution, the laws of the United States, and treaties made, or which shall be made, under their authority; to all cases affecting ambassadors, other public ministers, and consuls; to all cases of admiralty and maritime jurisdiction; to controversies to which the United States shall be a party; to controversies between two or more states, between a state and citizens of another state, between citizens of different states, between citizens of the same state claiming lands under grants of different states, and between a state, or the citizens thereof, and foreign states, citizens, or subjects.

In all cases affecting ambassadors, other public ministers and consuls, and those in which a state shall be party, the Supreme Court shall have original jurisdiction. In all the other cases before mentioned, the Supreme Court shall have appellate jurisdiction, both as to law and fact, with such exceptions, and under such regulations, as the Congress shall make.

The trial of all crimes, except in cases of impeachment, shall be by jury; and such trial shall be held in the State where the said crimes shall have been committed; but when not committed within any state, the trial shall be at such place or places as the Congress may by law have directed.

Section 3. Treason against the United States, shall consist only in levying war against them, or in adhering to their enemies, giving them aid and comfort. No person shall be convicted of treason unless on the testimony of two witnesses to the same overt act, or on confession in open court.

23 of federal crimes. The President can make treaties with foreign governments, but they must be approved by two-thirds of the Senate. The President chooses judges for the Supreme Court and other high officials. They must also be approved by the Senate. The President can make temporary appointments to federal offices when the Senate is not in session.

24 **24.** Every year, the President must give to Congress a report on the state of the nation. The President can call a special session of Congress if necessary. The President, or any other high government official, can be removed from office for any major wrongdoing.

25 **25.** The Supreme Court is the final authority in matters of law. Congress can also set up other lesser national courts. Federal judges hold their office for life unless proven guilty of any wrongdoing. Their pay cannot be lowered during their term in office.

26 **26.** The federal courts settle disputes concerning the Constitution and conflicts between the U.S. and other nations. They also settle legal questions of U.S. law and problems between citizens of various states. The 11th Amendment prohibited residents of one state from suing another state. Most of the cases appearing before the Supreme Court begin in the lower courts. All trials must be tried in the state where the crime originally occurred. The Supreme Court determines if those cases were tried correctly.

27 **27.** A person can only be convicted of treason for actions committed against the United States. A person cannot be convicted of treason for thinking treasonous thoughts.

Congress has the right to set the punishment for traitors. The family of convicted traitors cannot be punished.

28. Each state must recognize the legal actions and official records of every other state. Persons who move to another state must be treated the same way as the citizens of that state. A person charged with a crime, who flees to another state, must be returned to the state where the crime was committed. The clause referring to the return of fugitive slaves was canceled by the 13th Amendment.

29. Congress has the power to control all land belonging to the United States. It has the right to govern the Western territories and create new states. No new state can be made from part of an existing state without that state's consent. New states will be equal to the existing states. Every state will be guaranteed a republican form of government and protection from foreign invasion.

30. The Constitution can be changed, if necessary, by adding amendments. Three-fourths of all the states need to approve a proposed amendment. No amendment can deprive a state of its equal representation in the Senate.

31. The United States promises to pay all debts incurred by any previous government. The Constitution and all federal laws and treaties are the supreme law of the land. They have priority over any state laws that conflict with them. All federal and state officials must promise to support the Constitution. The Constitution became the supreme law of the land after nine of the original thirteen states approved it.

27 The Congress shall have power to declare the punishment of treason, but no attainder of treason shall work corruption of blood, or forfeiture, except during the life of the person attainted.

28 **Article IV. Section 1.** Full faith and credit shall be given in each state to the public acts, records, and judicial proceedings of every other state. And the Congress may by general laws prescribe the manner in which such acts, records, and proceedings shall be proved, and the effect thereof.

Section 2. The citizens of each state shall be entitled to all privileges and immunities of citizens in the several states.

A person charged in any state with treason, felony, or other crime, who shall flee from justice, and be found in another state, shall, on demand of the executive authority of the state from which he fled, be delivered up to be removed to the state having jurisdiction of the crime.

No person held to service or labor in one state, under the laws thereof, escaping into another, shall, in consequence of any laws or regulation therein, be discharged from such service or labour, but shall be delivered up on claim of the party to whom such service or labour may be due.

29 **Section 3.** New states may be admitted by the Congress into this Union; but no new state shall be formed or erected within the jurisdiction of any other state; nor any state be formed by the junction of two or more states, or parts of states, without the consent of the legislatures of the states concerned, as well as of the Congress.

The Congress shall have power to dispose of and make all needful rules and regulations respecting the territory or other property belonging to the United States; and nothing in this Constitution shall be so construed as to prejudice any claims of the United States, or of any particular state.

Section 4. The United States shall guarantee to every state in this Union a republican form of government, and shall protect each of them against invasion; and on application of the legislature, or of the executive (when the legislature cannot be convened), against domestic violence.

30 **Article V.** The Congress, whenever two thirds of both Houses shall deem it necessary, shall propose amendments to this Constitution, or, on the application of the legislatures of two thirds of the several states, shall call a convention for proposing amendments, which, in either case, shall be valid to all intents and purposes, as part of this Constitution, when ratified by the legislatures of three fourths of the several states, or by conventions in three fourths thereof, as the one or the other mode of ratification may be proposed by the Congress; provided that no amendment, which may be made prior to the year one thousand eight hundred and eight, shall in any manner affect the first and fourth clauses in the ninth section of the first article; and that no state, without its consent, shall be deprived of its equal suffrage in the Senate.

31 **Article VI.** All debts contracted, and engagements entered into, before the adoption of this Constitution, shall be as valid against the United States, under this Constitution, as under the confederation.

This Constitution and the laws of the United States which shall be made in pursuance thereof, and all treaties made, or which shall be made, under the authority of the United States, shall be the supreme law of the land; and the judges, in every state, shall be bound thereby, any thing in the constitution or laws of any state to the contrary notwithstanding.

The Senators and Representatives before mentioned, and the members of the several state legislatures, and all executive and judicial officers, both of the United States and of the several states, shall be bound, by oath or affirmation, to support this Constitution; but no religious test shall ever be required as a qualification to any office or public trust under the United States.

~~Article VII. The ratification of the conventions of nine States, shall be sufficient for the establishment of this Constitution between the States so ratifying the same.~~

TEN ORIGINAL AMENDMENTS: **THE BILL OF RIGHTS**

(These first 10 amendments were adopted in 1791.)

Article I. Congress shall make no law respecting an establishment of religion, or prohibiting the free exercise thereof; or abridging the freedom of speech, or of the press; or the right of the people peaceably to assemble, and to petition the government for a redress of grievances.

Article II. A well regulated militia being necessary to the security of a free state, the right of the people to keep and bear arms shall not be infringed.

Article III. No soldier shall, in time of peace, be quartered in any house without the consent of the owner; nor in time of war, but in a manner to be prescribed by law.

Article IV. The right of the people to be secure in their persons, houses, papers, and effects, against unreasonable searches and seizures, shall not be violated; and no warrants shall issue, but upon probable cause, supported by oath or affirmation, and particularly describing the place to be searched, and the persons or things to be seized.

Article V. No person shall be held to answer for a capital or otherwise infamous crime, unless on a presentment or indictment of a grand jury, except in cases arising in the land or naval forces, or in the militia, when in actual service, in time of war or public danger; nor shall any person be subject for the same offenses to be twice put in jeopardy of life or limb; nor shall be compelled, in any criminal case, to be witness against himself; nor be deprived of life, liberty, or property, without due process of law; nor shall private property be taken for public use without just compensation.

Article VI. In all criminal prosecutions the accused shall enjoy the right to a speedy and public trial, by an impartial jury of the state and district wherein the crime shall have been committed, which district shall have been previously ascertained by law, and to be informed of the nature and cause of the accusation; to be confronted with the witnesses against him; to have compulsory process for obtaining witnesses in his favor; and to have the assistance of counsel for his defense.

Article VII. In suits at common law, where the value of controversy shall exceed twenty dollars, the right of trial by jury shall be preserved; and no fact tried by a jury shall be otherwise re-examined in any court of the United States than according to the rules of the common law.

Article VIII. Excessive bail shall not be required, nor excessive fines imposed, nor cruel and unusual punishments inflicted.

Article IX. The enumeration in the Constitution of certain rights, shall not be construed to deny or disparage others retained by the people.

Article X. The powers not delegated to the United States by the Constitution, nor prohibited by it to the states, are reserved to the states respectively or to the people.

AMENDMENTS SINCE THE BILL OF RIGHTS

Article XI *(1798).* The judicial power of the United States shall not be construed to extend to any suit in law or equity, commenced or prosecuted against one of the United States by citizens of any state, or by citizens or subjects of any foreign state.

Article XII *(1804).* The electors shall meet in their respective states, and

---

31

32 **32. The first ten amendments grant basic human freedoms. The people have the right to freedom of religion, speech, the press, assembly, and petition. The states have the right to keep armed militias for protection. No individual can be forced to keep soldiers in his or her home against his or her will. And no government official can enter a person's home without showing reasonable cause that a crime has been committed.**

33 **33. All persons accused of a crime have the right to a fair and speedy trial. The government must formally charge someone with a crime before they can be brought to trial. Individuals cannot be tried twice for the same crime, and they cannot be forced to give testimony against themselves. In lawsuits of more than twenty dollars, the people involved have the right to a trial by jury. Excessive punishments cannot be given.**

34 **34. The people have rights that are not mentioned in the Constitution. The powers not given to the federal government are reserved to the states, or to the people.**

35 **35. A citizen of one state cannot sue another state in federal court.**

36

36. This amendment changed the way Presidential electors vote for the President and Vice-President. Now the electors vote for only one candidate in each office. If no candidate receives a majority of electoral votes, Congress decides the election. The House of Representatives selects the President and the Senate chooses the Vice-President. The Vice-President must meet the requirements needed for the Presidency.

37. These three amendments abolish slavery and protect the rights of all American citizens. They were passed following the Civil War. Any person who was born in the United States or who has been a naturalized citizen is a citizen of the United States. No state can take away the rights of a United States citizen. Many Confederate leaders were prohibited from holding office, but by 1872, most were allowed to return to political life. No United States citizen can be denied the right to vote on the basis of their race or color. The 19th Amendment changed this to include women as well. The 26th Amendment modified this to include all citizens over the age of eighteen.

36 vote by ballot for President and Vice-President, one of whom, at least, shall not be an inhabitant of the same state with themselves; they shall name in their ballots the person voted for as President, and in distinct ballots the person voted for as Vice-President; and they shall make distinct lists of all persons voted for as President, and of all persons voted for as Vice-President, and of the number of Votes for each, which list they shall sign and certify, and transmit, sealed, to the seat of the government of the United States, directed to the President of the Senate; the President of the Senate shall, in the presence of the Senate and House of Representatives, open all the certificates, and the votes shall then be counted. The person having the greatest number of votes for President shall be the President, if such number be a majority of the whole number of electors appointed; and if no person have such majority, then from the persons having the highest numbers, not exceeding three, on the list of those voted for as President, the House of Representatives shall choose immediately, by ballot, the President. But in choosing the President, the vote shall be taken by States, the representation from each State having one vote; a quorum for this purpose shall consist of a member or members from two thirds of the States, and a majority of all the States shall be necessary to a choice. ~~And if the House of Representatives shall not choose a President whenever the right of choice shall devolve upon them, before the fourth day of March next following, then the Vice-President shall act as President, as in the case of the death or other constitutional disability of the President.~~

37 The person having the greatest number of votes as Vice-President shall be the Vice-President, if such number be a majority of the whole number of electors appointed; and if no person have a majority, then from the two highest numbers on the list the Senate shall choose the Vice-President. A quorum for the purpose shall consist of two thirds of the whole number of Senators, and a majority of the whole number shall be necessary to a choice.

But no person constitutionally ineligible to the office of President shall be eligible to that of Vice-President of the United States.

Article XIII *(1865).* **Section 1.** Neither slavery nor involuntary servitude, except as a punishment for crime whereof the party shall have been duly convicted, shall exist within the United States, or any place subject to their jurisdiction.

Section 2. Congress shall have power to enforce this article by appropriate legislation.

Article XIV *(1868).* **Section 1.** All persons born or naturalized in the United States, and subject to the jurisdiction thereof, are citizens of the United States and of the state wherein they reside. No state shall make or enforce any law which shall abridge the privileges or immunities of citizens of the United States; nor shall any state deprive any person of life, liberty, or property, without due process of law, nor deny to any person within its jurisdiction the equal protection of the laws.

Section 2. Representatives shall be apportioned among the several states according to their respective numbers, counting the whole number of persons in each state, excluding Indians not taxed. But when the right to vote at any election for the choice of electors for President and Vice-President of the United States, representatives in Congress, the executive and judicial officers of a state, or the members of the legislature thereof, is denied to any of the ~~male~~ inhabitants of such state, being ~~twenty-one years of age, and~~ citizens of the United States, or in any way abridged, except for participation in rebellion or other crime, the basis of representation therein shall be reduced in the proportion which the number of such ~~male~~ citizens shall bear to the whole number of ~~male~~ citizens ~~twenty-one~~

years of age in such State.

Section 3. No person shall be a Senator or Representative in Congress, or elector of President and Vice-President, or hold any office, civil or military, under the United States, or under any state, who having previously taken an oath, as a member of Congress, or as an officer of the United States, or as a member of any state legislature, or as an executive or judicial officer of any state, to support the Constitution of the United States, shall have engaged in insurrection or rebellion against the same, or given aid or comfort to the enemies thereof. But Congress may, by a vote of two thirds of each house, remove such disability.

Section 4. The validity of the public debt of the United States, authorized by law, including debts incurred for payment of pensions and bounties for services in suppressing insurrection or rebellion, shall not be questioned. But neither the United States nor any state shall assume or pay any debt or obligation incurred in aid of insurrection or rebellion against the United States, or any claim for the loss or emancipation of any slave; but all such debts, obligations, and claims shall be held illegal and void.

Section 5. The Congress shall have power to enforce, by appropriate legislation, the provisions of this article.

Article XV *(1870)*. **Section 1.** The right of citizens of the United States to vote shall not be denied or abridged by the United States or by any State on account of race, color, or previous condition of servitude.

Section 2. The Congress shall have power to enforce this article by appropriate legislation.

Article XVI *(1913)*. The Congress shall have power to lay and collect taxes on incomes, from whatever source derived, without apportionment among the several states, and without regard to any census or enumeration.

38. Congress has the right to collect taxes on people's income. Congress does not have to base this tax on each state's population.

Article XVII *(1913)*. The Senate of the United States shall be composed of two Senators from each state, elected by the people thereof, for six years; and each Senator shall have one vote. The electors in each state shall have the qualifications requisite for electors of the most numerous branch of the state legislatures.

39. This amendment changed the way Senators are elected. Before, they were chosen by the state legislatures. Now they are elected directly by the people. If a Senator cannot complete his or her term, the state's governor may appoint a temporary replacement until an election can be held.

When vacancies happen in the representation of any state in the Senate, the executive authority of such state shall issue writs of election to fill such vacancies:

Provided, That the legislature of any state may empower the executive thereof to make temporary appointments until the people fill the vacancies by election as the legislature may direct.

This amendment shall not be so construed as to affect the election or term of any Senator chosen before it becomes valid as part of the Constitution.

Article XVIII *(1919)*. Section 1. After one year from the ratification of this article the manufacture, sale, or transportation of intoxicating liquors within, the importation thereof into, or the exportation thereof from the United States and all territory subject to the jurisdiction thereof for beverage purposes is hereby prohibited.

Section 2. The Congress and the several states shall have concurrent power to enforce this article by appropriate legislation.

Section 3. This article shall be inoperative unless it shall have been ratified as an amendment to the Constitution by the legislatures of the several states, as provided in the Constitution, within seven years from the date of the submission hereof to the states by the Congress.

40. This amendment prohibits the making, sale, and shipment of alcoholic beverages. It was later canceled by the 21st Amendment.

Article XIX *(1920)*. The right of citizens of the United States to vote shall not be denied or abridged by the United States or by any State on

41. The right to vote cannot be denied on account of a person's sex.

41 | account of sex.

Congress shall have power to enforce this article by appropriate legislation.

42 | **Article XX** *(1933).* **Section 1.** The terms of the President and Vice-President shall end at noon on the 20th day of January, and the terms of Senators and Representatives at noon on the 3rd day of January, of the years in which such terms would have ended if this article had not been ratified; and the terms of their successors shall then begin.

Section 2. The Congress shall assemble at least once in every year, and such meeting shall begin at noon on the 3rd day of January, unless they shall by law appoint a different day.

Section 3. If, at the time fixed for the beginning of the term of the President, the President-elect shall have died, the Vice-President-elect shall become President. If a President shall not have been chosen before the time fixed for the beginning of his term, or if the President-elect shall have failed to qualify; then the Vice-President-elect shall act as President until a President shall have qualified; and the Congress may by law provide for the case wherein neither a President-elect nor a Vice-President-elect shall have qualified, declaring who shall then act as President, or the manner in which one who is to act shall be selected, and such person shall act accordingly until a President or Vice-President shall have qualified.

Section 4. The Congress may by law provide for the case of the death of any of the persons from whom the House of Representatives may choose a President whenever the right of choice shall have devolved upon them, and for the case of the death of any of the persons from whom the Senate may choose a Vice-President whenever the right of choice shall have devolved upon them.

~~**Section 5.** Sections 1 and 2 shall take effect on the 15th day of October following the ratification of this article.~~

~~**Section 6.** This article shall be inoperative unless it shall have been ratified as an amendment to the Constitution by the legislatures of three fourths of the several States within seven years from the date of its submission.~~

43 | **Article XXI** *(1933).* **Section 1.** The eighteenth article of amendment to the Constitution of the United States is hereby repealed.

Section 2. The transportation or importation into any state, territory, or possession of the United States for delivery or use therein of intoxicating liquors, in violation of the laws thereof, is hereby prohibited.

~~**Section 3.** This article shall be inoperative unless it shall have been ratified as an amendment to the Constitution by conventions in the several states, as provided in the Constitution, within seven years from the date of the submission hereof to the states by the Congress.~~

44 | **Article XXII** *(1951).* **Section 1.** No person shall be elected to the office of the President more than twice, and no person who has held the office of President, or acted as President, for more than two years of a term to which some other person was elected President shall be elected to the office of the President more than once. ~~But this Article shall not apply to any person holding the office of President when this Article was proposed by the Congress, and shall not prevent any person who may be holding the office of President, or acting as President, during the term within which this Article becomes operative from holding the office of President or acting as President during the remainder of such term.~~

45 | **Article XXIII** *(1961).* **Section 1.** The district constituting the seat of government of the United States shall appoint in such manner as the Congress may direct: A number of electors of President and Vice-Presi-

42. This amendment changes the date for the President and Vice-President beginning their terms of office. The opening date for Congress was also moved. The amendment provides for what should be done in case something happens to the President-elect before taking office.

43. This amendment canceled the 18th Amendment, and made it once again legal to make and sell alcoholic beverages.

44. No person may serve more than two terms as President.

dent equal to the whole number of Senators and Representatives in Congress to which the District would be entitled if it were a state, but in no event more than the least populous state; they shall be in addition to those appointed by the states, but they shall be considered, for the purposes of the election of President and Vice-President, to be electors appointed by a state; and they shall meet in the District and perform such duties as provided by the twelfth article of amendment.

Section 2. The Congress shall have power to enforce this article by appropriate legislation.

Article XXIV *(1964).* **Section 1.** The right of citizens of the United States to vote in any primary or other election for President or Vice-President, for electors for President or Vice-President, or for Senator or Representatives in Congress, shall not be denied or abridged by the United States or any state by reason of failure to pay any poll tax or other tax.

Section 2. The Congress shall have power to enforce this article by appropriate legislation.

Article XXV *(1967).* **Section 1.** In case of the removal of the President from office or his death or resignation, the Vice-President shall become President.

Section 2. Whenever there is a vacancy in the office of the Vice-President, the President shall nominate a Vice-President who shall take office upon confirmation by a majority vote of both houses of Congress.

Section 3. Whenever the President transmits to the President *Pro Tempore* of the Senate and the Speaker of the House of Representatives his written declaration that he is unable to discharge the powers and duties of his office, and until he transmits to them a written declaration to the contrary, such powers and duties shall be discharged by the Vice-President as Acting President.

Section 4. Whenever the Vice-President and a majority of either the principal officers of the executive departments or of such other body as Congress may by law provide, transmit to the President *Pro Tempore* of the Senate and the Speaker of the House of Representatives their written declaration that the President is unable to discharge the powers and duties of his office, the Vice-President shall immediately assume the powers and duties of the office as Acting President.

Thereafter, when the President transmits to the President *Pro Tempore* of the Senate and the Speaker of the House of Representatives his written declaration that no inability exists, he shall resume the powers and duties of his office unless the Vice-President and a majority of either the principal officers of the executive departments or of such other body as Congress may by law provide, transmit within four days to the President *Pro Tempore* of the Senate and the Speaker of the House of Representatives their written declaration that the President is unable to discharge the powers and duties of his office. Thereupon Congress shall decide the issue, assembling within 48 hours for that purpose if not in session. If the Congress, within 21 days after receipt of the latter written declaration, or, if Congress is not in session, within 21 days after Congress is required to assemble, determines by two-thirds vote of both houses that the President is unable to discharge the powers and duties of his office, the Vice-President shall continue to discharge the same as Acting President; otherwise, the President shall resume the powers and duties of his office.

Article XXVI (1971). **Section 1.** The right of citizens of the United States, who are 18 years of age or older, to vote shall not be denied or abridged by the United States or any state on account of age.

Section 2. The Congress shall have power to enforce this article by appropriate legislation.

45 **45. The residents of the District of Columbia have the right to vote in Presidential elections. The District has three electoral votes.**

46 **46. No person can be denied the right to vote in national elections for failure to pay a tax. In 1966, the Supreme Court extended this right to include state elections as well.**

47 **47. This amendment determines what should be done if something happens to the President. If the President dies or cannot continue in office, the Vice-President becomes President. This person then appoints a new Vice-President who must be approved by Congress. The Vice-President may also become Acting President if the President cannot fulfill the duties of the office for a limited time.**

48 **48. All United States citizens over the age of eighteen have the right to vote.**

PRESIDENTIAL FACTS

President Term	Party	Vice-President	Birthplace/Born-Died	Facts
George Washington 1789–1797	None	John Adams	Westmoreland Co., Va./1732–1799	First president to appear on a U.S. postage stamp.
John Adams 1797–1801	Fed.	Thomas Jefferson	Braintree, Mass./1735–1826	Only president to be the father of another president—John Quincy Adams.
Thomas Jefferson 1801–1809	Rep.	Aaron Burr	Albemarle Co., Va./1743–1826	First president to be inaugurated in Washington, D.C.
James Madison 1809–1817	Rep.	George Clinton	Port Conway, Va./1751–1836	Was the only president to lead troops while in office—Battle of Bladensburg, Aug. 24, 1814.
James Monroe 1817–1825	Rep.	Daniel D. Tompkins	Westmoreland Co., Va./1758–1831	Was the first president to have been a senator.
John Quincy Adams 1825–1829	Rep.	John C. Calhoun	Braintree, Mass./1767–1848	Was the first and only son of a president to become president.
Andrew Jackson 1829–1837	Dem.	John C. Calhoun	Waxhaw Settlement, S.C./1767–1845	Was the only president to pay off the national debt.
Martin Van Buren 1837–1841	Dem.	Richard M. Johnson	Kinderhook, N.Y./1782–1862	Was both the eighth president and the eighth vice-president.
William Henry Harrison 1841	Whig	John Tyler	Berkeley, Va./1773–1841	Had 106 great-grandchildren, the most of any president.
John Tyler 1841–1845	Whig	——	Greenway, Va./1790–1862	Was the first president to have no vice-president during his entire term.
James K. Polk 1845–1849	Dem.	George M. Dallas	near Pineville, N.C./1795–1849	Was the first president to voluntarily retire after one term.
Zachary Taylor 1849–1850	Whig	Millard Filmore	Orange County, Va./1784–1850	Was the first president to have held no previous political office.
Millard Filmore 1850–1853	Whig	——	Locke, N.Y/1800–1874	Was the first president to have been an indentured servant.
Franklin Pierce 1853–1857	Dem.	William R. King	Hillsboro, N.H./1804–1869	Always insisted that grace be said before every meal.
James Buchanan 1857–1861	Dem.	John C. Breckinridge	near Mercersburg, Penn./1791–1868	Was the first and only president to never marry.
Abraham Lincoln 1861–1865	Rep.	Hannibal Hamlin	near Hogdenville, Ken./1809–1865	First president to be photographed at his inauguration
Andrew Johnson 1865–1869	Rep.	——	Raleigh, N.C./1808–1875	Was the only unschooled man to become president.
Ulysses S. Grant 1869–1877	Rep.	Schuyler Colfax	Point Pleasant, Ohio/1822–1885	His favorite breakfast was cucumbers soaked in vinegar.
Rutherford B. Hayes 1877–1881	Rep.	William A. Wheeler	Delaware, Ohio/1822–1893	Was the first president to visit the West Coast while in office.
James A. Garfield 1881	Rep.	Chester A. Arthur	Orange, Ohio/1831–1881	Liked to juggle Indian clubs to build his muscles.
Chester A. Arthur 1881–1885	Rep.	——	Fairfield, Vt./1830–1886	Had a French chef in the White House where dinners often lasted two to three hours.

President Term	Party	Vice-President	Birthplace/Born-Died	Facts
Grover Cleveland 1885–1889	Dem.	Thomas A. Hendricks	Caldwell, N.J./1837–1908	Was the first and only president to be married in the White House.
Benjamin Harrison 1889–1893	Rep.	Levi P. Morton	North Bend, Ohio/1833–1901	In 1891, was the first president to have electricity in the White House.
Grover Cleveland 1893–1897	Dem.	Adlai E. Stevenson	Caldwell, N.J./1837–1908	First president to be elected to two non-consecutive terms.
William McKinley 1897–1901	Rep.	Garret A. Hobart Theodore Roosevelt	Niles, Ohio/1843–1901	Always wore a red carnation in his lapel for good luck.
Theodore Roosevelt 1901–1909	Rep.	Charles W. Fairbanks	New York, N.Y./1858–1919	Was the first president to win the Nobel Peace Prize.
William H. Taft 1909–1913	Rep.	James S. Sherman	Cincinnati, Ohio/1857–1930	First president to serve in the Supreme Court.
Woodrow Wilson 1913–1921	Dem.	Thomas R. Marshall	Staunton, Va./1856–1924	Was the first president to cross the Atlantic during his term in office.
Warren G. Harding 1921–1923	Rep.	Calvin Coolidge	Blooming Grove, Ohio/1865–1923	Was the first president to visit Alaska.
Calvin Coolidge 1923–1929	Rep.	Charles G. Dawes	Plymouth Notch, Vt./1872–1933	Had a reputation of never wasting a penny or a word.
Herbert C. Hoover 1929–1933	Rep.	Charles Curtis	West Branch, Iowa/1874–1964	Was the first president to visit China.
Franklin D. Roosevelt 1933–1945	Dem.	John N. Garner Henry A. Wallace Harry S. Truman	Hyde Park, N.Y/1882–1945	Was the only president to be elected to four terms.
Harry S. Truman 1945–1953	Dem.	Alben W. Barkley	Lamar, Missouri/1884–1972	Was the first president to televise a speech from the White House.
Dwight D. Eisenhower 1953–1961	Rep.	Richard M. Nixon	Denison, Texas/1890–1969	Was the first president to appear on color television.
John F. Kennedy 1961–1963	Dem.	Lyndon B. Johnson	Brookline, Mass./1917–1963	Was the first Boy Scout to become president.
Lyndon B. Johnson 1963–1969	Dem.	Hubert Humphrey	near Stonewall, Texas/1908–1973	First president to be sworn in by a woman—Sarah Hughes, a Federal District Judge.
Richard M. Nixon 1969–1974	Rep.	Spiro T. Agnew Gerald R. Ford	Yorba Linda, Calif./1913–	Was the first president to resign from office.
Gerald R. Ford 1974–1977	Rep.	Nelson Rockefeller	Omaha, Nebraska/1913–	Was the first to become president without being elected.
Jimmy Carter 1977–1981	Dem.	Walter F. Mondale	Plains, Georgia/1924–	Was the first president to be born in a hospital—the Wise Clinic in Plains, Georgia.
Ronald Reagan 1981–1989	Rep.	George Bush	Tampico, Ill./1911–	Believed in knocking on wood for good luck.
George Bush 1989–	Rep.	J. Danforth Quayle	Milton, Mass./1924–	Played first-base for his Yale University baseball team.

State	Admitted into the Union	Capital	Area in Square Miles	Population 1980	Population 1988	Electoral Votes
Alabama (Ala.)	1819	Montgomery	51,609	3,890,061	4,102,000	9
Alaska	1959	Juneau	586,412	400,481	524,000	3
Arizona (Ariz.)	1912	Phoenix	113,909	2,717,866	3,489,000	7
Arkansas (Ark.)	1836	Little Rock	53,104	2,285,513	2,395,000	6
California (Calif.)	1850	Sacramento	158,693	23,668,562	28,314,000	47
Colorado (Colo.)	1876	Denver	104,247	2,888,834	3,301,000	8
Connecticut (Conn.)	1788	Hartford	5009	3,107,576	3,233,000	8
Delaware (Del.)	1787	Dover	2057	595,225	660,000	3
Florida (Fla.)	1845	Tallahassee	58,560	9,739,992	12,335,000	21
Georgia (Ga.)	1788	Atlanta	58,876	5,464,265	6,342,000	12
Hawaii	1959	Honolulu	6450	965,000	1,098,000	4
Idaho (Ida.)	1890	Boise	83,557	943,935	1,003,000	4
Illinois (Ill.)	1818	Springfield	56,400	11,418,461	11,614,000	24
Indiana (Ind.)	1816	Indianapolis	36,291	5,490,179	5,556,000	2
Iowa (Ia.)	1846	Des Moines	56,290	2,913,387	2,834,000	8
Kansas (Kans.)	1861	Topeka	82,264	2,363,208	2,495,000	7
Kentucky (Ken.)	1792	Frankfort	40,395	3,661,433	3,727,000	9
Louisiana (La.)	1812	Baton Rouge	48,523	4,203,972	4,408,000	10
Maine (Me.)	1820	Augusta	33,215	1,124,660	1,205,000	4
Maryland (Md.)	1788	Annapolis	10,577	4,216,446	4,622,000	10
Massachusetts (Mass.)	1788	Boston	8257	5,737,037	5,889,000	13
Michigan (Mich.)	1837	Lansing	58,216	9,258,344	9,240,000	20
Minnesota (Minn.)	1858	St. Paul	84,068	4,077,148	4,307,000	10
Mississippi (Miss.)	1817	Jackson	47,716	2,520,638	2,620,000	7
Missouri (Mo.)	1821	Jefferson City	69,686	4,917,444	5,141,000	11
Montana (Mont.)	1889	Helena	147,138	786,690	805,000	4

FACTS ABOUT THE 50 STATES

State	Admitted into the Union	Capital	Area in Square Miles	Population 1980	Population 1988	Electoral Votes
Nebraska (Neb.)	1867	Lincoln	77,227	1,570,006	1,602,000	5
Nevada (Nev.)	1864	Carson City	110,540	799,184	1,054,000	4
New Hampshire (N.H.)	1788	Concord	9404	920,610	1,085,000	4
New Jersey (N.J.)	1787	Trenton	7836	7,364,158	7,721,000	16
New Mexico (N.Mex.)	1912	Santa Fe	121,666	1,299,968	1,507,000	5
New York (N.Y.)	1788	Albany	49,576	17,557,288	17,909,000	36
North Carolina (N.C.)	1789	Raleigh	52,58	5,874,429	6,489,000	13
North Dakota (N.Dak.)	1889	Bismarck	70,665	652,695	667,000	3
Ohio	1803	Columbus	41,222	10,797,419	10,855,000	23
Oklahoma (Okla.)	1907	Oklahoma City	69,919	3,025,266	3,242,000	8
Oregon (Ore.)	1859	Salem	96,981	2,632,663	2,767,000	7
Pennsylvania (Penn.)	1787	Harrisburg	45,333	11,866,728	12,001,000	25
Rhode Island (R.I.)	1790	Providence	1214	947,154	993,000	4
South Carolina (S.C.)	1788	Columbia	31,055	3,119,208	3,470,000	8
South Dakota (S.Dak.)	1889	Pierre	77,047	690,178	713,000	3
Tennessee (Tenn.)	1796	Nashville	42,244	4,590,750	4,895,000	11
Texas (Tex.)	1845	Austin	267,339	14,228,383	16,841,000	29
Utah (Ut.)	1896	Salt Lake City	84,916	1,461,037	1,690,000	5
Vermont (Vt.)	1791	Montpelier	9609	511,456	557,000	3
Virginia (Va.)	1788	Richmond	40,817	5,346,279	6,015,000	12
Washington (Wash.)	1889	Olympia	68,192	4,130,163	4,648,000	10
West Virginia (W.Va.)	1863	Charleston	24,181	1,949,644	1,876,000	6
Wisconsin (Wis.)	1848	Madison	56,154	4,705,335	4,855,000	11
Wyoming (Wyo.)	1890	Cheyenne	97,914	470,816	479,000	3
District of Columbia		Washington	67	637,651	617,000	3

GLOSSARY

A

addicted dependent on a habit such as drugs or alcohol

advocates people who support a cause through speaking or writing

airlift system of transporting supplies when ground routes are cut off

aliens people who live in a country but who are not citizens of that country

Allies a partnership formed during World War I by the Soviet Union, Great Britain, France, and later joined by the United States; the partnership fighting against the Axis nations in WW II

amnesty pardon for political offenses against a government

anarchists people who are against all forms of government

anti-semitism violent hatred and prejudice toward Jews

appeal request to a higher court for review of a case

appeasement the policy of giving in to keep peace

arbitration settlement of a dispute by persons chosen to hear both sides and make decisions

archipelago a curving chain of islands

armistice a temporary peace agreement

assembly legislature

assembly line rows of factory workers and machines along which work is passed

Axis the World War II partnership of Germany, Italy, and Japan

B

baby boom the sudden and great rise in birthrate after World War II

balance of payments difference between what a country spends on and earns from exported goods and services

bigotry intolerance, prejudice

blitzkrieg sudden warfare intended to surprise the enemy and win a quick victory

blockade to prevent normal traffic from entering or leaving an area

blockhouses forts

blue-collar describing work in industry, such as factory jobs

bohemia area where people live unconventional lives

Bolsheviks Russian political group which later formed Communist party

bootleggers people who made, transported, or sold liquor illegally during Prohibition

breadlines where people stood in line waiting for free food during the Depression

C

capital money for operating a business

capitalism an economic system in which individuals or companies, rather than government, own most factories and businesses and laborers produce products for a wage

Central Pacific railroad that started in California and went east

chancellor high official of state

checkpoints places on a border where people are stopped for inspection by authorities

citizenship the right to live in and be protected by the laws of a country

civil disobedience opposition to a law through refusal to obey

civil rights those rights guaranteed to all citizens by the Constitution and other acts of Congress

coalition union of different groups with common objectives

communes groups of people living together who share money and chores

communists people who believe that government should own and control all land and industry

concentration camp where Nazis held as prisoners those considered enemies during World War II

conformity wanting to be like everyone else

conservative maintaining and opposing changes in established traditions

consumers people who buy goods and services for personal needs

consulate official residence where foreigners go to seek help or information in another country

containment a policy to stop the spread of communism

corporations large businesses in which a group of people manage the company

counterculture group with values markedly different from those of the mainstream

court-martialed brought to trial in the military system

craft unions unions for workers with a specific skill

creditor nation lender of money to other countries

D

D-day the invasion of Western Europe by the Allies on June 6, 1944

debtor nation when a country owes more money than it has loaned to other countries

deferments temporary delays of military service

deficit amount of money the government spends over and above what it collects from taxes

demilitarized kept free of armed forces

deported forced to leave a country which is not one's homeland

détente French word meaning "relaxation"

discrimination the act of showing favor toward or prejudice against people because they belong to a particular group

doves Americans against U.S. involvement in Vietnam

drafted called to serve in the armed forces

E

ecology the science of the relationship between living things and their environment

embargo a ban on commerce and trade

entrepreneur person who takes risks to organize and manage a business

environmentalists people working to solve problems affecting the earth and its resources

escalated increased, particularly in relation to war

Establishment the prominent figures of American culture and politics

evangelical spreading Christian teachings

F

fascist one who believes in rigid, militaristic, one-party dictatorship

feminists people who believe women deserve the same rights as men

filibuster tactic to delay the passing of a bill in legislature by giving long speeches

flappers young women of the twenties who dressed in a bold new style

Fourteen Points President Woodrow Wilson's plan for world peace after World War I

freedom rides black and white students riding together on buses to challenge segregation during the 1950s and 1960s

free enterprise economic system allowing private industry to operate with little government control

free trade business between nations that is carried out without major restrictions

front-porch campaign political campaign in which supporters go to hear candidate speak in his or her home

fundamentalism strict obedience to religious law

G

generation gap the lack of communication and understanding between older and younger people

genocide deliberate murder of entire nation or ethnic group

geothermal power from deep in the earth

ghetto area in which many people of the same ethnic background live—often crowded into old, run-down buildings

glasnost new policy of democratic freedoms allowed in the Soviet Union

guerrilla a soldier who relies on hit-and-run raids at unexpected times and places

H

hawks Americans who favored U.S. involvement in Vietnam

hippies 1960s young people who rebelled against traditional values

Holocaust the slaughter of Jews by Nazis during World War II

hostage prisoner

I

industrial unions unions for employees of a particular industry

inflation the process by which the prices of goods and services increases

international law set of rules to govern nations' relations with each other

investor one who puts money into a business to make a profit

isolationist believes in the complete separation of one country from another

isthmus narrow strip of land with water on each side connecting two larger bodies of land

K

kamikaze aerial attack of an enemy ship in which pilot kills himself

L

labor unions associations of workers to promote and protect the rights of their members

lend-lease U.S. policy allowing Britain to borrow weapons, or pay for them later during World War II

lobbied attempted to influence lawmakers

M

majority leader member of Congress chosen by dominant party to push bills through the Senate or House of Representatives

martial law temporary rule by military authorities, during which people have many of their liberties taken away

McCarthyism public accusation of disloyalty, often unfounded

microchip a tiny, square-shaped slice of material on which an entire integrated circuit is formed

migrate move

monarchy government or state headed by sole ruler like a king or queen

monopoly complete control of an industry, product, or service

Morse code system of communication devised by Samuel Morse using short and long sounds for letters

muckrakers journalists who wrote articles about injustice and corruption

N

National Guard state and federal military force used in civil emergencies

Nazis the German political party during Adolf Hitler's time in power; National Socialists

neutral not favoring either side

non-violent resistance a form of peaceful protest that avoids the use of physical force

O

on margin buying a stock with a small down payment, the rest to be paid later

open-border policy allows free passage between countries

orator forceful public speaker

P

pacifists people opposed to all war

patents written guarantees by government protecting the rights to produce, use, and sell an invention for a specified time

perjury lying under oath

pesticides chemicals used for killing weeds and insects

philanthropist person who works to help humankind

pogroms organized abuse and killing of a minority group

political activists people who work to change

governmental policies

prejudice strong feelings of dislike, usually against one of another ethnic group, gender, race, or religion

premier a head of government

progressive believes life can be improved by governmental reform

Prohibition the period from 1920 to 1933 when the manufacturing, sale, and transportation of liquor was illegal

propaganda the spreading of ideas to influence someone else's opinion

protectionism to place taxes and quotas on imports and exports

Q

quotas the number of people of a particular race or gender allowed

R

racketeers people involved in organized, illegal activities

rationing limiting goods during times of scarcity

recession a temporary falling off of business activity during a time of greater economic activity

recycling treating or processing materials to be used again

refineries factories that purify raw materials such as crude oil

relocation centers prison camps to which Japanese Americans were forcibly moved during World War II

reparations payments made for damages suffered

resettlement program finds new homes for refugees or immigrants

revenues income from city, state, or national taxes

right-wing the more conservative section of a political party

S

Sandinistas members of Nicaraguan revolutionary movement that took control of the country in 1979

segregation the practice of separating one racial, ethnic, or religious group from another, especially in schools or other public places

settlement house institution offering social and educational services

sexist favoring one gender over the other

sharecroppers people who live and raise crops on other people's land

silicon a material found in sand, used to make microchips

sit-down strikes when laborers protest against management inside their workplace by refusing to work or leave

socialism government ownership of factories and services with wages determined by workers' needs

socialists people who believe in government ownership of factories, railroads, mines, and other parts of an economic system

soviets councils of workers, soldiers, and peasants in the Soviet Union

speakeasy where people went to drink illegally during Prohibition (1920-1933)

speculation taking financial risks in hope of making a large profit

stereotyping assuming that all people conform to the roles society gives them

stock certificates shares of ownership in a business

stock market a place where shares of companies are bought and sold

stockpiled gathered together

strikebreakers in a labor disagreement, people who interfere with workers' efforts to protest against management

suburbs developed living areas on the outskirts of cities

summit highest level; for top officials only

supply-side economics a government plan of cutting taxes to increase consumer spending, intended to decrease the deficit

sweatshops places where employees work long hours at low wages in poor conditions

T

technological relating to the tools and processes used to produce goods and services

tenement set of rooms lived in as a separate apartment, later a name for run-down, over-crowded apartments

terrorists persons who use violence or threats, often to obtain political power

Third Reich the German empire under Adolf Hitler from 1933 to 1945

toxic poisonous, destructive

Treaty of Versailles the final agreement ending fighting for all nations in World War I

trust giant business made up of several individual companies in a single industry

U

undocumented without official status or legal papers

U-boats German submarines

Union Pacific railroad that started in Nebraska and went west

urban of a city

V

verdict the answer a jury gives a court concerning a legal case

Vietcong guerrilla members of the South Vietnamese communist movement

Vietnamization U.S. policy giving South Vietnam responsibility for carrying out the Vietnam war, while removing U.S. troops

Volstead Act law created by Congress creating penalties to enforce the Eighteenth Amendment

W

ward neighborhood political area

welfare payments government aid to the poor or unemployed

Western Front area extending for 450 miles across Belgium and northeastern France to the borders of Switzerland during World War I

white-collar describing jobs in offices

withdrawal the process of giving up a substance one is dependent on

Y

yellow journalism the use of unfair methods to attract or influence readers

Z

zones of occupation areas of a country controlled by the military

INDEX

A

Acquired immune deficiency syndrome (AIDS), 180, 183, 195-197

Advertising, 68, 97

Afghanistan, 187, 188

Africa; Italy and, 5; World War II and, 7

African Americans. *See also* Civil rights; Discrimination; Race relations; baseball integrated, 75; Carter, Jimmy and, 173; culture and, 72; education and, 80; housing and, 64-65; Kennedy, John F. and, 117; political achievements of, 182-183; Reagan, Ronald and, 188; voting behavior of, 82; World War II and, 29, 31, 81

Agnew, Spiro, 167

Agriculture. *See* Farmers; Farm workers union

AIDS (Acquired immune deficiency syndrome), 180, 183, 195-197

Alamogordo, New Mexico, 37

Alaska, oil pipeline in, 171

Albania, 5

Aldrin, Edwin "Buzz," 153-154, 177

Alienation, 101

Allied powers (WW II), 6-7. *See also* World War II

American Indian Movement, 83

Americans with Disabilities Act, 102

Andropov, Yuri, 189

Anti-semitism, 21-22

Apollo project (moon landing), 153. *See also* Moon landing

Appeasement policy (WW II), 12-15

Apple Computer Company, 199-200

Arab-Israeli War of 1973, 169

Arab oil embargo of 1973-1974, 169-170

Arias, Oscar, 193

Arima, Masafumi, 34

Arkansas, 86-87

Arms race. *See also* Cold war; Foreign policy; cold war and, 46; Reagan, Ronald and, 189; treaty with Soviet Union, 149, 163

Armstrong, Neil, 117, 152, 153-154, 177

Army. *See* Military; War

Arnaz, Desi, 66

Asia; immigration from, 210- 211; trade with, 216-217

Atomic bomb; China and, 161; Cold War tensions and, 149; Cuban missile crisis and, 119-121; Reagan, Ronald and, 189; World War II use of, 3, 7, 36-39

Auschwitz (Poland) death camp, 22

Australia, 6, 216, 217

Austria, 4, 11

Automobile; energy crisis and, 168-171; pollution and, 151

Axis powers (WW I), 6

B

Baby boom, 31, 63, 69

Back-to-the-land movement, 147-148

Baez, Joan, 140

Balance of payments, 208

Ball, Lucille, 66-67

Baseball, 75

Batista, Fulgencio, 118-119

Battle of Guadalcanal (WW II), 34

Battle of Leyte Gulf (WW II), 35

Battle of Midway Island (WW II), 34

Battle of Okinawa (WW II), 37

Bay of Pigs invasion, 108, 111, 119

Beatles (music group), 70, 140, 196

Begin, Menachem, 173-174

Bergman, Ingrid, 41

Berle, Milton, 66-67

Berlin, Germany; airlift to, 44, 51-53; blockade of, 46-47, 50-53

Berlin Wall, opening of, 180, 181, 202-205

Bernstein, Carl, 165

Berry, Chuck, 70-73

Blitzkrieg warfare, 5-6, 16-17

Blue-collar workers, 64

Bogart, Humphrey, 41

Boycotts; civil rights, 79-80, 88-89; farm workers union, 94

Brandenburg Gate (Berlin, Germany), 50

Brezhnev, Leonid, 162, 163, 189

Brown, Linda, 84-87

Brown, Oliver, 84-87

Brown v. *Board of Education*, 78, 84-87

Bulgaria, 204

Burger, Warren, 183

Bush, George; election of, 181, 185; foreign policy and, 204-205; Nicaragua and, 193

C

Califano, Joseph, 101-102

California; farm workers in, 92-95; Reagan, Ronald and, 187

Cambodia, 156, 157-158

Camp David Accords, 173-174

Canada; trade with, 209; World War II, 6

Capitalism. *See also* Class; Communism; Economic factors; Reagan, Ronald and, 187

Carson, Rachel, 108, 113, 122-125, 176

Carter, Jimmy, 61, 172-175; career of, 172-173; childhood of, 172; criticism of, 186-187; economic factors and, 173; election of, 147, 150, 172; energy crisis and, 170; foreign relations and, 173-175; hostage crisis and, 174-175, 188; human rights and, 177

Cartoons, 76-77

Castro, Fidel, 111, 118-121

Catholic church, Kennedy, John F. and, 109, 114, 116

Ceausescu, Nicolae, 203

Census, 215

Central America, immigration from, 212

Chamberlain, Neville, 12, 13, 14

Chavez, Cesar, 79, 83, 92-95, 105

Chemicals, 123-125

Chernenko, Konstantin, 189

Chicago, Democratic party convention of 1968, 112, 133

China; communism in, 47, 56, 58; diplomatic relations with, 160-163; Japan and, 5, 24, 37; Korean War and, 59-60; Nixon, Richard M. and, 149, 177; student demonstrations in, 180-181, 182; trade with, 207

Chinese immigrants, restriction of, 211

Churchill, Winston, 7, 39, 46

Cities; black mayors of, 183; growth of, 48; migration to, 31; racial violence in, 91; suburbia and, 62-65

Civil defense, 28

Civil disobedience, 89

Civil rights, 78. *See also* African Americans; Discrimination; Race relations; disabled people, 100-103, 183; discrimination and, 65; farm workers and, 92-95; Germany, 10; impact of, 82-83; interrelationships in, 106-107; Japanese immigrants, 7; Johnson, Lyndon B. and, 111; Kennedy, John F. and, 116, 117; King, Martin Luther, Jr. and, 81, 88-91; Montgomery, Alabama bus boycott, 79-80; public school integration and, 84-87; violence and, 112; women, 96-99

Civil Rights Act of 1964, 79, 98, 104, 126

Clark, Kenneth B., 85

Class. *See also* Economic factors; 1970 economic patterns, 150; suburbia and, 64

Clay, Lucius D., 51-52

Clean Air Act, 125

Cocaine, 196-197

Cold War. *See also* Arms race; Foreign policy; Berlin airlift and, 50-53; Berlin Wall and, 180; Cuban missile crisis, 118-121; Kennedy, John F. and, 111, 114; McCarthyism and, 54-57; start of, 46-47; tensions of, 149

Collins, Michael, 153

Communes, 140

Communication, television, 66-69

Communism. *See also* Capitalism; Class; Economic factors; Central America and, 191; Cuba and, 119; Eastern Europe and, 180, 181; economic factors and, 203-204; fear of, 47, 49, 54-57; Germany, 10; Kennedy, John F. and, 111, 114; Korea and, 58; Nicaragua and, 191; Soviet Union and, 46, 182; Vietnam and, 112, 131-133, 135, 149, 159

Community Services Organization (CSO), 93

Computer, 183-184, 198-201

Concentration camps (Nazi Germany), 21-23

Conformity, 49

Congress (U.S.). *See also* House of

Lend-Lease Bill and, 2; U.S. military assistance to, 17-19; World War II and, 6-7, 17, 32-34

Great Depression, 92; Germany and, 9-10

Great Society (Johnson program), 111-112, 128

Guadalcanal battle (WW II), 34

Guerilla movements, 114, 184-185, 190-192. *See also* Vietnam war

Gulf of Tonkin Resolution, 131

H

Haight-Ashbury district (San Francisco), 138

Hale, Clara, 184, 194-197

Hale, Lorraine, 195-197

Haring, Keith, 195

Hawaii, Pearl Harbor raid, 2, 7, 24-27

Health, Education and Welfare Department, 101

Health and disease; AIDS and, 180, 183, 195-197; atomic bomb and, 38-39

Health insurance, 111-112, 188

Hindenburg, Paul von, 10

Hippies, 138-141

Hiroshima, Japan, 3, 36-39, 119

Hispanics. *See also* Mexican Americans; political achievements of, 183

Hiss, Alger, 54-55

Hitler, Adolf; Allied invasion of Europe and, 34; Jewish extermination policy of, 20-23; Nuremberg, Germany rally of, 2-3; rise to power of, 4-5, 8-11; war threatened by, 12-13

Ho Chi Minh, 131

Holocaust, 4, 20-23, 173

Homelessness; party politics and, 183; Reagan, Ronald and, 188; U.S. census and, 215; World War II and, 31

Homosexuals, 83

Honecker, Erich, 204

Hong Kong, 216, 217

Hostage crisis (Iran), 147, 150, 169, 174-175, 187, 188, 189

Hostages, 189

House of Representatives (U.S.), impeachment and, 166

House Un-American Activities Committee (HUAC), 56

Housing; discrimination in, 64-65; Reagan, Ronald and, 188; suburbia and, 62-65; World War II and, 31

Human rights, 177

Humphrey, Hubert H., 128, 133, 136

Hungary, 20

Hunt, Howard, 165

I

IBM, 200

I.G. Farben Company (Germany), 22

Immigrants and immigration; Asian, 210-211; Democratic party and, 211-212; restriction of, 212-213; sources of, 183, 211, 212

Immigration Reform and Control Act of 1986, 180, 212

Impeachment, Nixon, Richard M. and, 166

India, 89

Indochina, Japan invades, 24. *See also* Vietnam; Cambodia

Inflation, 1970s, 150

Integration. *See also* African Americans; Civil rights; Race relations; of baseball, 75; King, Martin Luther and, 89; of transportation, 78, 79-80, 82, 88

Internment camps, Japanese Americans, 42-43

Interventionism, 149

Iran-Contra scandal, 184-185, 190-191

Iran hostage crisis, 147, 150, 169, 174-175, 187, 188, 189

Iraq, 169

Iron curtain, 203

Islam, 174-175

Israel; Camp David Accords, 173-174; Carter, Jimmy and, 150; war of 1973, 169

Italy; Allied invasion of, 7; Axis powers and, 6; fascist control of, 5; Germany and, 13

J

Jackson, Jesse, 183, 214

Jackson State University, 148

Japan; atomic bomb used against, 36-39; China and, 5; Pacific expansion of, 26; Pearl Harbor attacked by, 2, 7, 24-27; surrender of, 3, 39; trade and, 206-209; World War II and, 6, 34-35

Japanese immigrants, internment of, 7, 42-43

Jefferson Airplane (music group), 140

Jews; death toll among, 22-23;

Holocaust and, 4, 20-23; Nazi party and, 4, 9, 10; World War II and, 40

Jobs, Paul Steven, 198-199, 200, 201

Johnson, Andrew, 166

Johnson, Lyndon B., 83, 172, 187; childhood of, 126; Civil Rights Act of 1964, 117; Great Society and, 111-112, 128; political career of, 126-128; succeeds to presidency, 111, 126, 128; Vietnam war and, 108, 128-129, 130, 132, 133, 135

K

Kamikaze attacks, 34-35

Kansas, segregation in, 84

Kennedy, John F.; assasination of, 108, 111, 115, 117, 126, 139; Bay of Pigs invasion and, 119; child-hood of, 115; civil rights and, 89; Cuban missile crisis and, 110-111, 118-121; election of, 108, 109, 114-115, 116; environment and, 124; immigration policy of, 211-212; Johnson, Lyndon B. and, 127; New Frontier program of, 110, 116-117; political career of, 115-116; space race and, 153; Vietnam and, 112, 131

Kennedy, Joseph, Jr., 115

Kennedy, Robert F., 116; assasination of, 109, 112, 139; Vietnam war and, 133

Kennedy, Rose, 115

Kent State University, 148, 156-159

Khrushchev, Nikita, 118, 119-121

King, Coretta, 88

King, Martin Luther, Jr., 78, 81, 88-91, 91, 109, 112, 139

King, Yolanda, 88

Kissinger, Henry; China and, 160-163; Vietnam war and, 158-159

Korean War, 47, 58-61; armistice signed, 45; China and, 161; outbreak of, 44

Krenz, Egon, 204

Kunin, Madeline M., 183

Kuwait, 169

L

Labor. *See also* Economic factors; Labor unions; foreign trade and, 206-209; technology and, 44-45; wages and, 150; women and, 97, 99, 148; World War II and, 7, 29-30, 41

Labor unions. *See also* Economic

factors; Labor; farm workers, 82-83, 92-95, 105; Poland, 189

La Causa (farm workers strike), 92-95, 105

Language, immigration and, 213

Lawrence, William, 144, 145

Le Duc Tho, 159

Lend-Lease Bill of 1941, 2, 18-19

Lennon, John, 196

Levitt, William J., 62-65

Levittown, New York, 62-65

Leyte Gulf battle (WW II), 35

Libya, 189

Liddy, G. Gordon, 165

Little Richard (musician), 72

Little Rock, Arkansas, 78, 86-87

M

MacArthur, Douglas, 59, 60

Macintosh computer, 199-200

Magazines, 75; television and, 68; women's movement and, 97

Manchuria, 5, 24

Mandela, Nelson, 182, 215

Manhattan Project (atomic bomb project), 37

Mao Zedong, 177

Marshall, George C., 56

Marshall, Thurgood, 85

Marshall Plan, 44

Mass production, housing, 62-65

Materialism, 139

Mauchly, John William, 199

McCarthy, Eugene, 132, 133

McCarthy, Joseph, 47, 54-57, 187

McGovern, George, 164-165

Mead, Margaret, 140

Medical insurance, 111-112, 188

Mein Kampf (Hitler), 10

Mengele, Joseph, 22

Mexican Americans. *See also* Hispanics; farm workers union, 83, 92-95; Johnson, Lyndon B. and, 127

Midway Island battle (WW II), 34

Migration; to cities, 29, 31; Eastern Europe, 203-204; regions and, 183

Military. *See also* Korean War; Vietnam war; War; World War I; World War II; arms treaties, 121; Japan, 25, 27; Reagan, Ronald and, 184, 186-187, 188; Vietnam war, 131, 149; World War I, 29; World War II, 29

ILLUSTRATION CREDITS

2-3 (40). Hugo Jaeger, *Life* Magazine, © Time Warner, Inc.; 4. Graphic Photo Union; 8. UPI/Bettmann Newsphotos; 9. Bundesarchiv, Koblenz; 10. Yivo Institute; 11. Library of Congress; 12. The Bettmann Archive/BBC Hulton; 13. Robert Hunt Library; 14. Bundesarchiv, Koblenz; 15. UPI/Bettmann Newsphotos; 16. FPG International; 17. Bundesarchiv, Koblenz; 19. UPI/Bettmann Newsphotos; 20. The Imperial War Museum, London; 21, 23. AP/Wide World Photos; 24. National Archives; 25, 27. AP/Wide World Photos; 28, 29. Library of Congress; 30. Hansel Mieth (detail) *Life* Magazine © 1943 Time Warner, Inc.; 32. US Coast Guard; 33. UPI/Bettmann Newsphotos; 35. National Archives; 36. US Air Force; 37. UPI/Bettmann Newsphotos; 39. Franklin D. Roosevelt Library, Cambridge, MA; 41. National Archives; 44-45 (74). Courtesy Hearst Corporation; 47. Hiroyuki Matsumoto/Black Star; 48 (75). The Bettmann Archive; 49. UPI/Bettmann Newsphotos; 50. Bob East/Globe Photos; 52-55. UPI/Bettmann Newsphotos; 56. Erich Hartmann/Magnum; 57. David Levine, Reprinted with permission from The New York Review of Books. © 1965 NYrev, Inc.; 58. Rene Noorbergen/Camera Press London Pix Inc.; 59. US Department of Defense; 61. The Bettmann Archive; 62. Bernard Hoffman, *Life* Magazine, © Time Warner, Inc.; 63. Joe Scherschel, *Life* Magazine © 1958 Time Warner, Inc.; 65. (l) FPG International; (r) UPI/Bettmann Newsphotos; 66, 67. Photofest; 69. Hazel Carew/Monkmeyer; 70. UPI/Bettmann Newsphotos; 72. The Popular Culture Archives, West Redding, CT; 73. Courtesy RCA Records Label; 78-79 (104). Matt Heron/Black Star; 80. UPI/Bettmann Newsphotos; 81. *New Kids in the Neighborhood,* Norman Rockwell. Norman Rockwell Museum at Stockbridge, Printed by Permission of the Estate of Norman Rockwell. Copyright © 1967 Estate of Norman Rockwell; 83. Frank Johnston/Black Star; 84. (detail) Carl Iwasaki, *Life* Magazine © Time Warner, Inc.; 85. *The New York Times;* 87. UPI/Bettmann Newsphotos; 88. James Karales/Magnum; 90. *Dream 2: King and The Sisterhood,* 1988, Faith Ringgold. Courtesy Berenice Steinbaum Gallery, New York: 91. Robert Kelley, *Life* Magazine © Time Warner, Inc.; 92. Bob Fitch/Black Star; 93. George Ballis, Sun Mountain in Medicine Ways; 94. Phil Degginger/Bruce Coleman; 95. George Ballis, Sun Mountain in Medicine Ways; 96. Elliott Erwitt/Magnum; 97. Constantine Manos/Magnum; 98. John Olson, *Life* Magazine, © Time Warner, Inc. 99. UPI/ Bettmann Newsphotos; 100. Bob Daemmrich/Stock, Boston; 101. Philip Jon Bailey/Stock, Boston; 102. Charles Gupton/Stock, Boston; 103. Bob Daemmrich/Stock, Boston; 105. Courtesy Jessie de la Cruz; 108-109 (142). Elliott Landy/Magnum; 110. Declan Haun, *Life* Magazine, © 1967 Time Warner, Inc. 111. Library of Congress; 112. Steve Shapiro/Black Star; 113. © Simonpietri/Sygma; 114. Wayne Miller/Magnum; 115, 116. UPI/Bettmann Newsphotos; 118. Andrew St. George/Magnum; 119. Keystone Press Agency; 121. UPI/Bettmann Newsphotos: 122. Courtesy Houghton Mifflin Co. Photo by Brooks; 123. Museum of American Political *Life,* University of Hartford, West Hartford, CT. Photo, Robert Rubic; 125. Central Park Conservancy; 126-127. UPI/Bettmann Newsphotos; 129. Red Grooms. Moderna Museet, Stockholm; 130. AP/Wide World Photos; 134. Bernie Boston; 135. Owen Franken/Stock, Boston; 136. Library of Congress; 137. UPI/Bettmann Newsphotos; 138. Peter Simon/Stock, Boston; 139. © Peter Max, 1990. All Rights Reserved. Courtesy of AM X Art Ltd., New York, and The Peter Max Studio, NYC. 140. David McCullin/Magnum; 141. Owen Franken/Stock, Boston; 143. Courtesy the Peace Corps; 146-147 (176). Ellis Herwig/Stock, Boston; 148. Warren Morgan/Woodfin Camp; 149. Bruno Barbey/Magnum; 150. Drawing by Draper Hill. Reprinted by permission of *The Commercial Appeal,* Memphis, TN; 151. Cowell/Black Star; 152. Courtesy *Life* Magazine © Time Warner, Inc.; 153. NASA; 154 (177). Courtesy *Life* Magazine © Time Warner, Inc.; 155. Charles Harbutt/Actuality, Inc.; 156. Tarentum, PA, Valley News Dispatch; 157. Dennis Brack/Black Star; 158. Buffon/Sygma; 159. Nik Wheeler/Black Star; 160. AP/Wide World Photos; 162. Magnum; 163. Arthur Grace/Stock, Boston; 164. Dennis Brack/Black Star; 165. © 1974 Simon and Schuster, Inc.; 166-167. Fred Ward/Black Star; 168. Jason Laure/Woodfin Camp; 169. Jim Anderson/Black Star; 170. Edward Pieratt/Stock, Boston; 171. Lief Skoogfors/Woodfin Camp; 172. Jodi Cobb/Woodfin Camp; 173. Dennis Brack/Black Star; 175. Jim Anderson/Woodfin Camp; 180-181 (214). P. Durand/Sygma; 182. (t) Tannenbaum/Sygma; (b) (215) UPI/Bettmann Newsphotos; 183. AP/Wide World Photos; 185. UPI/Bettmann Newsphotos; 186. National Archives, Office of Presidential Libraries, Washington, D.C.; 187. Kobal Collection; 186. Vladimir Sichov, Courtesy William Collins Sons and Company, Ltd. 190. © Steele-Prekins/Magnum; 191. Cindy Karp/Black Star; 193. Dennis Brack/Black Star; 194. © Bachelier/Sygma; 195. Courtesy Tony Shafrazi Gallery, New York. Photo Brian Albert; 196. Gary Gladstone/The Image Bank; 198. Robert Knowles/Black Star; 199. D. Kirkland/Sygma; 200. James D. Wilson/Woodfin Camp; 201. Paul Shambroom/Photo Researchers; 202. Kainulainen Lehtikuva/Woodfin Camp; 203. Alexandra Avakian/Woodfin Camp; 204. Peter Turnley/Black Star; 205. Anthony Suau/Black Star; 206. Kevin Forest/The Image Bank; 207. Peter Menzel/Stock, Boston; 208. Bill Strode/Woodfin Camp; 209. Rick Browne/Stock, Boston; 210. David Burnett/Contact Press/Woodfin Camp; 213. Stephanie Maze/Woodfin Camp.